Word Smart Junior II

Word Smart Junior II

More Straight-A Vocabulary

by C. L. Brantley

Random House, Inc. New York
www.randomhouse.com

ISBN 978-0-375-76258-1

Editor: Scott Bridi
Production Editor: Diahl Ballard
Designer: Tina McMaster
Second Edition

Manufactured in the United States of America.

10 9 8 7

ACKNOWLEDGMENTS

I could not have written this book with the encouragement, love, and support of my husband, Drew. For all the times he cheered me up, urged me on, and went to the copy shop for me, I am deeply grateful.

I would also like to thank John Stanford for his expert advice on reading skills and vocabulary development, and for letting me use his students to test the words in this book. A big thank-you also goes out to all those students who took time out of their busy days to help me with this project. They are (in no particular order): Angie Oliver, Jessica Diaz, Angie Roman, Clint Bingham, Brandom Gomez, Bertha Nuñez, Tremayne Poole, Latasha Deary, Ann Honeycutt, Brooke Dlouhy, Rhea Brown, Nick Rodriguez, Jermaine "Cornell" Washington, Talishia Fisher, Leslie Salazar, Maria Gonzalez, Curtis Ruemke, Jr., Bevin Pitts, Travis Falk, Maria Yolanda Nuñez, Clarence Dewey Barber, Mary Quitarilla, Jacqui Ware, Candice Williams, Tim Bass, Isabel Velasquez, Amanda Welch, Keli Stewart, Jimmy Sanchez, and Valentino Reyes.

I'd also like to thank the editorial and production staff at The Princeton Review for all their time, effort, and expertise.

CONTENTS

Introduction

You have probably been learning vocabulary words in school for a long time now, right? Your teachers make you copy down the words, then you go home and look them up in a dictionary and write down the definition. Maybe you even have to write a sample sentence. Do you ever stop to think about why you are being taught vocabulary?

If you're like most people, you don't. You just do your homework as quickly as possible, and probably forget the words and their meanings by the time you hand in your assignment. Well, we want to change all that.

Don't worry, we're not going to tell you to ask for extra assignments, or make a bunch of flashcards, or read a hundred words out of the dictionary every night. Not that it would hurt you to do those things, but it wouldn't do much good either. That's because when you are just starting to build an adult vocabulary, a vocabulary that will help you succeed in high school, college, and beyond, the best way for you to learn new words is by *reading or hearing them in context.*

Here's How this Book Works

Word Smart Junior II is designed to help you learn as enjoyably as possible by reading important vocabulary words in context. There are eight chapters included here that follow the adventures of Bridget, a street-smart kid from New York, Babette, a mysterious French girl, Barnaby, a boy genius with a wild head of hair, and Beauregard, a huge black tomcat with a crazy past.

Around six hundred and fifty words are covered in this book. Whenever one of them appears for the first time, it will be in boldface (**like this**). If you come across a word you don't know, see if you can figure out its meaning by its context. Don't interrupt your reading by looking up every unfamiliar word unless you really can't figure out the meaning. Just try to enjoy the story from start to finish, then go back and look up the words you don't know.

USING THE GLOSSARY AND DOING THE QUIZZES

If you do have to look up a word right away, there is a glossary at the back of the book which defines all of the bolded words and uses them in sample sentences. Take a look in the glossary whenever you get confused.

At the end of each chapter there are some quizzes you can do to make sure you understood the words you have just read. The answers are in the back of the book. (Don't peek ahead of time!) If you miss some of the questions, look up the words you didn't understand in the glossary. Also, make sure you go over our special pronunciation guide at the beginning of each glossary entry, so you'll know how to say the words properly.

Okay, that's about all you need to know. Start reading, start learning, and prepare to impress the pants off everyone you know with your new, improved vocabulary!

Chapter 1
Seventh Inning Stretch

Trinidad! That island paradise where the deep green water glistens in the sun so brightly that the eyes are dazzled by beauty and shine! Soon, soon I will be there, and Consuela and I will cavort on the beach, dancing, prancing, and swirling about until we fall down on the sand....

At least, that's what I kept telling myself as I sat within the dreary, depressing confines of waiting area 27B at one of New York City's airports. My flight was hours late because of the weather; the rainfall outside was heavy. No, it was worse than heavy, it was **torrential;** it was as if rivers were flowing from the sky. I tried to remain patient. After pacing back and forth for a couple of hours, I decided to **repose** under a chair, where I curled up into a ball and closed my eyes, with my long, black tail tucked safely under me. But as I awakened from my short nap, the strangest thing happened....

Ah, but I am getting ahead of myself as usual. Allow me to introduce myself. My name is Beauregard, and I am a traveling gentle-cat from South Carolina. I suppose you might call me unusually **burly** for a cat. I am quite muscular, and stand over four feet tall when I walk on my back legs. I consider myself elegant, tasteful, and well-mannered, and I hope you will agree with me after you've learned a bit more about me. Because I'll be telling you a lot of this story, you could call me your **narrator.** Well, it's such an interesting and exciting story that I don't mind the job one bit.

As I was saying, I was on my way to Trinidad to visit a lovely cat named Consuela. She is such an **exotic,** unusual beauty! Her dainty paws are perfectly shaped. But alas, I did not get to see Consuela. As I opened my eyes after my nap, I heard a loud "POP." Only one thing and one person can make that sound: Bridget. I crawled out from under the chair and sure enough, there was Bridget, in jeans and a New York Knicks jersey, peeling the remains of a giant gum bubble off of her face. A second later, her neat black braids were flying out from under her baseball cap as she quickly **scampered** like a kitten toward a crowd of people.

✎ ✎ ✎ ✎ ✎

"**B**abette! Babette!" Bridget yelled. "Over here! Are you blind?"

Babette and Bridget were back together again. That settled it for Beauregard. These **foolhardy** young friends of his had a special talent for stumbling into trouble, and he wasn't about to let them try to **fend** off danger by themselves. Trinidad would have to wait—he had to protect them. Besides, he had been with them on more than one good adventure. Little did he know, this would be the biggest of them all.

"Bridget?" cried Babette, a tall young French girl, dressed fashionably in black from head to toe. She tilted her giant sunglasses down to get a better look around.

"Babette, I'm over here! Take those sunglasses off, you can't see a thing!" answered Bridget.

"Ah, there you are, *mon amie*. How are you?" Babette smiled, shoving her glasses firmly back in place.

"How am I? We haven't seen each other in months! I'm excited!" exclaimed Bridget, as she hugged her friend. "I'm glad your flight finally made it. Man, do I have plans for us. You showed me Paris and now it's my turn to show you New York. By the way, do you hear that strange noise?"

GATE H →

"Yes, it's a quiet purring, or a motor running, but it's barely **audible**."

"Hey, Babette, look over there under that chair! Could that be . . .?"

"Absolutely! Beauregard, our old friend," Babette declared with delight.

The two girls ran toward the cat, who, pretending to sleep, tried to stay completely still.

"Wake up, sleepyhead! It's us!" demanded Bridget.

Beauregard opened one eye, looked up at them, then closed his eye again.

"Now, Beauregard, do not be so **blasé**. Only the French can really pull that off, you know," teased Babette.

"Yeah," Bridget chimed in, "we know you're not completely **indifferent** to us. You like us a heck of a lot, or you wouldn't keep following us around. In fact, I think you're happy to see us."

Beauregard **murmured** something about "crazy kids" under his breath, came out from underneath the chair, and stretched.

"I couldn't quite make that out. Did he just say something?" Bridget asked. "Oh, I forgot, he doesn't talk—to us, anyway. Come on, Beauregard, we're going into town."

The long black cat blinked calmly and slowly **loped** along beside the girls, bouncing easily from paw to paw.

Outside the airport, Babette stood by the curb and began waving her arms.

"Taxi! Taxi!" she yelled. "Where are the taxicabs? This rain is **drenching** my new outfit. Soon it will be **saturated** with water; you'll have to wring me out!"

"Wait, Babette, we shouldn't take a taxi in this weather anyway," advised Bridget. "New York drivers seem to just forget how to drive when it rains. Every intersection gets jammed; there are **gridlocks** where traffic is stopped in all directions. We'll have to head underground: To the subway!"

Bridget led her friends to a shuttle bus that took them to the subway. Soon they were zipping along toward downtown New York. Babette and Bridget had a lot of catching up to do, so they **jabbered** happily, barely pausing for a breath, about school, their families—everything they'd done since they'd last met.

"Where are we going first?" asked Babette, finally. "I almost forgot to ask."

Bridget grinned. "It's a surprise. But don't worry, you won't have to wait long to find out. This is where we get off."

The train came to a stop and the friends got out and started making their way to the stairs that led outside.

"Uh oh, it's rush hour," remarked Bridget, as she looked around the crowded station. "All of these rain-soaked people are trying to get home. You may get **jostled** by the crowd, but just put your elbows out so you don't get hurt and meet me at the top of the stairs. Good luck!"

With that, Bridget began wriggling her way through the mass of people, with Babette and

Beauregard following close behind. A few minutes later, they stood together on the street and Beauregard began licking and straightening his fur.

"You have to **muster** up a lot of strength and courage to make it through a crowd like that," remarked Babette. "How do you do it every day?"

"You get used to it," shrugged Bridget. "But why are we **lingering** around the subway station? We have better things to do. Hey, I think it stopped raining!"

As Bridget held out her hand to make sure that no more drops were falling, a passing man dropped a quarter in her palm.

"Hey, mister, wait!" yelled Bridget, but the man had already disappeared into the crowd. "He thinks I'm a **panhandler,** begging for change. I guess I did have my hand out. Well, I needed a quarter for the pay phone anyway. Come on, there's one up ahead."

Bridget made a quick, secretive call, and then gestured to her friends to follow her.

"We're heading in here," she said, pointing to a tall brick building.

The lobby of the building was quiet and fancy. The three friends walked across the smooth marble floor to the elevator and pushed the button for the top floor. When the doors opened, the scene before them looked like something out of a science fiction movie: A strange looking shiny metal ship about the size of a sailboat took up most of the large open room, and scraps of metal, bubbling test tubes, and piles of scribbled notes littered the floor. A **rustle,** like the sound of windswept leaves, came from the far corner. One of the piles of paper was moving toward them!

Beauregard, always on the lookout for danger, crouched and then pounced on the rustling paper. After a short **scuffle,** which Beauregard won easily, the paper cried out for mercy.

"Aaaargh!" screamed the pile. A huge, bushy head of very light blonde hair appeared. The owner of the hair stood up, brushed off his slightly stained lab coat, and straightened his glasses.

"Barnaby!" yelped Babette, rushing toward the young scientist. "Are you okay?"

"Babette! Wonderful to see you! Why,um, yes, quite, quite, um, huh?" stammered the confused boy. "What just happened?"

"Take a look in the corner by the window," replied Bridget with a jerk of her head. "Beauregard is **skulking** around like a hunter stalking his prey. I think he hopes that another one of these piles of paper starts moving so he can attack it."

"I should have known," said Barnaby, smiling. "Well here we are, together again. Excellent! The last time you visited my laboratory, when I lived in Paris, I believe we had a bit of an explosion, didn't we? Yes, most of my notes and samples were lost under the rocks and **rubble** of the science building after it blew up when my gym sock experiment went **awry.** Not every experiment goes as planned, I told the university, but the other professors were very upset. They wouldn't listen to reason or any of my apologies. Basically, they ran me out of town. Luckily, this university here in New York offered me space to continue my work. I thought they might change their minds when I told them about the **catastrophe** in Paris, but they didn't **balk.** They not only gave me all of the equipment I needed, they gave it to me so quickly that I was back in action in just a week's time!"

"Well, speaking of gym socks and terrible disasters, Barnaby, it smells like you are up to your old tricks," remarked Bridget. "What *is* that awful **stench**? It smells like something died and is starting to **decompose.**" She held her nose in disgust.

Babette agreed, "Yes, and I believe I also notice the odor of old milk that's beginning to **curdle** and **congeal** into a thick, disgusting blob. It's a rather sharp and **pungent** odor, Barnaby, and one that's difficult to ignore."

"No, there's nothing rotting or **rancid** in here, Bridget, and nothing's curdling, Babette," insisted Barnaby. "What you both seem to think is a **horrid** odor is actually the sweet smell of success! I feel so **giddy** and excited when I think about it, I don't know whether to fall over or turn cartwheels."

Bridget rolled her eyes and thought about **chiding** her friend for stretching the truth, but she was used to Barnaby's wild inventions and grand claims. Most of them were just kooky ideas that never worked, but sometimes, she had to admit, the young scientist came up with something really amazing. The problem was, she could never tell what was **folly** and what was genius. She decided to bite her tongue and not scold him for now.

Barnaby took several long **strides** toward the metal ship.

"You see this?" he asked, pointing toward the craft. "This is my latest **prototype**—it's the first model of the first spaceship that can fly without using a **combustion** engine! That means that nothing gets burned. Whereas cars, airplanes, rockets, and space shuttles all burn incredible amounts of fuel, my new space shuttle doesn't burn any fuel at all. Humans are wrecking the planet when they dig for oil and gas and polluting the air when we burn those natural resources. But worse than that, combustion engines don't really work that well. I just can't believe that the world has put up with those dirty machines for so long!" The **indignant** inventor shook his fist in the air and then sighed with displeasure and continued.

"The new method of travel that I envision will make it possible for us to explore outer space and protect the world's environment at the same time. As you both have heard me say many times, the most **crucial** challenge that humans face is that of solving the problems and surpassing the limitations of our present means of transportation. If we don't try to do this, we are dooming ourselves to living in darkest ignorance."

Barnaby's speech was beginning to **exasperate** Babette. She stamped her foot with annoyance and impatience.

"Barnaby, please, enough **melodrama.** You're like one of those overly emotional actors in the American soap operas," she snapped. "Just tell us about your invention!"

Barnaby blushed, and Babette was immediately sorry that she'd spoken so harshly.

"I'm just eager to hear what you've made," she said gently.

"Yes, well, as you know, I have always been **intrigued** by the thought of **celestial** exploration. Exploring the heavens—ah, how many nights have I stared at the stars and dreamed of visiting distant worlds! Oops, there I go again. Sorry. Anyway, I started studying modern rockets, and after careful **analysis** of their design, I came to the conclusion that those rocket scientists at NASA have been doing it all wrong. Then, out of the blue, the solution came to me: I could use a **nautical** model for my spaceship!"

"Nautical?" asked Bridget. "You mean stuff like boats and sails and anchors and all that? That's kind of **quaint,** isn't it? I mean it's nice but it seems very old-fashioned."

"The idea may seem old-fashioned, but it really turned out to be very effective," insisted Barnaby. "I based my calculations on the latest research into the magnetic qualities of space dust. I have designed special ionic outer-space sails and a vacuum-valent anchor for normal planetary travel. Then there is the quasi-quantum quickener for time travel, but there are still some kinks in that. The strong smell you notice is from a very sticky, but highly conductive, plant mash I concocted. It took months for me to do all of this planning and construction, but finally I'm finished."

"Wow, Barnaby, that sounds great, but I'm afraid that most of what you said sounded like **gibberish** to me," sighed Bridget. "I just didn't understand a word. Vacuum ionic quantum whatchamajiggy, huh? You'll have to sit down and explain it to me step by step sometime, but not now. Now, we have bigger fish to fry."

"Fish?" asked Babette, completely confused. Beauregard, who had been stretched out on top of Barnaby's notes, perked up his ears at the word.

"Not real fish," explained Bridget. "It's just an expression. It means that we have more important things to deal with right now, namely, the Yankees game. The evil Boston Red Sox are in town, and the **rivalry** between the Red Sox and Yankees is ancient! They've been battling each other in the ballpark since before we were even born! Now that it has stopped raining, we *have* to go try to get tickets for the game. The only problem is that tickets are as **scarce** as hens' teeth."

"Hens?" Babette asked, as Beauregard once again cocked an interested ear.

"She means that tickets are rare, they're hard to come by," explained Barnaby. "Not only that, but I'm sure that prices are getting **exorbitant.** We'd have to cough up ridiculous amounts of money in order to get decent seats. But I have the strange feeling that we might be able to lay our hands on some tickets. Hmmm. How could we get some?"

Barnaby began pacing around the room and scratching his bushy head. Babette nudged Bridget and smiled knowingly. Something exciting **invariably** happened when Barnaby started scratching.

"Tickets, tickets, tickets," he murmured, scratching furiously. "Aha! I know! We can go to the box office and try to buy some!"

"Wait, Barnaby," Bridget said, "what is that thing that's stuck behind your glasses?"

"Oh. I wondered why I couldn't see out of my left eye," Barnaby said. "Let's see. Oh. Now that's interesting. It seems I have four tickets to tonight's Yankees game. Right above the home team dugout, too. They must have fallen out of my hair. I really should brush it from time to time."

"Don't you dare," said Bridget, as she hugged her friend. "Come on, we have to get back to the subway."

So Barnaby left his lab for the evening, and the friends scurried down to the subway with Beauregard trotting behind.

"Right above the dugout!" gasped Bridget excitedly, as they walked down into the station. "What a perfect **vantage** for catching foul balls. We couldn't be in a better position!"

A short while later, they were walking toward Yankee Stadium. The streets and parking lot were filled with excited, cheering fans and **peddlers** selling souvenirs, candy, and T-shirts from their carts. The sun was just beginning to set, and the late-summer evening was warm and pleasant.

"This crowd is so excited, Bridget," remarked Babette. "In France, we only see such a **hoopla** at soccer games. What a commotion!"

"I have to admit that even though I am a whiz at physics and chemistry, for some reason baseball **confounds** me," said Barnaby. "I love watching it, but I never understand what's going on. Bridget, Babette and I are counting on you to explain everything."

"Have no fear," declared Bridget, laughing. "With me as your guide, baseball will never **mystify** or **bewilder** you again. Let's get a move on, though, my throat is **parched;** I could drink a bathtub full of soda. And I want you guys to see the field keepers roll up the giant plastic **tarpaulin** that keeps the rain off the field. It's really cool!"

Once she made sure that Babette and Barnaby were in their seats, Bridget took off for the snack stand to get some food. Beauregard followed her, which was lucky, because Bridget bought far too many treats to carry by herself. She and Beauregard returned **laden** with drinks, popcorn, candy, and a dozen foot-long hot dogs that were fully loaded with dressings.

"You look like a couple of pack mules, all loaded down like that," joked Barnaby.

"Are you going to grab some of this, or what?" asked Bridget, who was struggling to keep it all balanced.

Babette and Barnaby eagerly took the giant drinks off of the cardboard tray on Beauregard's back and unloaded the food from Bridget's arms.

"You can't enjoy a baseball game without the proper **provisions**," said Bridget. "And now we have all the supplies we could possibly want: Dig in everyone! I bought every **edible** product that was available. You might argue that red licorice isn't fit to eat, but hey, I say if you can swallow it, it's edible."

They ate as if they hadn't had a meal in weeks; they only stopped slurping and chewing for long enough to cheer and holler for the Yankees. Bridget amazed everyone with her whistling abilities; she could stick two fingers in her mouth and produce a sound so loud and **shrill** that people at a distance of a hundred yards had to cover their ears.

"My, that is a piercing sound," said Babette, admiringly. "I just can't seem to do it."

"Don't feel bad, Babette," replied Bridget. "You have plenty of skills of your own. For example, you're **multilingual.** Exactly how many languages *do* you know?"

"Five," Babette said hurredly, and then stood in her chair and yelled "*J'aime les* Yankees! *Victoire pour les* Yankees!" Bridget looked at her friend enviously.

"Uggh," groaned Barnaby. "I feel like I weigh a ton. My stomach is **bloated** to three times its normal size. In **retrospect,** I see that eating that fifth foot-long hot dog was a bad idea."

"No sense regretting it now, Barnaby," said Bridget. "You need to get active. Wave your arms. Clap your hands. Let's hear some noise! Hey battabattabatta, hey... Ouch!"

"What happened?" asked Babette.

"Ow, it looks like a **shard** of fiberglass is sticking out from this seat and it just stuck me in the rear."

"How big a shard? Ooh, that's a pretty big splinter," remarked Barnaby, as he **sidled** over to Bridget with scientific interest. "There are probably germs all over these seats. We need to get you to the doctor for a shot of **penicillin** so you don't get an infection. That's the **prudent** thing to do; penicillin is great at killing germs."

"Slide back over to your seat, doc," laughed Bridget. "It only poked me, there's no blood."

"That's a relief," said Barnaby.

"Is it time for the **interval**?" asked Babette.

"Interval?" replied Bridget, confused.

"Yes an interval, you know, a space between things. You said that there was an interval between innings in which we would stand up and sing."

"Oh, you mean the seventh inning stretch," said Bridget. "Oh yeah. Look, it's time right now! This is when we get up and sing 'Take Me Out to the Ball Game.' I'll tell you the words quickly; it's an easy song to learn."

✎ ✎ ✎ ✎ ✎

But Bridget didn't sing. Something had caught everyone's attention. Just above the edge of the stadium a large object **loomed,** as big as a cloud. I couldn't make out exactly what it was.

The last rays of the setting sun **glared** so brightly that I couldn't see very well. Whatever the object was, I didn't like it. I was filled with a dark sense of **foreboding.**

Bridget lost no time in making use of her famous gum-chewing talent. She started blowing a bubble, bigger and bigger and bigger until a gust of wind lifted her off the ground. Babette, Barnaby, and I knew exactly what to do. We grabbed on to her legs for dear life and went sailing into the air. Just as we were taking off, a booming voice from the sky thundered through the stadium.

"Your Yankees or your lives!" the voice demanded. Then we heard an evil **cackle,** a **diabolical** laugh, that made us shiver with **dread.**

✍ QUIZ #1 ✍
Relationships

Decide what relationship the following pairs of words have to each other. If they have similar meanings, write "S" next to the pair of words. If they have opposite meanings, write "O" next to the words.

1. scarce : exorbitant   _____

2. catastrophe : disaster   _____

3. rancid : foul   _____

4. rival : ally   _____

5. foolhardy : prudent   _____

6. bewilder : confound   _____

7. drench : saturate   _____

8. indifferent : apathetic   _____

9. giddy : morose   _____

10. celestial : earthly   _____

11. dread : anxiety   _____

✍ QUIZ #2 ✍
Relationships

Decide what relationship the following pairs of words have to each other. If they have similar meanings, write "S" next to the pair of words. If they have opposite meanings, write "O" next to the words.

1. murmur : shriek _____
2. crucial : decisive _____
3. blasé : exotic _____
4. mystify : perplex _____
5. elegant: refined _____
6. exasperate : intrigue _____
7. indignant : resentful _____
8. burly : gaunt _____
9. parch : drench _____
10. lope : stride _____

✍ QUIZ #3 ✍
Fill in the Blank

For each sentence below, choose the word that best completes the sentence.

1. Mrs. Finster had such an unpleasant _____ that people would only tell her jokes that weren't funny.

   a. muster   b. cackle
   c. balk   d. jabber

2. After we thoroughly washed and waxed the 1972 Volkswagen, the car _____ like it was brand new.
   - a. congealed
   - b. glistened
   - c. rustled
   - d. scuffled

3. The colored glass statue of a rose was beautiful, but even a slight wind was enough to knock the _____ artwork on its side.
   - a. pungent
   - b. quaint
   - c. horrid
   - d. dainty

4. Hoping to get a free ice cream cone, the children continued _____ at the drugstore counter for hours after they had finished their burgers.
   - a. chiding
   - b. skulking
   - c. lingering
   - d. scampering

5. The _____ had no trouble selling his mini-refrigerators in California, but his trip to Alaska almost ruined him financially.
   - a. panhandler
   - b. peddler
   - c. melodrama
   - d. hoopla

6. After three days of heavy thunderstorms, the main street of our town transformed into a _____ of rushing water.
   - a. torrent
   - b. stench
   - c. gridlock
   - d. penicillin

7. The judge wanted to _____ the questions to the alleged burglary, but questions about the defendant's past continued to come up during the trial.

      a. confine   b. jostle

      c. glare   d. narrate

8. Although the hurricane had downed some seats and soaked most of the countryside, the _____ over the baseball field kept the infield dirt relatively dry.

      a. analysis   b. rubble

      c. combustion   d. tarpaulin

9. A cruel person, the chef uttered a(n) _____ laugh before placing the lobsters into the boiling water.

      a. audible   b. sidling

      c. diabolical   d. multilingual

10. Nancy felt it necessary to _____ excitedly around the room every day before English class started.

      a. fend   b. loom

      c. curdle   d. cavort

✍ QUIZ #4 ✎
Matching

Match each word on the right with the letter on the left that has a similar meaning.

1. prototype	A.	supplies
2. retrospect	B.	ship-related
3. provisions	C.	stand over
4. gibberish	D.	fragment
5. decompose	E.	nonsense
6. loom	F.	original model
7. dreary	G.	act of stupidity
8. shard	H.	looking back
9. nautical	I.	bleak
10. folly	J.	decay

✍ QUIZ #5 ✎
Matching

Match each word on the right with the letter on the left that has a similar meaning.

1. awry	A.	rest
2. shrill	B.	unchanging
3. bloat	C.	wrong
4. foreboding	D.	able to be eaten
5. repose	E.	sense of disaster
6. vantage	F.	astonish
7. dazzle	G.	burdened with goods
8. invariably	H.	good position
9. edible	I.	swell up
10. laden	J.	high-pitched

Chapter 2
Knuckleballs and Tentacles

Exactly what happened next, I'll probably never know. I remember that there was a bright light and a wave of sticky, hot air. For a minute it looked like the entire New York Yankees baseball team was flying through the air, like a band of athletic angels with mitts instead of harps. What a **spectacle!** You don't see things like that every day. Then I **swooned** and everything went black.

When I woke up, I found myself on a red velvet cushion on a chair at the head of a large banquet table.

The room I was in was so expensively furnished that it looked fit for **regal** visitors. The **grandeur** of the heavy red drapes along the walls was made more noticeable by the gold thread that was **embroidered** around its edges. Such lovely decoration! Precious gems embedded in the gold dishes on the table, drinking goblets, and platters on the table all sparkled in the candlelight. Every aspect of the room was delightful, but the part that really filled me with awe and admiration was the food. I hadn't seen a spread like that since the summer I spent at the court of the Sultan Subadai. That sultan really knew how to throw a party! I remember the time that he imported ten tons of caviar from Russia to fill his swimming pool, then hired the Spanish Olympic aqua-aerobics team to . . . but that's a story for another time. The question was, what were we doing in a fancy banquet hall?

✎ ✎ ✎ ✎ ✎

"Eek!" shrieked Bridget as she awakened from what must have been a trance. "What happened to my clothes?"

She stared down in horror at her pink satin dress, white lacy socks, and shiny, black, patent leather shoes. Babette and Barnaby laughed uncontrollably as their shocked friend examined her outfit. There were even ribbons in her hair!

"I see no reason for such **mirth,**" grumbled Bridget. "You'll quit your giggling when you get a load of the clothes you're wearing!"

"There's no need to be **testy,** Bridget. We did not mean to **vex** you by laughing, but . . . oh, no!" howled Babette, looking down with **dismay** as she realized that her stylish black outfit had been replaced by a serious, navy blue dress with a white sailor collar. "What a **prim** and proper, little-girl dress! I feel like a school principal! This is horrible. I **abhor** dresses."

"I hate them too," Bridget said. "I'd rather be dressed like Barnaby, even though he does look pretty goofy."

Barnaby's lab coat was gone, and in its place was a green satin jacket with black velvet lapels. A dashing silk scarf was tucked around his neck. Barnaby did not seem at all unhappy with his new clothes. After admiring himself in a large mirror that was hanging on the wall, he **swaggered** over to his friends with all the pride of a peacock.

"Yes, it seems there have been some wardrobe changes," announced Barnaby. "But what we need to know is *why*, and what's going on? What information can we **glean** from our surroundings? We must examine every detail for clues."

"Okay, Sherlock," joked Bridget. "I'd say that judging from the **opulent** furnishings and food, we are in the home of a very rich person."

"I think it's quite **ostentatious** and overdone," sniffed Babette with disapproval. "I think whoever brought us here is a **pretentious** snob without any taste or class. But we are definitely supposed to be impressed with the expense of all of this."

"Aren't you two forgetting something? Like the flying baseball players?" asked Barnaby.

"Oh, yeah," sighed Bridget. "Okay, so we're in the home of a very rich person who probably has a space ship that can make people hover above the ground. Great. Now what?"

Barnaby began poking around the curtains, looking for a way to open them.

"There has to be a way to look outside and see where we . . . ah, yes, here it is," Barnaby said as he pulled a long yellow cord. The curtains swung open to reveal the blackness of outer space to the right, and a swirling white mass of clouds to the left. Barnaby gasped, "What an **atmosphere**!"

"I'm so glad that you approve," boomed a deep voice. "I tried to make the room homey and comfortable, and like a room that you might see on your own planet."

Barnaby, Babette, and Bridget spun around
to face the door at the end of the banquet hall.
Standing there—or hovering, maybe—was the
strangest looking creature that they'd ever
seen. It had ten long **tentacles,** like the arms of
an octopus, and a huge green head with
droopy ears. It didn't have a nose as far as they
could tell, and its mouth was just a tiny
opening, but all around its head were nine
eyes that blinked and winked. A short, black
mane of hair, like a horse's, sprang from the
top of its skull and extended a short way down
its back. Around its shoulders (or what they
thought were shoulders) the creature wore a
little purple cape.

"That is the most **hideous,** frightful creature
I have ever seen," whispered Babette, to no
one in particular.

"Tut, tut, young lady," scolded the being.
"How rude. You wouldn't catch me calling
you **homely** or unattractive just because you
look different from me, or because you dress
like a principal." He turned to Barnaby and
said, "Young man, you were admiring the
room's atmosphere?"

"Umm, actually I was looking at Earth's
atmosphere, you know, its protective layer of
gasses, but the room is, umm, it's really, really
nice as well," **stammered** Barnaby.

"Thank you, young man," said the strange
being, holding out one arm toward the boy. "I

hope you have been enjoying the food—but how rude of me, I have not even introduced myself. I am Gorgas, an explorer from another galaxy. And you are . . .?"

Barnaby was frozen in place.

"Come, lad, there's no need to be shy and **timid,** I only want to shake your hand," urged Gorgas.

Bridget broke in, "Pardon him, Gorgas," she sensed that Barnaby needed a few seconds to get a grip on himself. "He's a scientist and he isn't used to social events. My name is Bridget, and these are my friends Babette, Barnaby, and Beauregard. Beauregard is the cat over there that's enjoying your chicken pot pie. We are all pleased to make your acquaintance."

Beauregard licked his whiskers, gave a polite little nod toward their host, and continued eating. Bridget took Gorgas's tentacle into her hand, bent her knees slightly, and dipped into a perfect **curtsy,** just like her mother had told her she should when meeting royalty. Bridget wasn't sure if Gorgas was a king, but she figured that it couldn't hurt.

"My dear, what lovely manners!" remarked Gorgas with pleasure. "What a delight!

In general I simply cannot **abide** ill-mannered people. I just cannot put up with them. And as for me, I would rather be torn limb from limb from limb from limb from limb than behave rudely. Might I add, Bridget, that you look quite **comely** in that **frock**. I knew you would look pretty in it."

"Thank you," said Bridget, because she knew that it would be impolite to give her real opinion of the outfit. "I hope I won't seem rude for asking, but we were wondering why exactly we were brought here."

"My apologies, Bridget, my dear, but it was an accident," said Gorgas. "You just drifted into my path. I had only meant to take possession of the baseball players, but once you arrived, I decided to try and make you feel welcome."

"Were you the one who said 'Your Yankees or your lives'?" asked Babette.

"That was just my idea of little joke," said Gorgas. "I'm afraid I'm a bit of a prankster."

"So you're saying that the **acquisition** of the Yankees was your goal," Bridget pressed on. "You seem to have quite a lot of money—one can't help but notice, why didn't you just buy the team?"

"I don't want to own them forever, young lady," explained Gorgas. "You see, part of my mission as an explorer is to **accumulate** information about other worlds. I must **amass** as much knowledge as I can. At any rate, for the past couple of weeks I have been watching television transmissions of baseball on my TV here in the spaceship. It's such a fascinating pastime! I must confess, though, that I am not confident that I truly understand all of the rules of the game."

"Oh, Bridget can **clarify** them for you. She's great at explaining things about baseball," said Barnaby, who had finally remembered how to talk.

Gorgas said snootily, "I'm sure Bridget has been a great help to *you*. How difficult it must have been for *you* to grasp those very complicated concepts."

"There is no need to **condescend** to Barnaby," snapped Babette. "You may think that you're super-intelligent because you've mastered intergalactic travel, but Barnaby is a brilliant inventor and scientist on Earth, and . . ."

"Well, excuse me, I would never dare to put on airs in front of a brilliant scientist," interrupted Gorgas. "I **presume** that Barnaby is quite capable of understanding the sport of baseball."

"You presume correctly, Gorgas," Bridget said, and folded her arms across her chest.

"In any event," Gorgas proceeded, "the rules of the game no longer interest me. I have another, more scientific, question to ask the Yankees. My **inquiry** will be about a certain amazing ability that is possessed by Lefty Zambisi, the starting pitcher—I must ask him about a trick that he performs, which I believe is called the 'knuckleball'…"

"The knuckleball is their secret weapon," Bridget said with excitement. "No other pitcher in the history of baseball has been able to throw a knuckleball with such control and **precision.** The ball always goes exactly where Lefty wants it to, directly over the plate. The beauty of this pitch is that the **trajectory** of the ball as it travels to the plate is impossible to predict. As soon as it leaves Lefty's hand, it could curve to the left or right or it could dip or wobble, but every time it crosses the plate it's safely in the strike zone. Batters go nuts! Whenever Lefty starts throwing knuckleballs, you know that the game will end in a **rout,** with the other team running for cover!"

"I can see that Lefty was right when he said you might be interested in our little experiment," said Gorgas. "He told me that you were offering him quite a bit of loud advice from the stands during the game, and suggested I ask you for help. He has a most unpleasant **disposition**—what a quick-tempered and gruff man! And I have never met anyone quite so **obstinate;** despite all of my begging and pleading, he absolutely refuses to show me how he throws his famous pitch."

"I'm sure it's not because of **spite** or meanness. He probably thinks you're a spy from another team or something," said Bridget.

"Well, I don't mean to **impose** upon you, Bridget, because you *are* a guest aboard my ship, but would it be too much trouble for you and your friends to come to the practice room with me? You see, that pitch is a miracle, it doesn't follow any known laws of motion in the universe. I must uncover the secret, for, uh, for the good of science. Yes, that's it, for the good of science," said Gorgas.

"Of course I'll come," Bridget replied. "Lead the way."

Bridget followed Gorgas as he slipped through the doorway. Barnaby, on the other hand, was going to have to be **coaxed.** He and Babette hung behind for a moment.

"Now Barnaby, come on," urged Babette gently. "I'm sure Bridget has a plan to get us out of here. I don't like Gorgas any more than you do, I think his way of talking is **stilted** and stuck up, and I don't think he's up to any good."

"Did you notice that he **exudes** some sort of slimy liquid from his tentacles? That's why I didn't shake his hand. Plus, there was something fishy about his reason for wanting to learn about knuckleballs. I don't like this," added Barnaby.

"We'll discuss it later, but now we have to hurry; we don't want to lose them," said Babette.

She and Barnaby jogged through the doorway. Beauregard, his belly full from feasting, followed sluggishly. They caught sight of Gorgas's purple cape swishing around a corner ahead of them, and ran to catch up.

"Here we are!" announced Gorgas, stopping in the doorway of a huge gym.

In the gym some of the Yankees were playing casual games of catch. A couple of them were practicing their swings in batting cages. Lefty Zambisi, however, sat on the floor with his arms crossed and his back against the wall, and when Gorgas entered the room, he groaned.

"Listen, fella, I've talked myself **hoarse** trying to get this through that giant green head of yours," rasped Lefty, rubbing his tired throat. "You will never throw my pitch, understand? I can't show you how to do it. I can't, I can't, I can't!"

"He certainly is **vehement**," remarked Gorgas to Bridget. "You might be right about his suspecting that I'm a spy." To Lefty, he said, "Listen, I've had about enough of your **defiance.** You *must* do as I ask. It is rude to refuse me a simple favor."

"Look, mister, can't you see that my energy is **flagging;** I'm tuckered out. Why don't you just leave me alone?" he whined.

Bridget sat down on the ground next to Lefty with a look of concern on her face.

"Gorgas," she said, "Lefty does seem tired. Remember, he just pitched seven straight innings and he's getting kind of old; he doesn't have the **stamina** that he used to have. Maybe if you went and got him a soda, I could see if I can bring him around to see your point of view. Don't worry, I'll **sway** him."

Gorgas strutted purposefully off and left them alone with Lefty.

"What is *this*, kid?" asked Lefty, narrowing his eyes at her. "I would never have suspected you of **duplicity**. I thought you were a diehard Yankees fan, and here you are spying for the enemy. Pretty two-faced, isn't this? And by the way, I am not getting old, and I have just as much staying power as I used to have."

"Stow it, Lefty, I'm no spy. I'm here to help you get off of this ship," snapped Bridget. "And I only made that 'old' comment to get Gorgas to leave us alone."

"Oh, yeah?" the pitcher said suspiciously, "Well, how do I know you're not lying?"

"We can **corroborate** her story, Mr. Zambisi," said Barnaby. "Babette and I can confirm that Bridget is the biggest Yankees fan around. Gorgas only transported us up here by accident, when he was transporting the team. Bridget is definitely not a spy."

"Bridget, I am so glad to hear that you have a plan to get us out of here. Gorgas is frightening me. He probably has plans to take over the world, enslave the human race, and declare himself Supreme Ruler of the Galaxy," said Babette.

"Come on, Babette, that's a **stereotype.** You've been watching too many sci-fi movies," scolded Bridget. "Not every alien with tentacles and a big green head wants to take over the world, you know. I think Gorgas is a little weird and I don't want to hang around here much longer, but I think he's pretty harmless, and I also think you're making too big of a deal out of this."

"I am not, I am not!" insisted Babette, with a **petulant** stamp of her foot.

"Easy, kid, no need to have a tantrum," joked Lefty. "If it makes you feel better, I agree with you: This Gorgas guy is trouble."

"I think so, too!" Barnaby blurted out.

Even Beauregard nodded his head slightly in agreement.

"Okay, okay. I know when I'm out-numbered," said Bridget. "I suppose we should figure out what to do next."

"I ought to confess that I never really thought Gorgas was a spy from another team," said Lefty. "But for some reason, I just don't want to explain my pitch to him. I realize that there's been a lot of **hype** in the media about my knuckleball, and a lot of folks are interested in learning how I do it. But Gorgas, he seems a little *too* interested in it, and he's so **persistent.** He's been pestering me about it for hours; he just won't let up!"

"Wait a minute, something just **dawned** on me," Barnaby broke in. "First of all, I admit that I'm not a baseball expert, but it looks to me like Gorgas has an **impediment** that would prevent him from being able to throw a knuckleball. He has no knuckles!"

"You sure *are* sharper than Gorgas," grinned Lefty. "For all of his brains, he didn't seem to understand that a person without knuckles can't throw a knuckleball. That's exactly what I told him from the very start, but he still doesn't believe me."

"What are we going to do?" asked Bridget. "We don't have time to sit and **ponder** the situation for hours. We have to think fast. Gorgas will be back with the soda any minute."

"Whatever you do, don't try to strong-arm him," warned Lefty. "My teammates and I tried to **pit** our strength against his, and we got licked. He is a **formidable** fighter, and is nowhere near as easy to beat as the Red Sox. Those weird tentacles of his are strong, and they have suckers on them!"

"Did you say suckers? Hmmm. Very interesting," remarked Babette. "No, we should not try to beat Gorgas with force. This situation requires **cunning** and **deception.** We must outsmart Gorgas and trick him into thinking that we're giving him everything he wants."

"What did you have in mind?" asked Barnaby, interested.

"Well, Gorgas seems to like Bridget very much, especially because she curtsied for him. Bridget, do you think you could continue to convince Gorgas that you are his **ally**?" asked Babette.

"Sure," said Bridget. "What do you think I should do?"

Babette quickly outlined her plan—and finished not a moment too soon. Gorgas returned with a large bottle of soda pop and plopped it at Lefty's feet.

"Well?" he boomed with the **imperious** tone of a powerful ruler. "Have you decided to tell me what I want to know? Or are you going to sit there **peevishly** refusing?"

"Go suck eggs, Gorgas," scoffed Lefty.

It would be hard to describe exactly how angry Gorgas got. He was **livid,** and his mouth, which was already little, tightened up until it was so **minute** it was barely even visible. Something was about to happen. The tension in that air was so thick that it seemed to have substance; it was nearly **palpable.** And suddenly Gorgas lost what little control he had. He threw a **tantrum** worthy of a three-year-old child who is deprived of dessert.

"You! You horrible, nasty, **odious** man!" howled Gorgas, waving his tentacles. "I have displayed an **inordinate** amount of patience with you. Much, much more patience than you have deserved. If you do not tell me how to throw a knuckle ball right this instant, I'll . . . "

"Gorgas!" shouted Bridget, so he would listen to her. "Let me have a word with you for a minute."

Gorgas heaved a great sigh, obviously disappointed that his outburst was interrupted, and took a few steps away with Bridget.

"Pardon me for that rather excessive display, my dear," said Gorgas.

"Well, I have good news," said Bridget with a smile. "All I had to do was **cajole** him a little to get him to reveal his secret. I used **flattery;** I told him what a great player he is and how much I admire him and a bunch of other nice things like that."

"Oh! You **crafty,** sneaky little thing, you. Good job. Oh, this is marvelous," squeaked Gorgas, bouncing up and down. "Please do go on."

"You'll never believe this, but he says he cheats. It has nothing to do with knuckles. He makes a little suction cup with his hand so that when he throws, the ball is delayed for a second before it comes loose. Batters can never figure out the timing so they can never hit the ball," Bridget explained.

"Did you say suction cup?" asked Gorgas.

"Yes, we could get a few suction cups for you and you could easily **emulate** his pitch. You could even do it better than him if . . . but, Gorgas, look at your arms!" cried Bridget, pretending to be surprised. "They are covered in suckers! They're perfect!"

"Aren't they lovely?" laughed Gorgas. "I will unlock the secret of that pitch at last! There's no stopping me now! Surely having more than one sucker will **enhance** the effectiveness of the pitch. No longer will it be called the knuckleball; we'll call it the Sucker Ball—the pitch for suckers!"

"What a great name," Bridget agreed enthusiastically, giggling to herself.

"My dear, I am greatly indebted to you. I am **obliged** to repay you for this fantastic favor you have done for me; my good manners simply prevent me from letting this pass unrewarded. What can I do for you?" Gorgas asked.

"Think nothing of it, Gorgas," Bridget said. "But if you insist on doing something for me, how about returning the Yankees to Yankee Stadium so that they can continue their game?"

"Of course I'll return the baseball players," agreed Gorgas.

"And while you're at it, my friends and I are ready to go back at any time," Bridget added. "In our regular clothes, too, if that's okay."

"Did you say at any time?" asked Gorgas, with what looked like a grin.

"Sure!" said Bridget.

"Very well, then. Children! Come here!" ordered the alien as he pulled a long stick that looked like a magic wand out from under his purple cape.

Babette, Barnaby, and Beauregard gathered around Bridget.

"You will now return to Earth—at *any time*, as requested," giggled Gorgas, and he waved the wand around them.

The four friends were suddenly bathed in a bright, hot light. The air around them grew heavy and they began to feel light-headed. The spaceship around them faded, the light dimmed, and as darkness surrounded them, they heard Gorgas's terrible laugh.

"Enjoy the seventeenth century!" he thundered.

✍ QUIZ #6 ✍
Relationships

Decide what relationship the following pairs of words have to each other. If they have similar meanings, write "S" next to the pair of words. If they have opposite meanings, write "O" next to the words.

1. timid : vehement   _____
2. prim : casual   _____
3. pretentious : humble   _____
4. accumulate : hoard   _____
5. stamina : constitution   _____
6. duplicity : fraud   _____
7. comely : hideous   _____
8. emulate : copy   _____
9. mirth : dismay   _____
10. flattering : spiteful   _____
11. ponder : contemplate   _____

✍ QUIZ #7 ✍
Relationships

Decide what relationship the following pairs of words have to each other. If they have similar meanings, write "S" next to the pair of words. If they have opposite meanings, write "O" next to the words.

1. petulant : pleasant _____
2. enhance : intensify _____
3. cunning : crafty _____
4. awe : scorn _____
5. odious : abominable _____
6. defiance : obstinance _____
7. palpable : unnoticeable _____
8. clarify : obscure _____
9. flag : signal _____
10. homely : opulent _____
11. tantrum : outburst _____

✍ QUIZ #8 ✍
Fill in the Blank

For each sentence below, choose the word that best completes the sentence.

1. Joanie's _____ requests—she called Thomas every hour for two weeks straight—finally got her the date she wanted for the prom.

   a. condescending   b. persistent
   c. formidable   d. peevish

2. The villagers _____ the bandits so thoroughly that most of the survivors never picked up a weapon again without starting to cry.

   a. exuded   b. coaxed
   c. routed   d. abhorred

3. The gift of the mammoth _____ was very thoughtful, because the king enjoyed using ice cubes that were nine inches thick.

   a. goblet   b. frock
   c. trajectory   d. curtsy

4. Because she always won, Katie _____ such a collection of marbles that it looked like she was carrying huge bunches of grapes in her pockets.

   a. swaggered   b. imposed
   c. vexed   d. amassed

5. The clock used at the Naval Command Center was so _____ that it only lost a second for every two hundred years of use.

      a. minute   b. regal
      c. precise   d. livid

6. Once my parents arrived home from vacation two days early, the _____ at my house party went from very good to very bad.

      a. tentacles   b. atmosphere
      c. mane   d. ally

7. Toby asked such a(n) _____ amount of questions that the teacher eventually asked him to just sit on his hands and let her finish at least one sentence.

      a. testy   b. ostentatious
      c. inordinate   d. obliging

8. Once he learned that he had just won the lottery, Morgan's sour _____ took a change for the better.

      a. acquisition   b. corroboration
      c. deception   d. disposition

9. The large glowing rock was _____ too deeply in the side of the cave for me to pry it out with just my hands.

      a. embedded   b. pitted
      c. cajoled   d. gleaned

✍ QUIZ #9 ✍
Matching

Match each word on the right with the letter on the left that has a similar meaning.

1. impediment
2. stereotype
3. spectacle
4. imported
5. sway
6. aspect

7. stilted
8. dawn
9. presume

A. oversimplified idea
B. movement back and forth
C. obstacle
D. element
E. the beginning
F. from another country
G. pompous
H. assume
I. impressive display

✍ QUIZ #10 ✍
Matching

Match each word on the right with the letter on the left that has a similar meaning.

1. imperious
2. stammer
3. embroider
4. grandeur
5. inquiry
6. swoon
7. hoarse
8. hype
9. abide

A. faint
B. live with
C. stutter
D. gloriousness
E. regal
F. gruff
G. investigation
H. exaggeration
I. stitch

Chapter 3

Popo the Bandicoot

Cats, as you probably already know, do not like being thrown into water. I am no different; I've noticed that having wet, matted fur strips you of every shred of your dignity. But wet fur was the least of our troubles. Gorgas had placed us in quite a **predicament.** Not only were we floating in the water off of the coast of what appeared to be a Caribbean island, but there was a naval battle going on less than a hundred yards away from us. We were all pretty shaken up, and fortunately some **flotsam,** probably wreckage from another sea battle, came drifting along, and we were able to grab hold of some boards and float.

One strange thing that we noticed immediately was that the ships in the battle looked like antiques. One was a Spanish **galleon,** a big ship with several sails that sailed the seas at least two or three hundred years ago, and the other was a smaller ship called a **schooner** that was flying the British flag—the Union

Jack, I believe they call it. The schooner was getting the worst of it. The galleon was bombarding it with frequent **volleys** of cannon fire, and one of its sails was in flames; it looked like the Spanish ship would **prevail** before long.

At what appeared to be the last possible moment, the schooner made a break toward a little **inlet** on the shore of the island. They raced for the cove at full speed, and we were directly in their path!

"Ouch, Beauregard, stop scratching me," complained Bridget, who had been floating silently, trying to figure out what to do next. "I said quit it! Hey, which way do you think that ship's heading?"

Barnaby looked up. "You mean that schooner?" he asked. "Considering its original **bearing,** and seeing its position now, I would say that it's headed straight in our direction!"

"Beauregard, please watch your claws," said Babette, rubbing her head. "Oh! Oh! That flaming ship is about to hit us! Paddle everyone; kick your legs! Hurry!"

Bridget and Barnaby started kicking and paddling—and not a moment too soon; the schooner whizzed by them, missing them by only a few feet.

"Thank goodness we're safe," sighed Bridget, as she watched the ship race to shore.

"Argh, that's what *you* think, matey," came a voice from above.

Bridget spun around and looked up. Right above her, attached to the front of the huge Spanish ship, hung a painted **figurehead,** carved in the shape of a beautiful woman with flowing gowns.

"I must be dreaming," said Bridget. "Did that figurehead just talk? And did it have a man's voice?"

"No, you sea-soaked nitwit. I'm over here," demanded the voice.

Standing on the deck of the galleon was a tall **buccaneer** with a striped shirt, a bandanna tied around his head, and a large gold hoop dangling from his left ear. The pirate's face was **ruddy** from sunburn and sea air and he wore an eye patch over his right eye.

"Wow, this is just like being in the movies," said Barnaby.

"Movies? What is a 'movies'?" asked the pirate. "No, I've no time to waste chatting with you. My name's Keelhaul McCall. *You* will call me Captain Keel. This is my boat—the *Ruffian*. I named it after myself, for sure as you're born, I'm the toughest outlaw on the seven seas."

Barnaby, Babette, and Bridget stared at him in fear, quite convinced that Captain Keel was the meanest **desperado** that had ever lived.

"My men will be taking you prisoner now. There must be some relations hereabouts who would pay a few sacks of gold to have them back," remarked the captain to his men, who were climbing down rope ladders toward the water. "And, mateys, bring me that **mangy** black cat, as well; we'll clean it up and add it to the collection."

Beauregard was deeply hurt. His fur was just wet, after all, it wasn't patchy, but his expression was not nearly as **doleful** as were Bridget's, Babette's, and Barnaby's.

"Argh, buck up there, me hearties," urged Captain Keel, his voice softening a little. "You're in for some real excitement. That schooner made a big mistake when it went to hide in that inlet; we're going to form a **blockade** and then **besiege** it until it hands over what's rightfully ours!"

"I thought it took a whole **armada** to surround and attack a ship in harbor," remarked Barnaby, as though he knew what he was talking about. "And you only have *one* ship."

"Aye lad, you're right, it would take a fleet of *most* sorts of ships," said the captain, "but the *Ruffian* is the finest ship I've ever commanded. The Spanish admiral I stole it from put up quite a fight, but like I told you, I am the **scourge** of the seven seas, and my reputation helps me win my fights: As soon as any captain sees the flag of my ship on the horizon his teeth start to chatter!"

"Pardon me, Captain Keel, but what is it exactly that you want from that schooner?" asked Bridget, with the **utmost** politeness and care. She didn't want to make the captain angry.

"The captain of that ship was the **perpetrator** of an outrageous **heist**! He stole from me!" thundered the pirate. "And he is the worst kind of thief—he's a pirate who steals from other pirates. He is the lowest of the low!"

"But that ship is flying the Union Jack, are you sure they're pirates?" asked Barnaby.

"Boy, don't you think I know what I'm talking about? Every pirate ship owns several different flags, and the one they fly depends on which people they want to trick. Sailing a pirate ship is all about **ruses,** you see? It so happens that there is a British colony in Trinidad. That **rascal** of a stealing pirate is hoping that the soldiers who live in that **garrison** there will think that a British ship is under attack and will send out a whole **regiment** to help them," explained Captain Keel. "Now boy, do I make sense to you, or do still think that you know more about pirating than old Captain Keel?"

Barnaby was forced to **concede** that Captain Keel did know more about pirating, and that in all the excitement over the battle, he'd just gotten a little carried away. But a disturbing new thought began to occur to him as he was calming down. He turned to whisper to Bridget and Babette. "Hey, what was that last thing that Gorgas said? You don't suppose that we're really…"

"In the 1600s?" whispered Babette. "I think we must be. The waters of the Caribbean are usually **teeming** with tourists and motorboats, and I don't see any! I don't see any large cities along that coast, and by the way, Trinidad used to be a British colony. It isn't anymore, or at least it isn't supposed to be."

Beauregard cast a **wistful** gaze toward the shore, thinking of Consuela and the vacation he had missed.

"It would seem that your friend the cat is **yearning** to go ashore," laughed the captain. "I don't blame him; there's great fun to be had in Trinidad, but all in good time. First, I have a proposition to make. That ship in the harbor holds a few things that are mine, and if you will fight with me and my men to get them back, you can join as members of our crew and share in the bounty that we win, and then I will let you go ashore. If you refuse, you will be my prisoners until I can get a good price for you…in one way or another."

Babette, Barnaby, and Bridget exchanged quick glances and found themselves in agreement.

"Under the circumstances we'll fight with you," said Bridget. "But just out of curiosity, what exactly are we trying to get back?"

"I suppose it's only fair to tell you the whole story," said the captain, who strolled along the deck. "It's like this. There's a secret place called Hanged Man's Island that only I know how to find. It's there I keep my **cache** of treasures, deep in an underground cave. I also store extra food and fresh water there, and whenever my men and I need to **replenish** our supplies, that's where we go. Ah, it's a lovely island. Sometimes, just sometimes, I would invite a couple of other pirates, who I deemed to be relatively good fellows, to join us there for fine food and entertainment at my **bungalow.** It's a simple cottage with a **thatch** roof that I made by myself from palm leaves, but you couldn't ask for a nicer place for a dinner party. There's even a **verandah** that wraps all the way around the house where you can sit outside and enjoy the beautiful **vista.** I may be a rough buccaneer, but I am also quite a **connoisseur** when it comes to good food and wine. I know how entertain, and believe me, after all the ships we've raided, I can afford the finest of everything."

"Aren't you afraid those other pirates will come back and take your booty while you aren't there?" asked Bridget.

"Well, little missy, I never was before. Have you never heard the old **adage** . . . now how did that one go, hmmm . . . oh, yes, 'there's honor among thieves'?" asked Captain Keel. "In my many years as a pirate, I always found that to be true. Pirates don't raid other pirates' islands or boats. Besides, before I ever brought anyone there, I made them make a **pact** saying that they would never to speak of the island to another soul, nor reveal its whereabouts. That's what makes Singapore Sam's **transgression** so much worse than mere thievery. He has sinned against a fellow pirate."

"Is Singapore Sam the captain of the schooner?" asked Babette.

"Aye, that he is," growled the captain. "He was my guest at Hanged Man's Island and he betrayed me. He stole something from me that is more precious than gold and rubies. And as soon as I get my treasure back, I'm going to completely smash his ship with my cannon fire. No, I'll do more than that, I'll **incinerate** it. There will be nothing left of it but **cinders** and ash!"

Barnaby was about to ask what the valuable treasure was, but Captain Keel had already started shouting orders to his men, rushing about the ship, and generally preparing for battle.

"All right, mateys, bring the *Ruffian* in as close as you can. I want her **nigh** onto that schooner; near enough that we can tie onto her and jump across to her decks and take back what's ours. Are you with me?" he demanded.

The band of pirates let out a cheer of enthusiasm and turned the ship into the cove. The wind filled the sails and in no time, the *Ruffian* was **adjacent** to the schooner. Captain Keel had **deployed** his men all along the length of the galleon and as soon as they tied on they began charging the deck of the other ship, waving their sabers and **muskets** and **bellowing** like bee-stung bulls. But the other crew was ready for them. The air was filled with the clang and clash of swords, angry shouts, and smoke from firing muskets.

The three friends found themselves in the **midst** of this furious battle.

Bridget ducked and shielded her head with her arms and yelled, "Run for cover!"

Barnaby followed Bridget into an empty water barrel, but Babette stood her ground and showed them all just how much damage an expert in karate, judo, and several other secret martial arts can do to a bunch of clumsy pirates. She started by flipping several men over her shoulder and into the water. The other pirates were **flabbergasted.**

"She's just a **scrawny** little skinny kid," complained a rather thick-skulled **lout,** scratching his head in confusion. "How can she do that?"

"Let's get her!" urged one of his crewman and, snarling, he charged toward her.

Babette quickly **hobbled** him with a sharp kick to his left leg. As he tried to limp away, she back-flipped toward him and delivered a powerful kick to his chin. He **reeled** backward from the blow and fell over the edge of the ship. As soon as they saw how easily Babette had dealt with him, most of the enemies **dispersed** in search of easier prey.

One foul-mouthed sailor, however, refused to be **daunted** by her amazing fighting abilities. He **gnashed** his teeth together so hard it seemed they might break, then he shouted out several **expletives** so shocking that Babette blushed.

"Please," she objected, "I find such terrible language **repugnant**."

"I don't care what you find," he shouted, "just as long as the shot of my musket finds you!"

With that, the pirate lifted the musket to his shoulder and took aim directly at Babette. As soon as they saw that this new confrontation involved a gun, Bridget and Barnaby, who had been cheering on their friend from their hiding place, came tumbling out of the barrel and ran toward the pirate to tackle him.

But they were too late; he had fired the gun. In what seemed like the blink of an eye, Babette calmly removed her sunglasses and held them up above her shoulder. The musket ball bounced off of the lens and **ricocheted** off of the figurehead, hit the main mast, and then rebounded to hit the pirate in the shoulder, which forced him to drop his musket.

"Ow!" he yelled, and turned to run.

"Those are some incredible sunglasses, Babette," remarked Bridget. "No wonder you always wear them."

Babette nodded mysteriously, and at the same time they heard a distant and enraged yowl that they recognized as coming from Beauregard. The three friends immediately ran over to see what was the matter. Captain Keel was **grappling** with a big man with a peg leg and Beauregard, who was stuck in-between them, was desperately trying to **extricate** himself from the fight by furiously clawing. To make matters more confusing, a beautiful parrot with bright green plumage, which was tied to the peg-legged pirate's shoulder, was flapping frantically about their heads.

"You monstrously nasty cat!" wheezed the peg-legged man in a **rasping,** gravely voice.

"Pieces of eight! Pieces of eight!" squawked the frightened parrot.

"Someone slap a **muzzle** on that bird's beak," grunted Captain Keel. "I'm tired of its talk. Say, young mateys, how about giving me a hand here? I'm running out of steam, and my back is killing me!"

Babette jumped in and made short work of the peg-legged pirate. After a couple of well placed kicks, he was tumbling into the sea with the rest of his crew.

"Ha, ha! You lily-livered cowards!" shouted Captain Keel in triumph, mocking and **flouting** at the swimming sailors. "That'll show you not to cross me, Sam! And I want you to know that I'm going to go over every inch of my galleon and make a careful **assessment** of the damages. You're going to pay **reparations** for all of your treachery!"

Singapore Sam and his soggy crewmen shook their fists and shouted angry curses, but Captain Keel just ignored them and turned to Babette.

"Ouch," he grumbled, rubbing his back, "my **rheumatism** must be acting up. That always happens when a storm is about to blow through. I can feel the weather in my bones."

"Are you sure your back isn't just sore from fighting?" asked Barnaby.

"Look, child, a little **exertion** never hurt Keelhaul McCall," growled the captain. "Can't you feel the **gale** that's whipping the sails? The wind is really picking up; we'd better hurry and collect the treasure."

Barnaby stared out toward the great **expanse** of ocean, which stretched as far as he could see. Sure enough, in the distance there was a **vivid** sunset that filled the sky with deep red, bright purple, and blue. The huge clouds glowed with such **radiance** that it almost hurt the eyes to look at them. Barnaby had read plenty of sailor stories and knew that a sunset like that meant trouble ahead.

"By the way, that was some job you did handling Sam's men," said Captain Keel to Babette. "I'd be proud to have you as a member of my crew."

"It wasn't really difficult," answered Babette modestly. "You see, their attack was so **haphazard** and disorganized. It's easy to defeat a group as sloppy as that one."

"Not so easy, me hearty," said the captain. "But let's discuss that another time. Now we must make sure that the *Ruffian* is safely **moored** so she won't blow away in the storm. Come with me—your friends, too. My men will secure the ship while we board the schooner. I think you'll be surprised at what we find there."

Surprise was not the word to describe what they felt; sadness and **despair** were more like it. The schooner's cabins were packed full of rare and unusual animals that were being kept in **wretched** conditions. Every **berth** contained at least two creatures, and the floors were completely covered with straw and **muck,** and looked like they hadn't been cleaned in weeks. The poor animals, frightened by the fighting, were bleating, howling, crying, and scurrying around in a **frenzy.**

"Captain Keel," said Bridget with horror, "I can't even find the words to tell you how much I **deplore** what you've done to these poor animals."

"Child, I'm as **appalled** as you are," said the captain, shaking his head. "This little schooner is far too small to **accommodate** all of these animals comfortably. These animals were perfectly healthy when I kept them. It looks like these cramped, dirty conditions have caused their health to **deteriorate** drastically."

Beauregard had begun to walk through the cabins. He stopped to look at the dodo bird from Australia and the indri from Madagascar. He paused by the bunk of the duck-billed platypus and the three-toed sloth. Dangerous **predators,** like the mountain lion and the polar bear, welcomed him and didn't seem interested in eating him at all. The big black cat even walked to the kitchen to check on the butterflies who were shut in the **scullery.** The animals all seemed comforted by his presence.

"But why did you capture all of these animals?" asked Barnaby.

"Well now, I'll tell you, but you probably won't believe me," the captain started. "You see, I was visited by a strange being from the heavens who came down and told me that many of these animals were being hunted and killed to the point that they were becoming nearly **extinct.** He told me that the environment was in danger of . . ."

"Keelhaul!" boomed a deep voice from the deck above. "Are you down there? Where are my animals?"

Bridget, Barnaby, and Babette exchanged **perplexed** glances. They were not sure what to think. Could it be Gorgas? Had he returned for them? What did he want with the animals?

"Quick, quick, now, let's all get up on deck," urged Captain Keel with fear in his voice.

The children followed the captain up the ladder and onto the deck. Standing or hovering near the mast was an alien with a huge green head, ten tentacles, and a dozen blinking eyes. The purple cape he wore flapped in the stiff evening breeze.

"Gorgas!" shouted Bridget. "What do you mean by sending us back three hundred years? That was not very polite!"

"Excuse me?" asked the alien. "Did you just call me Gorgas? How insulting. I am Vargas, a far wiser being. The fact that you have only two eyes must affect your ability to see clearly. Gorgas's hair is an unattractive black color, while mine, you will notice, is a fashionable and distinguished white."

The alien tilted his huge head to display a long mane of **hoary** hair.

"Vargas, sir, I was just explaining your plan to save the endangered ecosystems of the world to these crew members," offered the captain. "Why don't you tell them about all of the natural communities of animals and plants you will be preserving?"

"Ecosystem? What do I care about Earth's . . . oh, yes, that," said Vargas. "Well, there's been a slight change of plans, old boy. I'll tell you what, I'll still pay you those bars of gold, if you hand over one platypus and one of those birds whose feathers have that odd, pink **pigment.** I think they're called flamingos? Yes, I'd like a flamingo please."

Captain Keel climbed below the deck and returned with the animals. Vargas coiled his tentacles tightly around them.

"But what about the other animals, Vargas?" asked the captain.

"My dear fellow, that's your affair. I wouldn't dare tell you what to do with them," said Vargas. "Well, I hate to be **antisocial**—but I have more important things to do than sit around here chatting. Also, I need to use this boat, so I'm afraid you and all of the animals will have to jump overboard."

Vargas slithered over to Captain Keel and knocked him over the edge of the ship. He was heading toward Barnaby when a stampede of animals came rushing out from under the deck in a tidal wave of feathers and fur with Beauregard leading them! Vargas was so taken **aback** that he dropped the platypus and the flamingo.

Beauregard wasted no time. He jumped straight at the surprised alien's head!

Vargas was either sweating or **secreting** something slippery from his scalp, because I had a terrible time hanging on. But no matter. I only needed to keep my grip for a couple of seconds; just long enough for Popo the bandicoot to do his job.

A bandicoot, in case you don't know, is a rather large East Indian rat. And what, you might well ask, was I doing in cahoots with a rat? Ordinary cats, I must admit, do not look fondly upon rats and their **brethren,** mice. But I am a free-thinking cat, and I try to view all animals equally. Even dogs. Besides, it was Popo who came up with the plan to steal Vargas's wand. Apparently, the little bandicoot had once seen Vargas pull a stick just like Gorgas's out from under his cape. My job was to distract the alien while Popo scrambled under his cape to fetch it.

At first, Vargas was so upset that Barnaby was clinging to his head that Popo had no trouble scurrying under his cape in search of the wand, and he slipped off as soon as he had scrambled safely away. Babette, always quick and as **nimble** as an acrobat, flipped across the deck with lightning speed and sent Vargas flying into the sea with one of her kicks. As soon as we were free of the alien, Popo, who assured me that he knew exactly what he was doing, began waving the wand.

The schooner slowly rose out of the water and into the air. The strong winds from the coming storm blew around us, **circulating** faster and faster. Before we knew it, we were caught up in a funnel of wind. And there was no telling where the **cyclone** would drop us.

✍ QUIZ #11 ✎
Relationships

Decide what relationship the following pairs of words have to each other. If they have similar meanings, write "S" next to the pair of words. If they have opposite meanings, write "O" next to the words.

1. ruffian : desperado   _____

2. disperse : amass   _____

3. appall : please   _____

4. musket : rifle   _____

5. connoisseur : novice   _____

6. perplex : mystify   _____

7. expletive : curse   _____

8. adage : motto   _____

9. deteriorate : improve   _____

10. brethren : siblings   _____

11. scourge : savior   _____

12. antisocial : friendly   _____

✍ QUIZ #12 ✍
Relationships

Decide what relationship the following pairs of words have to each other. If they have similar meanings, write "S" next to the pair of words. If they have opposite meanings, write "O" next to the words.

1. regiment : garrison   _____

2. extinct : thriving   _____

3. wistful : yearning   _____

4. pact : treaty   _____

5. prevail : fail   _____

6. flabbergasted : composed   _____

7. predator : prey   _____

8. rasping : scratching   _____

9. muck : slime   _____

10. nimble : clumsy   _____

11. despair : hopelessness   _____

12. repugnant : attractive   _____

Fill in the Blank

For each sentence below, choose the word that best completes the sentence.

1. I thought the seaside cottage looked beautiful, although we did have to replace the _____ on the roof before we moved in.

   a. bungalow   b. verandah

   c. thatch   d. scullery

2. Believing the fish to be swimming closer to the bottom than usual, the fishermen _____ their nets deeper than they would usually.

   a. confronted   b. deployed

   c. exerted   d. grappled

3. Spending thirty minutes outside building a snowman with my family gave my face a _____ glow.

   a. ruddy   b. mangy

   c. scrawny   d. hoary

4. Luckily for the bank teller, the _____ caused when the robber's bullet hit the bank vault, a camera, and a potted plant eventually ended up striking the burglar's own arm.

   a. volley   b. muzzle

   c. ricochet   d. plumage

5. I had hoped to _____ my new magazine all over the world, but unfortunately only my parents seemed interested in reading it.

    a. bombard   b. gnash
    c. circulate   d. extricate

6. After the powder keg exploded, the only evidence left that there was once a raft at all were some pieces of torn sail and _____.

    a. buccaneer   b. schooner
    c. figurehead   d. flotsam

7. Because the vessels in the Lithuanian _____ outnumbered their enemy by nine to one, the Lithuanians were almost certain of their upcoming victory.

    a. galleon   b. armada
    c. blockade   d. heist

8. Because the next convenience store was 173 miles away, my brother and I decided to _____ our supply of Twinkies for the road trip.

    a. replenish   b. besiege
    c. flout   d. bellow

9. After the last-second touchdown, the _____ fans rushed the field and began tearing down the goalposts.

    a. vivid   b. wretched
    c. adjacent   d. frenzied

10. Fearing high winds and a possible hurricane, we _____ our boat to the pier with the strongest rope we could find.

        a. incinerated   b. unfurled

        c. conceded   d. moored

11. When Sally saw that her blind date was made of papier-mâché, she knew that she was the victim of a horrible _____.

        a. ruse   b. lout

        c. gale   d. midst

12. Chris was embarrassed by his sister at school because she _____ a horrible scent whenever someone made her angry.

        a. secreted   b. deplored

        c. reeled   d. hobbled

✍ QUIZ #14 ✍
Matching

Match each word on the right with the letter on the left that has a similar meaning.

1. nigh   A. view
2. cinders   B. joint disease
3. vista   C. water passage
4. doleful   D. environment
5. ecosystem   E. violation
6. utmost   F. almost
7. rheumatism   G. manner

8. accommodate   H. ash
9. inlet   I. help
10. transgression   J. bind
11. bearing   K. bright glow
12. predicament   L. sad
13. radiance   M. greatest degree

🖎 QUIZ #15 🖎
Matching

Match each word on the right with the letter on the left that has a similar meaning.

1. aback   A. secret supply
2. cache   B. discouraged
3. expanse   C. twister
4. pigment   D. surprised
5. teem   E. law breaker
6. haphazard   F. swarm
7. daunted   G. ship bed
8. assessment   H. open space
9. reparations   I. analysis
10. cyclone   J. prankster
11. perpetrator   K. dye
12. berth   L. repayment
13. rascal   M. disorganized

Chapter 4

Dr. Borges and the Library of the Infinite Fiction

Where we wound up was unlike any place or time I had ever seen. At first it looked like we had been sucked into a **void.** I thought we were back in outer space, but then I realized that there were no stars. We knew one thing for sure, and that was that we weren't anywhere on Earth. There was nothing **terrestrial** about it.

The schooner was drifting through the black emptiness and we all waited in silence, wondering whether we had been plunged into a deep **abyss** or hurled to the absolute end of the universe. Then, in the distance, a large, glowing object appeared. It was a tower, a huge ivory tower that far exceeded any tower we'd ever seen. It was covered in **exquisitely** beautiful and **elaborately** detailed carvings of flowers, animals, and historical scenes. Their detail was amazing; the art was more breathtaking than the work of Earth's greatest masters. We were drifting right toward it, which caused us all great alarm; there didn't appear to be any door or other means of access to the tower, and I feared that we would just crash straight into it.

Everyone aboard the ship, including the animals, stood as still as statues, **transfixed** with wonder and fright. Just as we were about to smash into the tower, my tail began twitching in uncontrollable **spasms.** I tried unsuccessfully to stifle a yowl of fright that was threatening to escape my throat and there I stood, twitching and yowling rather embarrassingly while everyone else hit the deck and covered their heads.

But at the last moment a **rift** appeared in the tower. It was a narrow **fissure,** but its dimensions were such that we were just able to fit through it. I heaved a mighty sigh and stopped screeching. My terror was **quelled**—for the moment, that is.

🙶 🙶 🙶 🙶 🙶

"**W**hoa!" yelled Bridget, with relief. "I thought we were going to have to **evacuate** the ship!"

"What good would it have done to jump off?" asked Barnaby, who, like Bridget, was still lying down on the deck. "There would have been nowhere else to go!"

"On the **contrary,** young man!" echoed a strange voice.

Barnaby, Babette, and Bridget stood up and looked around them. They were in the most gigantic library they'd ever seen. There were shelves that spiraled like corkscrews along the walls as far up as they could see, but this library was not neat and orderly like any libraries they had visited before.

The shelves were extremely **cluttered;** they were crammed with a random arrangement of papers, notes, magazines, postcards, and books. Creeping, flowering vines and other plants were growing out of the shelves, and on some shelves the **foliage** was so thick that you couldn't even see what was on them. But the strangest thing was that the whole library

was in **flux,** objects were changing and moving around them at all times. New papers appeared on shelves as others disappeared, some books became thinner while others grew fat, or all of the contents of one shelf would suddenly move to another. A flower suddenly blossomed with amazing speed: The three friends felt dizzy just looking around.

"Uh, what do you mean, on the contrary?" asked Barnaby, determined to keep hold of himself this time.

"I mean that what you said before is quite wrong," replied the voice in a **peculiar** accent. "The reason that I **contradict** what you said is because if you *had* jumped off of the ship, there would have been somewhere to go, which is here! But I don't mean to be **contentious.** I do hate to **quibble** or argue."

"Who are you, where are you, and where are we?" asked Babette.

"Patience, please. I'm coming down," said the voice, which did sound a little closer.

Babette looked up. Something was rustling along one of the shelves above her, and slowly circling down the spiral. Finally they saw a man rumbling toward them on a rolling library ladder, which was attached at the top to a smooth, shiny brass rail that was **burnished** by many years of use. It came to a halt beside the ship and the man jumped off.

At first glance, he looked very old. He had a
long, pointy white beard and although his
hairline had **receded,** he still sported a shock
of bushy, white hair. He looked oddly familiar
to Babette. He wore a rumpled, brown tweed
jacket and thick glasses that were pushed
down low on his nose. His face was wrinkled,
but the way he jumped off the ladder and
walked toward them was so **spry** that it
seemed like he couldn't be as ancient as they
had at first thought.

"My, my," he remarked, "I am surprised you
could travel in such a **dilapidated** ship. You
really should take better care of it. It's
practically falling apart!"

"It's not really our ship," offered Bridget.

"Ah, yes, you're the pirates then," said the
man, stroking his beard.

"Well, not exactly, but sort of, I guess," said Bridget. "My name is Bridget, and these are my friends, Babette, Barnaby, and Beauregard. I'm afraid I don't know any of the names of the other animals. We just rescued them."

"Lovely!" exclaimed the man. "My name is Dr. Borges, and this is my library. Do you mind if I come aboard and visit the animals? I so rarely get visitors."

Dr. Borges did not wait for permission. He climbed onto the deck with ease, and began to chatter, click, whinny, and hoot like a lunatic at every animal he saw. He kept it up for quite a while and the animals seemed to find him very amusing.

"He seems to be **fluent** in the language of every animal!" remarked Babette with admiration. "It must have been hard to master so many languages."

"Wonderful!" laughed Dr. Borges as he approached the three children. "That little flamingo **fledgling** over there—that little one just old enough to fly—just told the funniest joke about a chicken crossing a road. It's amazing that he has such a sense of humor after what they've all been through. Those dragonfly **larvae** were **ailing** from sea sickness."

"How can you talk to larvae?" asked Barnaby. "They aren't even fully developed insects yet."

"You should be the last person to doubt that young creatures have opinions," replied Dr. Borges. "Most **organisms,** from tiny bugs to giant whales, have opinions. In any event, the main complaint from these fellows is that they've been taken from their homes and are finding their new surroundings uncomfortable. They're glad that you rescued them, of course, but they are still unhappy to be so far away from their homes.

"That polar bear, for example, is from the icy **tundra** of the arctic with its vast plains of snow. The Caribbean sun was melting him! And that poor sheep was beginning to shed all of her beautiful **fleece** in the heat."

"It is a lucky thing that we came along," agreed Barnaby. "I also noticed that the animals from **arid,** desert climates weren't reacting well to the dark and damp in the hull of the ship. It's very difficult for an animal to **thrive** outside of its normal climate."

Just then, a tiny canary **alighted** on Dr. Borges's shoulder and twittered something in his ear.

"Yes, I suppose you must be curious about the library," said the librarian in response.

"Curious? Yes, we are curious too," Babette said eagerly. "Dr. Borges, just standing here in your library has been a very strange experience. I believe I am suffering from

delusions. My eyes might be playing tricks on me, but it seems like your tower is growing and changing all around us!"

"I have noticed that as well," added Barnaby, "but I can't even begin to **fathom** what might be causing it."

Meanwhile, Bridget, who was always very easily distracted, had wandered off and was poking around in some of the bookshelves.

"Hey, Doc!" she called. "This is quite a **copious** collection you have. I've never seen so many different kinds of books; you have very **eclectic** tastes in literature; there are biographies, histories, medical books, essays, college term papers, letters, and tons of great **fiction.** I think fiction is my favorite **genre.** I mean, poetry and plays and factual books are fine and all, but made-up stories are the best kind."

"Well, my collection might seem eclectic, but this is actually not an accurate representation of my tastes," explained Dr. Borges. "This library is just a **cumulative** collection from my lifetime."

"You mean that stuff keeps getting added to it?" asked Bridget.

"That's exactly what you see going on around you," he said, nodding. "Additions are being made to some volumes when new knowledge is gained, and information that has been proved to be inaccurate is being removed from other volumes. The **philosophy** section is always growing the fastest. It seems people never tire of writing about the meaning of life and truth and all that. New volumes might be added to a series, or a new chapter **appended** to an old book. Most things seem to get longer and more detailed—rarely are things **abridged.** Actually, that introduces an interesting **paradox,** which I have wondered about ever so long."

"What kind of paradox?" asked Bridget with interest.

"You see, this is the Library of the **Infinite** Fiction. It's infinite because it's endless; it goes on forever. It has existed forever, here on the edge of time and space, and contains a record of all the thoughts and experiences that have ever occurred in the whole universe. Everything that has ever been written, everything that you can even imagine being written, is here. Even things that haven't been written yet are here," said the librarian. "And yet, it keeps growing."

"Hey, it can't be infinite *and* be growing at the same time," Barnaby said, thinking out loud, "because something that's infinite already extends far beyond the realm of the imagination in size."

"That's the paradox! An infinite, yet growing library—it contradicts itself," exclaimed Bridget. "It's a paradox just like that old song that goes, *'You've got to be cruel to be kind.'*"

Bridget began singing the song and dancing around wildly, and Dr. Borges immediately joined her, singing in a **reedy** voice that squeaked like a clarinet. Bridget started in on the second verse while running and doing cartwheels, but Borges begged her to stop.

"Please, I **implore** you, no more," gasped the librarian, who was turning red in the face. "Not that I don't like your singing, but I'm afraid I find it impossible to **repress** the urge to dance whenever I hear music. I just can't stop myself. The problem is, I'm not used to dancing anymore. Whew! Give me a couple of minutes to **recuperate**. I'm beat."

Bridget stopped her **romping**. She was still giggly and excited about the paradox, but out of respect for the old librarian, she tried to appear **tranquil**. After a few seconds, however, her curiosity got the better of her.

"Dr. Borges, what did you mean when you called this the Library of the Infinite *Fiction*? There's a lot more than fiction here," asked Bridget.

"The explanation is a bit complicated, but I'll try to make it clear," he began, as his face started to become a normal color again. "You see, the history of time and all of the events in the universe are like a big story. And, in a way, we all make it up as we go along. Or, if you look at it another way, we are all characters in the story that's unfolding. Either way, it's an unending tale."

"You're right, that is a **convoluted** explanation," said Barnaby suspiciously. "Is that another one of your paradoxes? We are characters and authors at the same time? Why don't you tell us what's *really* going on?"

"Barnaby, there is no need to be **insolent**," whispered Babette. "Show a little respect for your elders. A man as smart as he is deserves some **reverence**."

Dr. Borges smiled an **indulgent** smile, as if Barnaby's little outburst amused him more than it offended him.

"It seems I would have a hard time making a **disciple** out of you!" laughed the librarian. "You wouldn't want to be a follower of an old man who can't even provide a **coherent** explanation of how his own home operates. Such a sharp scientific mind you have! However, young man, there are more ways to study the universe than merely looking at tiny **molecules** of matter under microscopes."

"There are no events so strange, no facts so odd, no **phenomena** so weird that science can't come up with a workable explanation for them," **asserted** Barnaby with confidence, even stomping his foot to make his point more **emphatic.**

"Well, now, Barnaby, I'd have to agree that scientists can come up with **viable** explanations for a lot of things," smiled Dr. Borges. "I'm sure you can **cite** many examples to prove your point—as you see it. I admire the strength of your **convictions.** It's good to have strong beliefs, and I wouldn't want to be accused of trying to **debunk** yours. You know, you remind me of a boy I once knew, long, long ago."

Dr. Borges sighed and shook his bushy head.

"Anyway, why don't we just call my explanations **avant-garde,** okay? I am, after all, always slightly ahead of my time," he said. "For the sake of simplicity, let's just say that some of the books in this library are **prophetic.** They tell of events that have not happened yet. I was just reading one a little while ago, which is how I found out that a pirate ship was heading my way. That's how I knew to open the tower. But the book contained other **revelations** that I must tell you about. For example, the book revealed that you and your friend Beauregard must rescue Earth from destruction! More than once, in fact."

"Wait a minute, now, Dr. Borges," said Bridget. "We're just kids. I can't imagine a possible **scenario** that would involve us saving the world. Are you sure that revelation was reliable?"

"I am absolutely certain of its **authenticity,**" replied Dr. Borges. "Do you, or do you not, know of a couple of ten-armed travelers named Gorgas and Vargas?"

"Uh oh," said Barnaby. "I'm almost afraid to hear this."

"Maybe we should have gone to the Metropolitan Museum of Art instead of the Yankees game," groaned Bridget.

The librarian continued, "You see, Gorgas and Vargas are the bitterest of rivals. They used to be private investigators back on their home planet of Smeltvlat. People from planets all around would hire them to track down lost people and property. But what started as simple professional competition turned into a **monstrous,** horrible battle that has spread ruin and **devastation** across many planets. They began betting with each other, challenging each other with impossible tasks that were designed to prove which one was the best at tracking down rare and unique things; they would stop at nothing to win these bets. The people of Smeltvlat finally got sick of their games and kicked them off of the planet. Now these dangerous **pariahs** are looking for a new world to call home."

Babette, Bridget, and Barnaby listened with horror.

"Sure, at first their little scavenger hunts were harmless," Dr. Borges went on. "But gradually, Gorgas and Vargas both developed a taste for power and wealth, as you have already seen.

Unfortunately for the people of Earth, they've decided that your planet is full of the weirdest plants, animals, sports, food, clothes, and customs in the whole universe. They have agreed that the one who can capture the most bizarre specimens in the shortest amount of time will win the right to rule Earth."

"I told you that Gorgas was after world **dominion**!" shrieked Babette.

Bridget and Banaby were too shocked to speak.

"I know that this is a lot to chew on," said the librarian. "You must believe that Gorgas and Vargas would never give up this battle. Either of them would rather destroy your planet than turn it over to his rival. But you will have a hard time stopping them. Yes, a very hard time. Most, most difficult . . ."

Dr. Borges scratched his head and paced.

"It is a good thing that Popo thought to steal that wand from Vargas," he said, still pacing and scratching. "You'll need a way to travel back and forth through time. They could be anywhere. Let's see, I had something around

here that might help you. Maybe I left it in this **nook** over here. Let me see . . ."

"How can there be a hidden corner in a circular building?" asked Babette.

Barnaby just shrugged. He wasn't about to start worrying about contradictions again.

"Nope," mumbled the librarian. "Hey, maybe I . . . ouch! My foot!"

Babette and Bridget almost fell over with surprise. A long metal tube, shining with a soft golden **luster,** had just fallen out of Dr. Borges's hair and hit his foot.

"Hey, I know how you feel," laughed Barnaby, patting his own mop of hair as the librarian hopped on one foot.

"Aha! Here it is," said Dr. Borges, stooping down to pick up the tube. "It's a **kaleidoscope,** you see, but not an ordinary one. With most kaleidoscopes, you look in one end and twist the tube and see beautiful shapes and colors shifting around together. But this one shows you different places and people shifting around together. It shows you the future, and sometimes the shapes and colors aren't that beautiful. Here, give it a try!"

He handed the tube to Barnaby, who held it up to the light and twisted the bottom. At first, he saw nothing but smoke and clouds. But slowly a figure began to **manifest** itself. It was Gorgas! He was slithering up the side of a steaming volcano. But he wasn't the only big green monster that the kaleidoscope showed.

"I don't know if this will sound **plausible** to you," said Barnaby, placing the tube on a shelf, "but you have to believe me because it's true. Gorgas is back in the time of the dinosaurs. I have no idea what he's up to, but we'd better stop him."

Beauregard, who had been having a wonderful deck party with his animal friends, picked up the kaleidoscope and looked for himself. He returned to visit with Popo the bandicoot briefly, then returned to his human friends.

And in his mouth was Popo's magic wand.

✍ QUIZ #16 ✎
Relationships

Decide what relationship the following pairs of words have to each other. If they have similar meanings, write "S" next to the pair of words. If they have opposite meanings, write "O" next to the words.

1. recede : shrink _____
2. elaborate : plain _____
3. plausible : likely _____
4. thrive : devastate _____
5. stifle : repress _____

6. fiction : reality   _____

7. contentious : congenial   _____

8. assert : contend   _____

9. dilapidated : exquisite   _____

10. contrary : stubborn   _____

✍ QUIZ #17 ✍
Relationships

Decide what relationship the following pairs of words have to each other. If they have similar meanings, write "S" next to the pair of words. If they have opposite meanings, write "O" next to the words.

1. pariah : outcast   _____

2. ailing : recuperating   _____

3. infinite : boundless   _____

4. quibble : bicker   _____

5. tranquil : agitated   _____

6. coherent : chaotic   _____

7. fissure : rift   _____

8. insolent : courteous   _____

9. reverence : disgust   _____

10. avant-garde : innovative   _____

✍ QUIZ #18 ✍
Fill in the Blank

For each sentence below, choose the word that best completes the sentence.

1. The scientists hoped their new invention could use electricity to extract all the _____ of gold from sea water.

   a. molecules   b. organisms

   c. foliage   d. fleeces

2. Although many researchers had already _____ his idea as pure make-believe, Professor Strock still insisted his "Gravity-is-a-Lie" theory was true.

   a. implored   b. abridged

   c. debunked   d. transfixed

3. Difficult as it was, climbing out of the north side of the canyon was the only _____ option for escape, because the enemy army was advancing from the other three directions.

   a. convoluted   b. indulgent

   c. spry   d. viable

4. Once the rash began to _____ themselves all over Tina's face, the doctors knew for certain that she had the chicken pox.

   a. manifest   b. romp

   c. cite   d. burnish

5. Police _____ the initial riot that began in the plaza, but by the end of the day the mob had come to life again and overrun the entire city.

    a. alighted   b. quelled

    c. appended   d. contradicted

6. All the lights in the building continued to flicker on and off due to the _____ in the city's electrical supply.

    a. genre   b. tundra

    c. flux   d. abyss

7. After retiring from her job, Viola started playing racquetball for eight hours a day to fill the _____ created in her daily routine.

    a. dimension   b. paradox

    c. void   d. phenomena

8. We packed extra canteens of water because we knew we were about to hike across one of the most _____ regions of the country.

    a. terrestrial   b. copious

    c. eclectic   d. arid

9. "Do as little as you possibly can" is Brannart's _____ about work, which explains why he has been fired from over 2,000 jobs.

    a. scenario   b. philosophy

    c. dominion   d. larvae

10. After shooting a hole-in-one the first time she ever picked up a golf club, Shanice showed that she had potential even though she was a _____ player.

    a. elaborate   b. emphatic

    c. peculiar   d. fledgling

11. The dictator's _____ were so strong that he could not be convinced that cutting down all the trees in the region would hurt the environment.

    a. delusions   b. spasms

    c. convictions   d. rifts

12. Melissa's room was so _____ that she had to use a bulldozer to clear a path from her front door to her bed.

    a. cluttered   b. dilapidated

    c. contrary   d. contentious

13. When we have a fire drill in our school building, all of the students and teachers are required to _____ the premises.

    a. evacuate   b. recede

    c. quibble   d. fathom

✍ QUIZ #19 ✎
Matching

Match each word on the right with the letter on the left that has a similar meaning.

1. clutter
2. kaleidoscope
3. luster
4. fledgling
5. access
6. fluent
7. monstrous
8. revelation
9. emphatic
10. disciple

A. admittance
B. shifting series of events
C. gigantic
D. forceful
E. pupil
F. sudden insight
G. gloss
H. baby bird
I. graceful
J. mess

✍ QUIZ #20 ✍
Matching

Match each word on the right with the letter on the left that has a similar meaning.

1. spasm	A. odd
2. peculiar	B. adding up
3. authentic	C. misconception
4. cumulative	D. predicting future events
5. reedy	E. beliefs
6. prophetic	F. muscle twitch
7. fathom	G. genuine
8. convictions	H. leave
9. evacuate	I. understand
10. delusion	J. thin

Chapter 5
Volcano of Doom

While Dr. Borges was meeting and mingling with the animals on the deck of the schooner, I overheard him telling them that all their **travails** were over. He assured them that he would put an end to their hardship and return them. all to their rightful times and places—after throwing a big party for them. Popo was happy to let us have the wand, even though it was actually his. He's such an **altruistic** bandicoot and is always putting the need of others before his own.

Barnaby took Vargas's wand from my hand, picked up the kaleidoscope, and turned to thank Dr. Borges for all his help—but that crazy librarian was busy dancing on the deck with a bunch of songbirds. He kind of reminded me of my Uncle Bojangles. When Bojangles heard music, he couldn't **refrain** from dancing either. I remember one time at a Christmas party back in South Carolina, he jitterbugged for nine hours straight, and everyone thought he must have drunk some of the water from under the tree. But actually, the band leader had . . . well, that's a story for another time.

As I was saying, Bridget, Babette, and I gathered around Barnaby while he moved the wand in small circles. We weren't exactly sure how to work the stick, so we all just concentrated on traveling back to the Mesozoic era, which was a period of time that took place over 180 million years ago. The Mesozoic era! Just thinking about it **evoked** pictures of terrifying dinosaurs roving aimlessly across a **stark,** grim land. Actually, I must admit, I didn't know what type of **terrain** to expect, but for some reason, I expected a lot of rocks and no trees.

But what I didn't expect was that traveling back in time would be so completely unsettling. At first, we just felt the hot, sticky air that we usually felt when the wand was doing its magic, and everything went black. But then we found ourselves flying in circles amidst a swirl of color and light, as a blaring noise, like jet engines and jack hammers, nearly deafened us. Every few seconds, a weird, ghost-like **apparition** of a person or animal would pop out of the swirl, look at us, and disappear. After that, things really got strange. It looked like Bridget, Babette, and Barnaby were being stretched like taffy. Their heads and legs started to **elongate,** then their chests started to **distend** and swell outward. I saw that my tail had stretched out several yards below me. Just as

I had thought we had been stretched until we would snap, something went "Pop!" and we found ourselves falling through the sky toward Earth.

"Bridget, I sure hope you are still chewing that gum of yours!" yelled Barnaby. "Because I clearly don't know how to work this wand, so we won't be getting any help right now from it!"

But Bridget was way ahead of him. She was already blowing a huge, pink bubble and waving her arms to tell her friends to grab on to her. Within seconds, the four of them were drifting downward at a comfortable speed under Bridget's bubble balloon.

"That settles it," huffed Babette as she grasped Bridget's left foot with both hands. "After this is over, no more traveling backward in time. I want to live in **chronological** order, so that the past is the past and the future is the future and we all know in which direction we're heading."

"I don't mind mentally **regressing** to my early childhood and playing with toys from time to time," agreed Barnaby, holding tight to Bridget's right leg. "That's fun. But really going back one or two hundred million years is not fun at all."

The unhappy travelers **slackened** their grips as they approached the ground and let themselves slip to the grass. Beauregard, who had been draped around Bridget's neck, came tumbling after them.

"Oof!" grunted Bridget, falling on top of the pile of her friends and sucking her gum back into her mouth.

She wiped her jeans off, put her hands on her hips, and scolded her friends gently.

"Complaining like this isn't going to get us anywhere, so you'd both better start thinking positively," she **admonished**. "Dr. Borges said we had to save the world, so let's get our acts together."

"Bridget is right," said Babette, who fluffed her hair and looked as fashionable as usual. "We have a serious mission, and we must **strive** with all our might to complete it."

"You know, this place is kind of odd," remarked Barnaby, as he looked around. "Do you notice anything?"

Babette and Bridget carefully looked over the **panorama** that presented itself to them. The view certainly was unusual. In the distance was an ocean. The land right around them was **lush;** it was absolutely covered in grass and flowering plants. They stood at the **summit** of a high hill and could see a long way in every direction. In the direction of the ocean they could see smoke rising from a volcanic island. On land, to their left, rose another mountain that was also smoking. Beneath them the ground rumbled softly.

"It seems like there are several volcanoes nearby," noted Bridget. "But we knew that already. I don't see any dinosaurs, but I can't say I'm unhappy about that."

"I know it's probably a small point, but volcanic activity was very common in the early part of the Mesozoic era, about 200 million years ago," explained Barnaby. "If I remember the latest scientific research, flowering plants and giant dinosaurs like the ones I saw in the kaleidoscope don't show up until much later: Like twenty or thirty million years later. But, hey, I'm more of a chemist that a dinosaur expert. I could be wrong."

"Let me ask you this, Barnaby," began Bridget. "Were scientists ever able to travel into the past to get **confirmation** of their hunches? Are they absolutely certain? Can they even give a **definitive** explanation for why the dinosaurs died out?"

"Well, there are some popular ideas about what happened. For example, we know that the climate changed dramatically and the dinosaurs couldn't adjust to it," replied Barnaby. "But we don't really know what caused that. Most explanations that scientists have are just **conjecture;** there's just not enough proof to support any one theory."

"It would seem that you're in a fine position to make some theories of your own," laughed Babette. "But you'll never get any of those **academic** friends of yours back at the university to believe that you actually traveled back in time and saw things for yourself."

Barnaby sighed, "Yes, those professors and scholars already consider me either insane or dangerously **incompetent** because I keep blowing things up. I tell them over and over that I know exactly what I'm doing and that I'm perfectly capable of conducting an experiment, but sometimes, in the name of science, risks must be taken in order for the common good to be served and the people of the world to be able to advance. It's like in kindergarten when Mrs. Chiz said . . ."

"Barnaby?" said Babette, nudging him with her elbow. "You're starting to **ramble** again."

"Sorry. I do tend to go on and on and get off track when I'm talking about my experiments," apologized Barnaby. "I really am sorry."

"Come on, Barnaby, there's no need for **contrition**," chirped Bridget. "We usually love listening to you yak. The only problem is that right now we have no time to lose. Something's terribly wrong here; there should be dinosaurs running all over the place. And for some reason, that volcano over there seems like the key to the mystery; something is **impelling** me to go check it out."

"Not some*thing*," giggled Babette, pointing. "Some*one*."

Bridget looked behind her to discover that Beauregard was indeed butting his head into her back to push her toward the volcano.

"Okay, I get the picture," said Bridget. "Let's get a move on."

Babette, Bridget, Beauregard, and Barnaby began a quick march over the hills toward the smoking volcano. As they drew closer, the smell of burning earth came **wafting** toward them on the wind. The beautiful greenery of the hills was **marred** here and there by long, ugly, black strips of **charred** land. The further they walked, the more the hills and smaller **knolls** were burned and **scorched,** and the warmer the air grew.

"That volcano must have blown its top pretty recently," remarked Barnaby. "Let's hope the eruptions are only **sporadic** and not regular."

"I'm with you," agreed Bridget nervously. "We have plenty to worry about, but I have to admit that my **principal** fear is that we're going to get blasted by this volcano."

"I have heard that they do start to rumble before they . . . hey!" said Babette, as they reached the top of another hill. "Do you see that down in the valley?"

In the valley below them and spilling up into the hills, hundreds of dinosaurs of all types had **congregated.** There were tyranosaurs and brontosaurs, and pterodactyl were swooping and perching all over the place. Every giant reptile for miles around must have been gathered there. They were making a lot of noise, but they seemed fairly peaceful, for dinosaurs.

"It doesn't look like they're in this valley to **forage** for food. Or to fight each other, either," observed Barnaby. "What on earth could they be doing here?"

His question was answered immediately. High on a rocky **crag,** just at the other end of the valley, Gorgas appeared, mane and purple cape flapping proudly in the breeze. The dinosaurs quieted quickly and looked at him.

"**Yonder** mountain is the Volcano of Doom!" his voice rang out across the crowd as he gestured with one tentacle to the volcano behind him.

His booming voice was so frightening that even the giant meat-eaters were **cowed** into respectful silence. Gorgas cleared his throat and blinked his many eyes thoughtfully.

"Uh oh, I think he's about to launch into an **oration**," said Bridget.

"Maybe his speech will give us a clue about what he's up to," added Babette. "Why don't we sneak around this side of the crowd and come up behind him and then take him by surprise?"

Bridget and Barnaby agreed. They began to make their way around the edge of the dinosaur mob as carefully and quietly as possible.

"Mighty dinosaurs," shouted Gorgas, "this pure, **pristine,** and untouched land is yours. Do you not want to keep it that way? You live in a blooming paradise of peace. But your **utopia** will become an **inferno** and you will all be burned to crisps, unless you listen to me. I have seen the future, and I see a great **cataclysm,** a horrible disaster, coming that will wipe out your entire population—unless you stop it, unless you do as I say!"

A low roar came from the crowd.

"Do as I say, or the creatures of the future will burn your remains for fuel!" he thundered again. "Your dead **carcasses** will be buried deep beneath the ground and millions of years from now these creatures, which are called humans, will call you **fossils** and use the oil and gas you turned into to fill their gas tanks and heat their homes. You will make for a rather nasty fuel, too, if you ask me, and messy, but, whoops, oh, no offense, that was not the point I wanted to **convey** at all. What am I trying to get across, again?"

"Looks like Gorgas rambles too," whispered Barnaby as they tip-toed along. "He'd better get to the point, these dinosaurs are already starting to look confused. Their brains are not very large, and they have trouble following complicated instructions."

"Oh, yes, yes," continued Gorgas, clearing his throat again. "Do you not wish to

proliferate and multiply in number, spreading young dinosaurs across the globe? If so, hear my plan. See that bright, glowing, orange river of hot, melted rock trickling down the side of the mountain?" He pointed behind him enthusiastically, "Well, that is the **magma** that will destroy you sooner or later unless we all work together to construct a large tube, like a U-shaped drinking straw. We'll stick one end in the volcano and the other end in the ocean and **siphon** all of the magma into the water! It could work! Or, if you think that's too hard, we could just **bore** a big hole in the side of the mountain and let most of the magma just spill out. Of course, that could get kind of messy. Anyway, the important thing is that you dinosaurs must take charge of this situation immediately. Yes, take the **initiative**! Bore the hole! Bore it today!"

The dinosaurs seemed **flustered,** nervous, and confused. Grunts of "Huh?" and "What is he talking about?" rose from the crowd. Ordinarily, Gorgas had the **charisma** and personality that was necessary to stir up a crowd. He had clearly studied the art of **rhetoric,** because his speech was well-structured and usually quite convincing, but this crowd just didn't seem to get his drift. Finally, a **stately,** dignified older brontosaur stepped forward and tried to clear things up.

"Dinosaurs, bore?" asked the huge, gentle creature.

Before Gorgas could think of a reply, Barnaby, Bridget, Babette, and Beauregard scrambled up onto the crag behind him.

"Hold it right there, Gorgas," warned Bridget. "Just what do you think you're doing?"

"Oh! Well, my dear, what a surprise!" yelped Gorgas. "Um, I was just doing a small experiment. I had heard that dinosaurs were not the most **industrious** reptiles, and I wanted to see what it would take to make them better, harder workers. I call it my Mesozoic **motivation** project—I really want to get the reptiles going, give them something to do. All for the sake of science, of course."

"Aw, come off it, Gorgas," scoffed Bridget. "We know all about your competition with Vargas. What we can't figure out is why you are trying to **induce** these dinosaurs to drain the volcano into the ocean. Don't you realize what kind of disaster that would cause?"

"Vargas? Vargas is a **scoundrel** and a villain and a cheat!" insisted Gorgas. "Whatever he told you is a lie. What did he tell you?"

"He told us nothing. We found out on our own," said Babette. "We discovered your plans to gather strange specimens and rule the world, and we know why you and Vargas were **exiled** from the planet Smeltvlat. There's no sense in denying it. And we are here to tell you that you might as well give up. We will make sure that you never succeed!"

In the valley below, the dinosaurs grumbled impatiently.

"Dinosaurs, bore?" repeated the old brontosaur slowly, but loudly.

"My goodness, such **meddlesome** children," said the alien, shaking his head and taking no notice of the crowd of reptiles. "Why can't you stay out of my affairs? Well, if you must know, Vargas was ahead of me in gathering odd creatures, so I knew I had to do something out of the ordinary. I decided to do a little research into the **DNA** of you Earth creatures. DNA, you see, is like a tiny handbook made out of chemicals. It's inside each and every one of the cells in your body. DNA explains how you developed and how you work. I knew that giant reptiles once roamed this planet, and I figured that these ancient reptiles were the **predecessors** of all modern Earth creatures. I just couldn't understand why so few of you had reptile **traits,** like cold blood and scaly skin. Then I took apart the DNA and looked at the **genes.** Your genes come from your parents and grandparents. And eventually it was pretty clear to me that dinosaurs had nothing to do with humans, or cats, or polar bears. Or bandicoots, for that matter."

"All I can figure, the only reasonable **inference** I can make about why you are talking to these dinosaurs, is that you want to save them from dying out so that their genes will survive into modern times. If dinosaurs survive into modern times, then there's no telling what might happen," said Barnaby, scratching his head in puzzlement. "But why drain the volcano? What good would that do, unless . . . oh! I see! Scientists know that a shift in climate wiped out the dinosaurs. You think that these volcanic eruptions are spewing enough dust and ash into the air to cause that shift! And you want to stop the volcanoes to keep the dinosaurs alive!"

"It doesn't take a super-intelligent being to know that there is a **correlation** between high volcanic activity and large changes in climate," remarked Gorgas. "Any fool would notice the connection."

"Gorgas, I certainly don't mean to be rude, but you have come up with the silliest **notion** I have ever heard," said Bridget, rolling her eyes. "How did you think of such a half-baked idea? If you drain all the magma into the seas, the sea creatures will die, the water will dry up, all of the plants will die so that the dinosaurs will have nothing to eat, and then they'll all die, and the . . . then . . . then Earth will be nothing but a dried up hunk of rock!"

Bridget's eyes opened wide as she realized how horrible Gorgas's plan really was. Gorgas noticed her shock and laughed his threatening, **baleful** chuckle.

"But, Gorgas, this must not be!" wailed Babette. "Earth is a beautiful planet filled with so much life! You must not destroy it!"

"Calm yourself, my dear, there is no need to get all **sentimental** and emotional just yet;" said Gorgas. "Bridget does not know for sure that the oceans will dry up. Perhaps there will be enough water, and the dinosaurs will live on. In that case, strange new creatures will appear in the future, and I will win the contest. If the planet does dry up, well, that's a pity. But at least Vargas won't win, either."

Barnaby kept scratching his head and thinking as he whispered to Bridget, "We need a plan, and fast. These dinosaurs are getting cranky, and Gorgas doesn't seem to have control of them at all. Wait! That's it! Now if only we had a loudspeaker or a **megaphone** so that they could all hear me."

"Um, Barnaby," whispered Bridget. "What is that big cone-shaped thing sticking out of your hair?"

Barnaby patted his hair and, sure enough, discovered a megaphone sticking out of it.

"Great! I thought I had one of these around somewhere!" said Barnaby. "Quick, Bridget, Babette, Beauregard, jump down into that deep **crevice.** That crack in the rocks is the perfect place to hide. I think we're going to need some protection."

All of the friends quickly followed Barnaby and huddled together.

"Now," explained the young scientist. "I hope this works. Have you noticed that the dinosaurs are nervous and excited? They don't understand what Gorgas said, but I think they are ready for some kind of action. All that brontosaur seemed to get out of Gorgas's speech was the word 'bore.' It looks like the dinosaurs think that Gorgas is calling them boring."

"That's not very nice," remarked Babette.

"No, it isn't," agreed Barnaby. "But I think I can use that misunderstanding to get the dinosaurs to take care of Gorgas for us. All I need is a simple message that they can understand. But I'll have to be a pretty good **ventriloquist** to pull this one off."

"Is that what the megaphone is for? You are going to say something and make it look like it's Gorgas who's talking?" asked Babette.

"That's the idea," he said. "I just hope I can do a good enough job faking his voice. Well, here goes . . ."

Barnaby cleared his throat, paused for a moment to think, then held the megaphone to his mouth.

"Dinosaurs! Dinosaurs hear me!" boomed Barnaby. "Dinosaurs bad. Dinosaurs stupid. Dinosaurs boring. Hate dinosaurs. Dinosaur bore! Dinosaur bore!"

A chorus of roars rang out in the valley. The dinosaurs began to get the message. And as far as they were concerned, Gorgas was insulting them. The giant brontosaur, no longer gentle, moved forward and hip-checked the crag with his tough **flank.** Barnaby, Babette, Bridget, and Beauregard covered their heads as rocks and dirt fell around them. Again the brontosaur rammed his side into the crag, and this time, the rock was **jarred** so violently that Gorgas went tumbling into the crowd of angry reptiles. It looked like he was done for.

The children and Beauregard had to sit still for some time while the angry roars and stomping continued. Barnaby even had time to **ruminate,** which was one of his favorite activities. The thing he was **musing** about this time was the fate of the poor dinosaurs.

"You know," he began, "I feel sorry for these dinosaurs. Maybe they understood a little more of what Gorgas said than we think they did. Maybe they know now that some day— millions of years from now, but still some day—their kind will disappear. I do feel some **empathy** for them. After all, for a while there, I knew just what it felt like to worry about disappearing. It was like I felt what they felt."

"I feel kind of bad, too," said Bridget. "But in all of the science fiction movies I watch, the most important **directive** time travelers get is that they should not change the things that happen in the past, because there's no telling how it will affect the future. Speaking of which, we should get out of here before we accidentally change history."

Barnaby nodded sadly and pulled the wand out of his pocket, but he didn't get a chance to use it. Before he could even wave it in one circle, Babette, Bridget, Beauregard, and he were caught up in a whirlwind of light and noise like the one they'd traveled in before. And they had a pretty good idea of who was controlling this one.

✍ QUIZ #21 ✍
Relationships

Decide what relationship the following pairs of words have to each other. If they have similar meanings, write "S" next to the pair of words. If they have opposite meanings, write "O" next to the words.

1. scoundrel : rogue _____

2. academic : uneducated _____

3. cataclysm : devastation _____

4. lush : stark _____

5. motivate : discourage _____

6. muse : ruminate _____

7. proliferate : decrease _____

8. charisma : appeal _____

9. bore : burrow _____

10. pristine : marred _____

✍ QUIZ #22 ✍
Relationships

Decide what relationship the following pairs of words have to each other. If they have similar meanings, write "S" next to the pair of words. If they have opposite meanings, write "O" next to the words.

1. elongate : distend   _____
2. char : scorch   _____
3. industrious : lazy   _____
4. stately : humble   _____
5. oration : speech   _____
6. congregate : scatter   _____
7. fluster : soothe   _____
8. empathy : identification   _____
9. rhetoric : eloquence   _____
10. contrite : proud   _____

✍ QUIZ #23 ✍
Fill in the Blank

For each sentence below, choose the word that best completes the sentence.

1. Despite all his kind requests, Farmer Jones was unable to _____ his sheep into leaving the north meadow.

   a. impel   b. mingle

   c. slacken   d. cow

2. Because a fine layer of moss covered all the tiny pebbles along the riverbank, we were extra careful when crossing the slippery _____.

   a. utopia   b. panorama

   c. terrain   d. inferno

3. A professor at the local university told Wilhelm that the _____ he found in the cave was the leg bone of a Tyrannosaurus Rex.

   a. fossil   b. carcass

   c. gene   d. DNA

4. The walls of the city, which were four hundred feet high and twenty feet deep, were the _____ line of defense against foreign invaders

   a. chronological   b. principal

   c. sentimental   d. altruistic

5. Because the twenty-four ounce strawberry smoothie tasted so good, it was difficult for Jim to _____ from drinking it all at once.

      a. jar   b. convey

      c. flank   d. refrain

6. My father would _____ about the weather for hours until mom hushed him because it was his favorite topic.

      a. strive   b. ramble

      c. rove   d. exile

7. It was a hard climb, but when we reached the _____ of Mount Fuji, the view from the top was worth it.

      a. crag   b. knoll

      c. summit   d. crevice

8. The _____ look from the class bully scared Christian so much that he decided to beat himself up rather that face the bully on the playground.

      a. incompetent   b. sporadic

      c. meddlesome   d. baleful

9. Although the lawn mower was out of fuel, we used a _____ to get gas out of pickup's tank so we could mow the front lawn.

      a. predecessor   b. megaphone

      c. ventriloquist   d. siphon

✍ QUIZ #24 ✍

Matching

Match each word on the right with the letter on the left that has a similar meaning.

1. magma	A. ghost
2. conjecture	B. lava
3. yonder	C. cause to happen
4. induce	D. guess
5. apparition	E. idea
6. definitive	F. go backward
7. notion	G. characteristic
8. regress	H. at a distance
9. inference	I. conclusion
10. trait	J. conclusive

✍ QUIZ #25 ✎
Matching

Match each word on the right with the letter
on the left that has a similar meaning.

1. forage	A.	connection
2. travail	B.	first step
3. era	C.	period of time
4. waft	D.	order
5. correlation	E.	proof
6. evoke	F.	float gently
7. confirmation	G.	criticize
8. initiative	H.	search for food
9. admonish	I.	difficult task
10. directive	J.	summon

Chapter 6
Judge, Jury, and Jailer

Traveling through time must not be something you ever get used to. You would think that on the third time around, the process wouldn't stretch and **distort** our bodies so much, and maybe we wouldn't feel quite as dizzy. But the side effects of time travel did not **diminish.** If anything, they got worse.

When we came out of our tailspin, Bridget, Babette, Barnaby, and I found ourselves sitting in a big wooden jury box in an old-fashioned courtroom. It looked like we were the only ones there. I can't tell you how relieved I was to see sunlight streaming through the glass windows. At least it seemed like we were on Earth at some time in the recent past. I took a peek outside to see if I could get any clues about where we were, and almost yelped with joy to see a tall magnolia tree with branches **abounding** in big, creamy, white blossoms. In fact, the blossoms were so plentiful that you could barely see the dark green, waxy leaves. I knew there was something about the sunlight that reminded me of the South, but the magnolia tree was the **clincher.** There is practically no surer way to know you are in the South than to see a magnolia tree.

The kids were starting to come to their senses, and I was about to push them toward the door of the courtroom, when a terrible wail sprung up from across the room. There, in the prisoner's box, sat Gorgas. Several of his eyes were blackened, his mane was tangled, and his purple cap, usually bright and fresh, was **dingy** and dirty. His tentacles were chained together. He looked so **frail,** weak, and helpless, it was almost enough to make you feel sorry for him. Of course, we didn't care much for Gorgas. But Vargas—now he could really hold a grudge, as we were about to find out.

✎ ✎ ✎ ✎ ✎

"All rise for the Honorable Judge Vargas," announced Vargas, as he entered through the doors of the courtroom.

The alien wore a powdered, white wig on top of his already white mane. The wig kind of looked like George Washington's hair. Instead of his cape, he wore a long, black robe. He **sauntered** up to the front of the room as slowly and casually as his tentacles would carry him, as if he had not a care in the world. Behind Vargas came a **procession** of furry little creatures who looked like coconuts with arms and legs, walking in a straight line as if they were in a parade. Gorgas let out another wail. Apparently, Vargas leading a **cavalcade** of walking coconuts was the last thing he wanted to see. Bridget, Babette, and Barnaby, who were too confused to do anything else, stood up.

"Not you, Gorgas," snarled Vargas as he passed the prisoner. "Don't stand up. **Sprawl** face down on the floor, with your tentacles spread wide, like a sorry criminal should."

"But Vargas, I am chained! I cannot spread my arms to show you the respect you deserve," whimpered Gorgas, reaching out to Vargas as best he could through the bars of the prisoner's box. "Oh, mighty one, come here and let me touch the hem of your robe so I can kiss the **fringe.** You are so wise and great! Please, be merciful!"

"Enough!" barked Vargas, whipping his robe away and **rebuffing** Gorgas's efforts to come near him. "Don't **fawn** over me. You'll get no special favors by praising me, and your prayers and **supplications** disgust me."

"But how can you **spurn** me this way? We have known each other for so long!" continued Gorgas, rattling his chains. "What have I done to deserve such **scorn**?"

"I'm glad you asked," replied Vargas, with a **wry,** crooked smile. "Ladies and gentleman of the jury—hey, you Vizwatts; sit down and be quiet! Remember, you're at the trial of the century!"

The little coconut creatures had been tumbling and rolling around the aisle, but they jumped to attention when the judge spoke and they took their seats.

"That's better. Now then, ladies and gentleman of the jury, this person, one Gorgas by name, stands accused of the most unheard of crime in the galaxy," Vargas began. "In fact, some of his crimes are truly **unprecedented,** which means that this evil creature was the first to mastermind and perform the horrible crimes. Hopefully, we will be able to punish him in a measure that is equal to the evilness of the crimes he has committed."

"But, **magistrate,** sir, if these crimes are totally new and are unknown to the justice system, how can you be sure that they're against the law?" asked Bridget, who had learned a lot about the law by watching reruns of *Law and Order* while she was sick in bed with the chicken pox. Not that she wanted Gorgas to go free, but she was curious.

"Fine, fine. I will list some of the more common charges against Gorgas. We will deal with his stranger crimes later," sighed Vargas. "And please, don't call me a magistrate. Magistrates only deal with small trials. This, as I have said, is the trial of the century! I am an important judge."

"Sorry, your honor," said Bridget.

"See that you remember that. As I was saying, even long ago, when he was a child on Smeltvlat, Gorgas had a criminal mind. He had a fine, rich family who hired the best Karloffian **governess** to take care of him and teach him. Karloffian nannies are as strict as they come, but even when Gorgas was a very young Smeltvlatian, he did everything he could to disobey her. He refused to clean up his room, he never ate everything on his plate, and he refused to stop reading his comic books when it was time to go to bed. Horrifying, isn't it?" asked Vargas.

"Well, lack of tidiness isn't exactly a crime on Earth . . . " began Barnaby.

"No, of course not," snapped Vargas. "I'm only trying to show you what a bad sort of person he is now. He never possessed any of the **virtues** that you might hope to find in a child, like cleanliness, respectfulness, or generosity. In fact, aside from fairly good manners, I don't think he has developed any positive qualities at all. But he did not commit his first real crime until he was a teenager. You see, by law, all youngsters on our planet had a **curfew.** They had to be at home and indoors by the time the third moon rose above the horizon. Of course, Gorgas thought that the law wasn't meant for him. He would break curfew and stay out at the arcade, whooping it up with his friends until the fifth or sixth moonrise."

"My, that is naughty," remarked Babette.

"But that's only the beginning," insisted Vargas. "The rest of his life can only be described as a crime **spree.** He committed crime after crime, all with great enjoyment. While he was a private investigator, his favorite crime was **larceny.**"

"I was not a thief!" shouted Gorgas. "I never stole anything from my clients. Back then, I had **integrity.** I would never lie, cheat, or do anything dishonest."

"Oh no?" boomed Vargas. "How about all of the clients you stole from me? Now that's larceny, pure and simple. Then, of course, there were the charges of **corruption** brought against you while you were mayor of Tralala. Apparently, Gorgas was a very wicked mayor who could be paid to do almost anything. What do you have to say about that? Well? Can you defend yourself?"

The Vizwatts excitedly chittered like monkeys and rolled themselves around on the hard, wooden benches.

"Order! Order in the court! Stop that, you crazy Vizwatts!" demanded Vargas. "Well, Gorgas? I also seem to remember a certain election year. You were the **incumbent,** trying to get reelected mayor. And the **candidate** you were running against—Welmok, I think it was—mysteriously disappeared. Kidnapped, so the rumor went, by a bunch of thugs you hired. You thought you had it made. You won the election, of course, but then, at your **inauguration,** just at the point in the **ceremony** when you are supposed to swear to obey the law, Welmok showed up, all roughed up and dusty. And he had quite a story to tell; it was amazing how fast you tried to get out of town!"

"Did he get caught?" asked Bridget. "What happened?"

"Oh, the usual," complained Vargas. "A committee was formed to look into the whole affair. There were people from both political parties, Gorgas's and Welmok's, on the committee, so it was **bipartisan.** But bipartisan doesn't always mean fair. The committee met for months, but nothing was ever decided. They couldn't seem to come to a **consensus** about what should be done. The members would gather, some person would **drone** on and on about how we needed to get to the bottom of this, and then everyone would fall asleep. Then the next day, the same people would **convene** again, and the same thing would happen. Finally, Gorgas decided to hire people, his so-called "friends," to come in and **vouch** for his honesty. These well-paid witnesses swore up and down that Gorgas was innocent. And the committe believed them! They let Gorgas go free!"

"I was innocent!" shrieked Gorgas. "It was you who kidnapped Welmok, but you wanted it to look like I was the criminal! You did everything you could to **incriminate** me and get me thrown in jail. You're the kidnapper!"

Boos and hisses echoed through the courtroom as the Vizwatts showed their displeasure with Gorgas.

"Be careful what you **allege,** Gorgas," warned Vargas. "You know that you have no proof to back up that claim."

But Gorgas continued, pleading to the children, "I know I have no proof of the allegation I just made, but who else could it have been? My evidence against him is only **circumstantial,** it's true. There were no witnesses, no hard facts. But Vargas hates me. He practically led a **crusade** against me to have me thrown out of office when I was first elected. He was like a soldier with a mission;

he even had an army, so to speak. It was a **coalition** of ice-cream truck drivers, butterfly collectors, and welders. Why such different groups would want to make friends in order to form an **alliance** against me is, to this day, a mystery. But Vargas got them to work together and they did everything they could to drag me down."

"Um, Gorgas and Vargas, I must admit, this is all very interesting," began Bridget politely, "but, if it's all the same to you, we'll be on our way. This seems to be a private matter between you two."

Bridget, Babette, Barnaby, and Beauregard had not set foot out of the jury box before Vargas stood up and bellowed. "Stay where you are! The trial has not even begun. You, with the braids, do you know how to use a stenography machine?"

"A what?" asked Bridget.

"No matter, no matter," said Vargas. "Come sit down here by this machine and type down everything anyone in this room says. That's the official way to do things here on Earth, correct? You, with the sunglasses, how do you feel about swearing in the witness? He must take an **oath** saying that he will tell the truth. It probably won't do any good to ask him to promise, but he must anyway. Here's a Bible for him to put his tentacle on."

Vargas had slithered off of the judge's chair and was busily **bustling** around the room like a last-minute holiday shopper trying to get everything ready.

"Well, don't you have to be a **parson** or preacher to do that? Swear someone in, I mean?" asked Babette.

"Nonsense. Regular humans do it all the time. I have seen it on your television programs," said Vargas.

"He's right," said Bridget.

"Okay, then," said Babette, taking the Bible and shrugging her shoulders.

"What about me?" asked Barnaby. "What should I do?"

"Oh, yes. Here, take this legal pad. I might need to **dictate** a letter or something. If I do, I'll say, 'Take a letter,' and then you must write down everything I say. Got it?" asked Vargas.

Barnaby nodded.

"Right. Very well, then, swear in the witness," commanded the wig-wearing alien.

Babette stepped up to Gorgas and held out the Bible. Gorgas placed one tentacle on top of it, but he did not look happy.

"Do you swear to tell the truth, the whole truth, and nothing but the truth?" asked Babette.

"What do you mean by truth?" asked Gorgas, narrowing his eyes in a **guarded,** cautious way. "You cannot be too careful about making these things clear up front. I must say, Vargas, this does not look like it will be a fair, balanced trial. You hate me, and these children, I fear, are none too fond of me either. In fact, I suspect that in this courtroom there is a general **bias** against me. So much, alas, for the fair lady, Justice! My heart overflows with sadness. It is a true, true shame."

"I will tell you what the shame is, Gorgas," snapped Babette. "The shame is the **affected** manner you have. Quit putting on airs. You sound like a character in an old, British play."

The Vizwatts giggled and bounced in the aisles with amusement. Babette stared coldly at them, then returned her attention to Gorgas.

"Now, Gorgas, you must be **forthright.** Come straight to the point and say what you have to say. **Frankness** is the key, so you must be straightforward and hide nothing," Babette explained. "Do you swear?"

"Oh, very well," huffed Gorgas, a little put out by Babette's comments.

"Thank you," said Vargas, who was just shuffling out from under a table. "I will now explain the case against Gorgas."

"Hey, isn't that a new wig?" asked Barnaby. "That one seems a lot curlier than the last one. And it seems to have every color in the **spectrum**. Are judges supposed to wear rainbow-colored clown wigs?"

"What a **keen** eye you have! Such sharp powers of observation. You notice every **nuance** of my clothing," remarked Vargas, obviously pleased with Barnaby's comment.

"There aren't many nuances to a clown wig," replied Barnaby. "The fact that you're wearing one isn't a subtle detail; it would be pretty hard to miss. But why the change?"

"You see, I am the lawyer now," explained the alien. "The other wig is for when I am the judge. And I have a nice, blond page-boy wig for when I'm the jailer."

"This is not a trial!" yelled Gorgas, struggling against his chains. "It's a **parody** of a trial. A rotten, weak imitation of the real thing. Vargas, you filthy, stinking, oozy-headed . . ."

"Tut, tut!" scolded Vargas. "There's no reason why we can't keep the **discourse** in this court polite. Please **endeavor** to watch your language and converse nicely. I know it is hard for you, but please try as hard as you can."

Gorgas had been bearing Vargas's insults well, but his patience was wearing thin. By the way he was scowling, it was clear that his fear had given way to **wrath.** The angry alien was planning something.

"Vargas, come on. I know we have had our differences. Why don't we just settle this fairly?" he offered. "Because we cannot seem to come to an agreement, let's ask these children to **arbitrate.** They will listen to our arguments and make a decision, and we will do what they think is the fairest thing. If it turns out that I have certain, um, **assets**—money, property, or anything of value—that should belong to you, well, I will gladly **bestow** them upon you, along with a thousand apologies."

"I admire your proposed **largess,** Gorgas," sniffed Vargas. "I have never known you to give gifts so generously. So, are you saying that you trust the humans, who dislike you even more than they dislike me, to do our **reckoning** for us? You think that they can settle our accounts and figure out who owes who, what?

"I trust their **discretion** completely," claimed Gorgas. "They are free to make their own decision. And I'm sure it will be wise."

"Hah!" snorted Vargas. "Then you are a bigger fool than I thought you were. No way. What a laugh. You, little girl with the braids. Read back what Gorgas just said. I want to hear it again."

Bridget looked down at the roll of paper coming from the stenography machine. She had been trying to type down everything, but, of course, she didn't know how to type. And besides, a stenography machine is not like a typewriter.

"Uh, Vargas, I'm afraid it's a little **garbled** and jumbled up," confessed Bridget. "It doesn't make much sense. I'm not much of a typist."

"Well, I suppose the memory of his idiocy will have to **suffice**," sighed Vargas. "Yes, the memory will have to do. Sorry to **foil** your little plan, Gorgas, but I am looking forward to playing the part of the **dynamic** lawyer, full of fire and excitement. The lawyers on the television programs from Earth are so thrilling and impressive, don't you think?"

Gorgas grumbled, stared at the ground, and refused to answer.

"Come, now, there's no use acting **sullen**," teased the alien lawyer. "I know you too well. Usually when you're angry, you have a lot to say. In fact, I'd miss all the goofy things you say if you weren't around. That's why I'm not going to execute you or banish you when I become Ruler of Earth. My **reign** over this planet will be kind and generous. No, I just intend to shave your head."

Gorgas howled with anger and struggled against his chains. Vargas laughed and swirled around so that his robe flew up around him. All the little Vizwatts jumped up and started spinning around with him until they fell down from dizziness.

"Yes, when I am Ruler of the World, my first **decree** will be that all criminals must have their heads shaved. A shaved head is the worst shame a Smeltvlatian can suffer. Calm down, Gorgas, you're acting like I mean to **mutilate** you or something. It's not like I'm going to cut off your tentacles. It's just your silly, little, black mane!"

Gorgas stopped struggling for a split second and cast a quick, **furtive** glance toward Vargas. He did not want anyone to notice that he had seen Vargas's spare wand and keys underneath his robe.

"Vargas, I'm not sure all of this carrying on is good for your **karma**," remarked Bridget. "You know, doing bad things damages your life force. And in your next life, you could come back as a cockroach or something really horrible. If you believe in that sort of thing, anyway."

"Karma, schmarma," said Vargas. "I'm a Smeltvlatian, so I'm **exempt** from your human rules of behavior. They don't apply to me, and I don't have to go along with them. You have too many rules anyway, for a . . ."

Suddenly a wail and a loud thump came from the prisoner's box. Gorgas had collapsed!

"Oh, dear, this is no fun," whined Vargas. "If he faints, terrorizing him just isn't as fun. You, science boy, put down that notepad. Can you **diagnose** him for me?"

"Well, I'm not a doctor, so I don't really think I can figure out what's wrong," explained Barnaby. "Besides, he's an alien, and I know nothing about alien health problems."

"Fine, then. I'll try to deal with him. The rest of you, see if one of these tables has wheels on its legs. Maybe we can use it as a **gurney,** you know, one of those rolling beds that they have in hospitals," said Vargas, as he bent over Gorgas. "Let's see, what seems to be the pro . . ."

Gorgas moved like lightning, and Vargas learned too late that his enemy's fainting spell was only a **pretense,** a **shrewd** and clever act to lure him into a position so that the keys and the wand could easily be taken out from underneath his robe. They **bandied** blows for a few seconds, knocking each other around with their tentacles. But Gorgas had the benefit of surprise. In a few seconds, he was free and holding Vargas at bay with his own wand.

Gorgas paused for a moment to **relish** his victory and enjoy the sight of Vargas with his clown wig all tangled up. Then he began his speech.

"Vargas, I **resent** the insulting way you have treated me and all the lies you have told," he began. "I am most displeased. But I will be **vindicated.** Oh, yes, my name will be cleared. Once the people of Smeltvlat find out what a dangerous criminal you are, they will **shun** you forever. No Smeltvlatian will ever speak to you again. Then they will forget about all of the little things I did, and welcome me home."

Bridget, Barnaby, Babette, Beauregard, and all the Vizwatts had hoped that the battling Smeltvlatians would not notice them sneaking toward the door. No such luck.

"Hold it right there!" commanded Gorgas. "You silly Vizwatts can go. But you kids are coming with us, and bring that cat. We have some scores to settle."

✍ QUIZ #26 ✍
Relationships

Decide what relationship the following pairs of words have to each other. If they have similar meanings, write "S" next to the pair of words. If they have opposite meanings, write "O" next to the words.

1. resentment : ire   _____
2. oath : pledge   _____
3. keen : blunt   _____
4. cavalcade : procession _____
5. bustle : saunter   _____
6. wrath : animosity   _____
7. shun : embrace   _____
8. frank : covert   _____
9. spurn : rebuff   _____
10. dingy : immaculate   _____

✍ QUIZ #27 ✍
Relationships

Decide what relationship the following pairs of words have to each other. If they have similar meanings, write "S" next to the pair of words. If they have opposite meanings, write "O" next to the words.

1. consensus : accord   _____
2. alliance : coalition   _____
3. largess : philanthropy _____

4. fringe : center   _____
5. shrewd : candid   _____
6. relish : distaste   _____
7. furtive : guarded   _____
8. integrity : virtue   _____
9. bias : fairness   _____
10. dynamic : lethargic   _____

✍ QUIZ #28 ✍
Fill in the Blank

Match each word on the right with a word on the left that has a similar meaning.

1. While everyone agreed that Doug's _____ of Principal Evans during the talent show was funny, it didn't stop Doug from getting two days of detention.

          a. crusade   b. inauguration
          c. parody   d. ceremony

2. Delia Washington was the favored _____ to be elected as the next mayor of Toledo.

          a. magistrate   b. parson
          c. candidate   d. governess

3. The secretary of state hoped to _____ a peaceful settlement between the two sides before a full-scale war erupted.

          a. arbitrate   b. vindicate
          c. incriminate   d. endeavor

4. Once Jim Halbof, regarded by everyone as the most honest person in the world, _____ for Romero's character, Romero was elected Mayor by a landslide.

    a. alleged   b. vouched
    c. distorted   d. diminished

5. Sent to his room an hour earlier than usual, the boy's _____ mood quickly changed to joy when he discovered his new train set waiting for him there.

    a. forthright   b. bipartisan
    c. sullen   d. discreet

6. Because Shelby was born and raised in Palestine, Texas, it was obvious to everyone that her English accent was _____.

    a. affected   b. circumstantial
    c. wry   d. unprecedented

7. When the evening paper ran a picture of the governor accepting a million dollar bribe, the citizens knew that _____ in the government was everywhere.

    a. larceny   b. corruption
    c. curfew   d. karma

8. The king had a revolution on his hands after he _____ that all peasants had to work an extra three hours a day to build his new castle.

a. bandied
b. decreed
c. sprawled
d. diagnosed

9. When she became a world famous singer, Glydia hoped to _____ a great gift of money to the Juilliard School of Arts, where she was first trained.

a. dictate
b. garble
c. reckon
d. bestow

✍ QUIZ #29 ✍
Matching

Match each word on the right with the letter on the left that has a similar meaning.

1. assets
2. mutilate
3. suffice
4. nuance
5. convene
6. fawn
7. incumbent
8. drone
9. spectrum
10. spree

A. gather
B. deform
C. fun outing
D. flatter
E. band of colors
F. subtle difference
G. personal resources
H. holder of office
I. satisfy
J. continuous low hum

Matching

Match each word on the right with the letter on the left that has a similar meaning.

1. exempt
2. clincher
3. abounding
4. gurney
5. reign
6. supplication
7. frail
8. pretense
9. discourse

A. unsupported claim
B. movable hospital table
C. weak
D. excused
E. plentiful
F. begging
G. conversation
H. rule
I. decisive act

Chapter 7
Showdown 2026

I probably don't have to tell you that I wasn't looking forward to another trip through time and space. The last couple of jaunts had left my head fuzzy and my eyes **bleary.** To tell the truth, I'm not sure that the whole process is even **hygienic**—it certainly did nothing to promote my health or cleanliness. After each time jump, I was left with a strange, sticky **residue** on my fur, as if I had been dipped in oil. I noticed it on Babette, Barnaby, and Bridget too. They looked sweaty, but the sweat had an odd, greenish tinge to it that made their healthy faces take on a sickly **hue.** I remember wishing I had a scrub brush so I could **scour** that green mess off their faces. After that, perhaps, a nice **astringent** to make sure every last bit of slime was gone and leave their skin fresh and **taut.** Nice tight skin is the key to a good complexion, you know. But, the situation being what it was, I was forced to try to lick them clean.

As it turned out, we had been in the Sacajabogue City courthouse in Louisiana, in the year 1926. It was a small, pretty town in the southern swamps. Too bad we didn't get a chance to really take a look around. I have often wondered what the natives thought of the crazy little alien coconut creatures. The courtroom Vizwatts took Gorgas at his word and ran away as fast as they could. I noticed them rolling through the bushes and blackberry bramble to get away. Perhaps they got caught in some dark **bog** on the edge of town. The earth in south Louisiana is so wet and spongy that whole horses used to get stuck in it. Or maybe the Vizwatts made friends and settled down. I guess we'll never know.

We, on the other hand, got dragged forward in time about one hundred years. At least, that's what Gorgas told us. When I came to, I was in the corner of what used to be called an artist's **loft,** a big, open room on the top floor of a building. For some reason, it looked familiar, but I couldn't tell why. The room looked like a science lab. Strewn everywhere were bottles full of bubbling liquids, sheets of metal, and scribbled notes. But it was much fancier that most labs I'd seen. In a corner, by one of the tall windows, was a beautiful wooden desk—probably **mahogany,** judging from its rich, reddish-brown color. Fine furniture and rugs filled the room. The skyline that I saw through the windows looked familiar, too. Familiar, but different; I couldn't quite place it.

In the center of the room stood a tall man with a long, thin nose and pale hair. He was so **gaunt** that it looked like he must not have eaten for a month. His skin was dull, yellowish, and **sallow.** He wore a lab coat, sort of like Barnaby's, and seemed to be having some sort of argument with Gorgas, who was standing close by.

"What do you mean, it's not ready?" demanded Gorgas. "Didn't I make you rich? Before I came along, you were a poor, struggling scientist. Now you are a **prosperous entrepreneur,** owner of your own successful company."

"Yes, I agree, the **revenues** my business has enjoyed have been large. I could never have tried such a **venture** without the large, cash **subsidy** you gave me," said the skinny scientist.

"I was very honored to be the **recipient** of such a big gift. But, please, let me explain. I didn't say the Death Ray wasn't ready. I just said that I wasn't sure I could give it to you."

Bridget, Babette, and Barnaby, who had been rolling around on the floor dizzily, pushed themselves up to their feet, looked around, and tried to get their bearings. Vargas, his clown wig now gone, was still unconscious.

"Hey," whispered Barnaby. "I feel like I've been here before."

"I know what you mean," said Bridget, nodding.

Babette jerked her head toward Gorgas and asked, "What do you think is going on?"

"You had better have a good explanation for this, Niels," growled Gorgas.

Niels, the scientist, blinked calmly and replied, "Well, of course. You see, you have another one of your kind with you here. I hope you are not upset, but I really cannot **differentiate** between the two of you. You both have nine eyes, ten legs, moist heads. Aside from your hair, which could easily be dyed and cut, I can't tell you apart. I have to be very careful about handing over my inventions. How do I know you are the one who **commissioned** me to build the Death Ray? How do I know it wasn't him, the one with white hair, who hired me?"

"So, you think all Smeltvlatians have a **uniform** appearance? Well, I suppose I can't **reproach** you for your poor skills of observation, because you aren't to blame. Humans do tend to miss a lot of details," sighed Gorgas. "But, no matter. I forgive you. Now hand over the keys to the Death Ray."

"Wait one second!" groaned Vargas, untangling his tentacles and standing up. "Niels, he is lying. It was I who paid you. I'll prove it, too. Remember how I visited you that time when you were stumped? You couldn't figure out a certain problem, and you were about to give up. You told me that science really wasn't for you, and that all your life, you really wanted to be a tap dancer. But you had to give up your dream because you had no sense of **rhythm** so you couldn't dance in time to any music. Right?"

"Yes, how glad I was to have a **confidant.** I needed someone to tell my secrets to, someone to trust," said Niels sadly. "I thought all my work had been for **naught,** but you helped me by showing me that my work was worth something. So who is this other guy and what should I do?"

"What should you do?" snapped Gorgas. "Don't listen to this fellow. I am your employer. Listen, remember how you lost your lucky pen in this huge room, and I helped you do a **painstaking** search of the entire place, crawling across every inch of the floor, even though I had no idea what your lucky pen looked like?"

Niels seemed confused.

"Yes, yes, I remember that, too," he agreed. "You couldn't find it. It didn't turn up again for months. Hmm. I'm afraid I don't know exactly what to do, here. Which one is the real you?"

"I almost hate to get involved in this **controversy**," began Bridget, "but isn't it possible that they both hired you to create a Death Ray?"

"Who are you and what exactly do you mean?" snapped the scientist.

"My name is Bridget, and these two are Babette and Barnaby. I can't say we're happy to be here, but we might as well help you out if we can," she replied. "What I was suggesting was that Gorgas and Vargas, without realizing what the other had done, may have both hired you to create a Death Ray. You couldn't tell them apart, so you thought it was only one alien. I can tell you one thing—unless you made two Death Rays, we're probably going to have trouble."

Niels nodded. "I think you may be onto something. Gorgas and Vargas, eh? I never knew his, uh, their names. But, say, what are you doing here?"

"We should ask you the same thing," chimed in Babette. "Do you realize what kind of aliens you are mixed up with? The two of them are responsible for some of the most **abominable** crimes in the galaxy. In fact, they nearly destroyed Earth for the sake of sport. And you're making a Death Ray—whatever that is—for them?"

Vargas did his best to look sad and helpless. A twisty little **tendril** of white hair fell over a couple of his eyes, making him look almost boyish.

"How can you believe that, Niels?" asked Vargas sadly. "Can't you see that these children and I are being held prisoner by that terrible creature?"

"That doesn't make any difference," said Barnaby. "They may be two separate aliens, but they have the same **mode** of action, the same way of doing things. They are both **wily**, crafty, and sneaky through and through. And bad to the bone—if they have bones. I'd call them evil **incarnate.**"

"Those are strong words, Barnaby," commented Niels. "You really think they embody all that is evil?"

"Look, he's not kidding around," Bridget jumped in. "They are competing with each other to rule the world, and they would rather destroy the planet than lose the game. We have to stop them."

Niels stroked his chin and thought about his predicament. He did not appear to be convinced. Gorgas stood by patiently.

"I'm not sure. I'd like some **tangible** proof—something I can touch and see and hold in my hands," he said. "I'm sorry, but I have a cautious **temperament.** That's just the way I am."

"We don't have time to argue about this," insisted Babette, stomping her foot. "I tell you, every time we see these aliens something bad happens. It is an alarming **trend.** I feel certain that the pattern will continue if one of them gets a Death Ray. You must not hand it over."

Gorgas heaved a sigh and held up his wand.

"My dear, you base your argument on a shaky **premise,**" he said. "You act as if Niels here has a choice. I'm afraid he doesn't. Niels, I am bored with this discussion. Let us **dispense** with the chit chat and get down to business."

Gorgas shook a couple of his tentacles threateningly. Niels stroked his chin and shook his head.

"It looks like you kids were right," said the scientist. "It does seem that he would be **apt** to use the Death Ray for evil. Such mood swings he has! One minute he's acting like my friend, and the next he wants to beat me up."

"Yes, you're right, Niels," urged Vargas, inching closer. "Gorgas is a **volatile** being; he could lash out at any time. Give the Death Ray to me."

"That's enough, Vargas!" boomed Gorgas. "Niels, you disappoint me. But no matter. I will punish you later. The Death Ray is around here somewhere. I will find it myself."

Gorgas slithered over to the lab area and began snooping around, opening drawers, looking behind curtains, and overturning piles of paper. Vargas, no longer guarded by his enemy, quietly sneaked over to the desk and began searching as well. The two Smeltvlatians were so focused on finding the invention first that neither of them took any notice of the humans.

"I owe you kids an apology. It's true, these aliens are creeps," Niels huffed. "I was feeling guilty about cheating them, but now I'm glad."

"Cheating them?" asked Bridget, confused. "You mean that . . ."

"That's right. There isn't any Death Ray," he explained. "Oh, I tried to design one, but I guess I'm just not good at weapons. I used the money they gave me to create a **vaccine** that prevents nonrhythmitis, which is the condition that kept me from being a tap dancer. I wanted to make sure that no child would ever again suffer from the devastating lack of rhythm that cost me my dream."

"That's definitely better than a Death Ray," said Bridget. "Is the vaccine a pill? What's it made of?"

"No, it's not a pill," explained Niels. "You have to shoot it under the skin with a **hypodermic** needle. As far as what it's made of, it's a pretty complicated **concoction.** I don't want to bore you with a lot of medical **jargon,** so I won't list all of the ingredients."

"No offense, Niels, but do you think we could discuss this later?" asked Barnaby. "I'd really like to hear about it, but Gorgas and Vargas are going to get tired of searching soon, and they'll be coming back to you for answers. We need a plan."

"I think I have an idea," said Babette, "but we'll have to **orchestrate** our actions carefully; we're going to have to act as a team to pull this off. Bridget, do you still have your gum?"

"Naturally," grinned Bridget.

"Niels, is that your lucky pen in the pocket of your lab coat?" asked Babette.

"Er, yes . . . " replied Niels.

"Okay, here's what we're going to do," began Babette.

The humans gathered in a huddle and whispered frantically as the aliens continued to search. Gorgas tore at the tape on an unopened **parcel** that was sitting on the **threshold** only to discover it was a package of chocolate chip cookies that had been sent by Niels's mother. Vargas had even overturned a filing cabinet, but they'd found nothing. Finally, Niels interrupted their search with a laugh.

"Look at you two!" he cried. "Scrambling around on the floor. You won't find what you're looking for, you know. You'll never find it. Not in a million years."

"Niels, I've had enough of you," warned Gorgas, moving threateningly toward the tall scientist. "I'm going to sock you in the jaw."

"W-wait!" cried Niels, nervously backing away. "I mean, you won't find it because I have it. It's right here!"

Niels reached into his pocket and pulled out his lucky pen. It was a **nondescript** ballpoint pen, nothing special or unusual about it. It was black and it had one of those little buttons on the top that you push to bring the tip in and out. The only mark on it was a tiny picture of a skull, which was the **logo** of a local chemical company. It was just an ordinary pen, but the aliens were fascinated.

"Ah, so small and elegant!" cooed Vargas. "It is the perfect **covert** weapon—dreadfully destructive, yet so easily hidden. Please, Niels, give it to me."

"Nope. Because I can't decide between you, you will have to decide for yourselves," said Niels, tossing the pen to the middle of the room. "Fight for it. Come on, fight for it. What are you, chickens?"

Niels did not have to **goad** the aliens for long. In an instant, they were in the center of the loft, circling carefully around the pen on the floor, waiting for a chance to bend over for it without getting knocked in the head by a tentacle. Vargas, who had taken a letter opener from the desk, seemed to have an advantage. But Gorgas was quicker. He distracted Vargas by waving one of his left tentacles and made a grab for the Death Ray with a right.

"Ha, ha!" he crowed with triumph. "Here we are at last, Vargas. And it is I who have the Death Ray and you only have a letter opener!"

"Curses!" shouted Vargas, backing away.

Gorgas pointed the pen and Vargas and began hitting the button. Click. Click. Click, click. Click, click, click. Nothing happened. He tried again. Click. Click. Still nothing. Vargas seized his chance and charged at Gorgas full speed. They fell to the floor, a big oozy ball of tentacles.

"Now, Bridget!" urged Babette.

Bridget ran toward the fighting pair, pulling her gum in a long string from between her teeth. Working like lightning, she began to wrap the gum like a rope around and around the aliens. Before they knew what was happening, they were tied up tightly with gum, unable to even wiggle one tentacle. Babette and Barnaby relieved the aliens of their wands, their back-up wands, and their weapons—the pen and the letter opener.

"My dear!" objected Gorgas. "Please release me! Didn't you see, Vargas was the **assailant.** I was just the victim of his attack."

"Ooh, Gorgas, how I **revile** you!" growled Vargas. "You never stop. Please, children, do what you want with us, but don't leave me tied to someone I hate so much."

"You know, guys, I'm a nice person," said Bridget. "I have this personal **creed** I like to live by, which is that on a **fundamental** level, everyone is good. At their core, no one is evil. Sure, they may develop some bad habits and do some bad things, but everybody deserves a second chance."

"That's a lovely **ideology,** my dear," agreed Gorgas eagerly. "What a beautiful belief system. You'll see. Vargas and I will **forge** an agreement and become friends. I swear, we will reach an **accord,** or my name isn't Gorgas!"

"You didn't let me finish," replied Bridget, shaking her head. "I have always held that idea dear. I **cherish** the belief that people will do the right thing, if only you show them how. But my experience with you two has **infused** me with a deep mistrust for aliens on scavenger hunts. I have no faith in you."

Vargas squirmed and objected, "You are right to dislike us, after all the things we've done. I don't know how it happened. I used to be the most **ingenuous** young Smeltvlatian, just as open and honest as I could be. Then, because of Gorgas and all that he did to me, my honesty began to **atrophy** and my sense of fair play withered away."

Vargas tried to smile at Bridget, but it came off looking more like a silly **simper.**

"Perhaps, here on Earth, there is some sort of **therapy** I could go through, some treatment to restore my better qualities," he continued. "You see, I can be made well again, unlike some people I know."

"I see what you are hinting at!" growled Gorgas. "But if you're trying to **insinuate** that I cannot be cured, you are wrong! My dear Bridget, Vargas may **profess** a desire to reform, but his claim is false. I, however, truly want to fly right from now on."

"You just don't get it," said Barnaby. "We are not going to believe you. The things you have done are not **trifles,** they are serious crimes! We're not going to let you get away with them. Niels, why don't you **whet** the razor so it will be nice and sharp?"

"Actually, Barnaby, it's an electric razor. Straight razors are too dangerous," whispered Niels.

"Oh. Well, whatever," said Barnaby. "Gorgas, Vargas, you'd better get ready. We're going to shave your heads and send you back to Smeltvlat!"

"No! Not that!" shrieked the aliens.

"Yes, that," said Barnaby. "Niels, do you want to do the honors?"

"Why, certainly," said Niels, stepping forward with his battery-driven razor. "Get ready, you two."

It was a good thing Bridget's gum was so carefully wrapped around the two aliens. They screamed and yelled as Niels shaved their heads, but they could not move. After it was over, the aliens, who never were very attractive in the first place, were downright ugly. The **dour,** gloomy expressions on their faces did not improve their appearances.

"You will pay for this!" they both shouted.

Babette stepped forward and held out one of the wands she'd taken from Gorgas.

"Barnaby has explained to me that using this wand is simple," she began. "I only have to concentrate on what I want your destination to be, and it will do the rest. But first, Bridget, please pin the note on them."

Bridget came forward and taped a note to the tied up aliens. It read, "People of Smeltvlat: Please **ensure** that these criminals are punished to the full extent of the law." Once the note was attached, Babette closed her eyes and began moving the wand in slow circles. The aliens howled like wolves and in a matter of seconds, they were gone. They left behind nothing but their shaved hair and a small, oozy puddle.

"All right!" cried Bridget, happily exchanging high fives with everyone. "That was some plan, Babette. It was perfect—the **optimal** solution to our problems."

"I'm not so sure," sighed Babette. "These wands worry me. They are so powerful, I fear what would happen if they fell into the wrong hands. I think we should destroy them."

"Destroy them? But how are we supposed to get home? Niels, what year is this and where exactly are we?" asked Bridget.

"It's 2026 and we're in New York City. I guess you come from the past, huh?" he responded.

"Yes," sighed Bridget, as she sadly sunk into a chair and gazed out the window. "At least we're in New York. My family is probably out there somewhere. I can't go back to them now. They probably think I've been missing for years! But Babette is right. Those wands should be destroyed."

The look of **desolation** on Bridget's face moved Niels deeply. She looked so lost and miserable. He was about to hug her when a terrible crash came from across the room.

"Beauregard!" shouted Bridget, jumping out of her chair. "What are you doing?"

The giant black cat had been trying to climb a large **tapestry** that was hanging on the far wall. The thick, wool drape was carefully stitched with a picture of Earth as seen from outer space. Unfortunately, the tapestry did not hold his weight, and it came toppling down on top of him. But instead of a wall behind the curtain, there was an **alcove,** a little curved room that dipped back about a dozen feet. Inside the alcove was a metal space ship about the size of a sail boat.

"Hey, wait a second . . . that's my ship!" cried Barnaby, clapping and running toward it. "I knew this place looked familiar. This is my old laboratory! And that's the space ship I was showing you before we went to the Yankees game!"

"You designed that ship?" asked Niels with surprise. "It was here when I rented this space. I have spent years trying to figure it out. It's so advanced!"

"Why thank you! Bridget, don't you see? Our troubles could be over," Barnaby explained. "This ship is capable of time travel."

"Really?" asked Bridget, perking up.

"Absolutely. Hey, Babette. Hand me those wands. I'll hold them while you, you know, karate kick them or something," said Barnaby.

Babette gathered the Smeltvlatian wands and Barnaby held them bunched up in front of him. Babette took a moment to center herself, then with one mighty "Hiyah!" chopped them all in two with the edge of her hand.

"So much for that," said Barnaby. "Now then, everybody help me **lug** that ship out here. It's so heavy that it'll take all of us to drag it out. I need to examine it and see if I can get it going."

Bridget, Babette, Barnaby, Niels, and even Beauregard pulled the ship into the middle of the loft, and Barnaby jumped in the hatch on top and got right to work. After a few minutes, he jumped out with a puzzled look on his face.

"Remember how I told you that there were some problems with the quasi-quantum quickener?" asked Barnaby. "Well, there still are. The **configuration** of the controls is a little messed up and laid out wrong. I put all the buttons in reverse order. But that's not a big problem. I can't seem to **synchronize** the steering clock with the probe clock. They should always show the same time and tick together exactly the same way, but the probe clock is running fast. Finally, there seems to be some sort of **fluctuation** in the engine system; one minute I have plenty of power and the next, the power **wanes** and I'm left with almost nothing."

"I hope you won't think I'm intruding," said Niels, "but as I said, I have spent years studying your ship and the notes you left behind. I think I might have solved your power problem."

"Oh?" asked Barnaby, hopefully.

"Yes, I did several experiments to find out what you were using to fuel the ship," began Niels. "You were using a mash made of bananas, correct? The sugar from the fruit was released slowly as the fruit decayed, and the ship **derived** its energy from the sugar. Well, that's fine for normal planetary travel, but for time travel you need something with more kick than just fruit sugars. Happily, I was able to discover that the **element** you were missing was chocolate."

Niels walked over to the threshold of the loft, picked up the box Gorgas had opened, and brought it to Barnaby.

"I had my mother bake these up special," he explained. "They are chocolate chip cookies that are designed to **integrate** into the system the exact amounts of sugar and chocolate that you need to travel through time. Just set up a reserve tank for the cookies and keep the fruit mash for space travel. What do you think?"

"Niels, you're the greatest!" cried Barnaby, hugging his fellow scientist around the waist. "I'm glad you believed in my project. No one in my time takes me seriously; they all think I'm crazy. Ah, well. Now, if only I could figure out how to get these clocks to run correctly."

"Let me at them," said Babette, rolling up her sleeve. "I have a way with machines."

Barnaby led her into the ship. And sure enough, one good whack was all those clocks needed to straighten up and tick and tock together. The friends were finally ready to go home.

Bridget, Barnaby, Babette, and Beauregard gathered around to say farewell to Niels. He seemed a little sad that they were leaving.

"I am sorry to see you go," sighed the scientist. "I get so little company. It's lonely. I wonder what will become of me, now that the aliens aren't funding my research."

"I think I can help you with that," said Barnaby, pulling his kaleidoscope out of his pocket. "Here, look through this and tell me what you see."

"Wow!" said Niels. "I see myself wearing a **garland** of roses around my neck. Someone is giving me an award for my vaccine! And now, now I see an invitation to join the most **elite** science club in the world, the Geneva Group. Only the finest, most respected scientists are asked to join. And now, but this is hazy, I think I see . . . no . . . wait . . . yes! I see myself dancing, tap dancing in a musical production! This is great!"

"That's your future, Niels," said Bridget, smiling warmly. "See? You have nothing to worry about."

Niels handed the kaleidoscope back to Barnaby and hugged all of the kids good-bye.

He even patted Beauregard on the head. They all piled into the ship and Niels opened one of the large windows.

"Thanks for your help!" chirped Bridget as she climbed in. "We have to go now, we have a Yankees game to finish."

Barnaby fastened the hatch and strapped everyone in, then he sat down behind the controls and heaved a deep sigh.

"Keep your fingers crossed," he cautioned. "Let's hope that those cookies pack a serious punch!"

✍ QUIZ #31 ✎
Relationships

Decide what relationship the following pairs of words have to each other. If they have similar meanings, write "S" next to the pair of words. If they have opposite meanings, write "O" next to the words.

1. fundamental : trifling   _____

2. integrate : fuse   _____

3. nondescript : usual   _____

4. cherish : despise   _____

5. wane : wax   _____

6. tendril : sprout   _____

7. wily : devious   _____

8. covert : overt   _____

9. reproach : praise   _____

10. assailant : mugger   _____

11. prosperous : impoverished   _____

✍ QUIZ #32 ✐
Relationships

Decide what relationship the following pairs of words have to each other. If they have similar meanings, write "S" next to the pair of words. If they have opposite meanings, write "O" next to the words.

1. tangible : actual   _____

2. jargon : lingo   _____

3. revile : adoret   _____

4. forge : fabricate   _____

5. abominable : commendable   _____

6. optimal : worst   _____

7. hue : tone   _____

8. volatile : inert   _____

9. bog : mire   _____

10. taut : tense   _____

11. hygienic : sanitary   _____

✍ QUIZ #33 ✍
Fill in the Blank

For each sentence below, choose the word that best completes the sentence.

1. The tents within the rebel camp were of such _____ appearance that it was almost impossible to tell them apart.

   a. dour   c. uniform
   b. bleary   d. rhythmic

2. Normally an easily frightened person, Nigel was _____ into taking skydiving lessons by the ceaseless taunts of his older sister.

   a. derived   b. insinuated
   c. goaded   d. orchestrated

3. Because the assault team all had to reach the perimeter of the enemy base at exactly the same time, everyone worked to _____ their movements as closely as possible.

   a. fluctuate   b. concoct
   c. differentiate d. synchronize

4. Vincent's love of cruel practical jokes and a vicious _____ earned him more bloody noses than any other person on the planet.

   a. creed   b. logo
   c. premise   d. temperament

5. The new _____ was so fast and powerful that I could actually watch the pimples vanish into nothingness.

        a. vaccine   b. astringent
        c. hypodermic   d. residue

6. With no visible landmarks for miles, it was easy to believe that the _____ grasslands stretched on forever.

        a. sallow   b. desolate
        c. elite   d. gaunt

7. The _____ who invented the world's first disposable car (costing only $300) became a millionaire overnight.

        a. entrepreneur   b. recipient
        c. revenue   d. subsidy

8. After watching the entire basketball season without ever leaving his house, Robert realized that his leg muscles had begun to _____.

        a. infuse   b. atrophy
        c. whet   d. lug

9. We placed the _____ on our front door to show all carolers that they were welcome to come sing to us.

        a. alcove   b. mahogany
        c. parcel   d. garland

10. Luckily, a(n) _____ was reached between the fourth graders before the spitwad fight got too out of hand.

a. ideology	b. controversy
c. accord	d. trend

✍ QUIZ #34 ✍
Matching

Match each word on the right with the letter on the left that has a similar meaning.

1. commission		A.	claim knowledge
2. incarnate		B.	nothing
3. profess		C.	point of entering
4. bramble		D.	thorny shrub
5. naught		E.	scrub thoroughly
6. configure		F.	grant authority
7. loft		G.	space under a roof
8. element		H.	distribute
9. threshold		I.	given human form
10. dispense		J.	part of a whole
11. scour		K.	fit parts together

✍ QUIZ #35 ✍
Matching

Match each word on the right with the letter on the left that has a similar meaning.

1. painstaking		A.	likely
2. confidant		B.	tiny amount
3. apt		C.	honest
4. mode		D.	decorated cloth
5. tinge		E.	trusty companion
6. ensure		F.	risk
7. tapestry		G.	manner
8. simper		H.	treatment
9. ingenuous		I.	smirk
10. therapy		J.	involving much care
11. venture		K.	guarantee

Chapter 8
Like the Cheshire Cat . . .

Bridget is the most naturally adventurous of the children, but she is also the first to grow tired of her travels. I remember her telling me once that she thought the best part of visiting new places was coming home. Not that she didn't like exploring. She just liked home most. As soon as Barnaby closed the hatch, Bridget started beaming as though it were her birthday.

I wasn't so sure that there was a reason to be smiling just yet. This was, after all, the first voyage the ship had ever made. It hadn't even been properly **christened.** Traditionally, there is a **ritual** that new ships go through before they sail. Someone declares the ship's name and then smashes a bottle of champagne across the bow. I decided that if we actually made it back to our correct time and place, I would personally christen the ship "Mr. Lucky."

I had no idea what to expect from time travel in Barnaby's boat. Gorgas and Vargas, for all their faults, had at least tried out their wands before they started zapping us around in time. To use an **analogy** that I learned while traveling through Asia with the Peking circus, what we were about to do was like juggling knives blindfolded. We didn't know what we were doing, and we had no idea where we might get stuck.

Barnaby did seem to have good control of the ship at first. He eased us out through the open window, which was luckily of the right **proportion** to let us through. We **hovered** in the air, just hanging out for a second, as Barnaby tried to **compute** our route with the help of the ship's calculator. He twisted a few knobs, punched a couple buttons, and eased a lever forward.

Then, things got really weird.

✐ ✐ ✐ ✐ ✐

"Whoa! What's going on?" gasped Barnaby, looking down.

It didn't seem as if the ship had moved at all, but for a minute all the light around them was **refracted,** so that the white light was split into a rainbow of color that swirled in circles. Then it stopped. The building they had just flown out of was still standing, but everything else was different. There were horses and carriages instead of cars in the dusty street below and the buildings were all made of wood and brick. The shining skyscrapers were gone.

"Umm, I think we went too far back," said Bridget, looking down through a window.

"Can you fix it?" asked Babette.

"Oh, I see," said Barnaby, tinkering with his controls. "We were moving in **increments** of ten years instead of one year. We went back centuries instead of decades. Let's see, now. Okay, I think I have us back on track. Is everyone ready?"

Barnaby eased back on a lever and the light swirled again. This time, when they could see clearly again, Bridget almost squealed with joy. They were hovering outside the same building, but everything around her looked like the New York City she grew up in.

"This looks right!" she said clapping.

"Babette, what does the probe clock say?" asked Barnaby hopefully.

"It says we're back," smiled Babette. "We can even make it to the Yankees game—but we might be a little late."

"Great! I'm going to have to crash through the window of my laboratory," warned Barnaby. "I don't want to land this ship on the street. Hold on!"

Barnaby rammed his ship into the window and the glass gave way with a crash. The boat slid across the floor, knocking over tables and cabinets until it finally came to a stop in a huge pile of paper. Bridget quickly unfastened the hatch and jumped out. Her eyes shone brightly as she danced around clapping.

"We're back! The world is safe from Smeltvlatian scavengers and we can still catch the Yankees game," she said excitedly. "What could be better?"

Just as she asked the question, there was a knock at the door.

"Open up, Barnaby, it's Dean O'Malley," called a rough, hoarse voice.

"Uh oh," groaned Barnaby. "Not the dean! I'm really in trouble now. He's in charge of my department. Wait until he sees this mess!"

"Don't worry, we'll think of something," said Bridget, too happy to worry about anything.

She skipped over to the door and flung it open.

"Welcome, welcome, Dean O'Malley!" cried Bridget. "My name is Bridget and this is Babette. The cat's name is Beauregard. We are friends of Barnaby's. Please come on in, because we have so much to tell you."

"My, what an **ebullient** personality you have," said the dean in a **husky** voice. "Are you always so bubbly and excited?"

The dean was not what Bridget expected. He was a short man, and so **stout** that he almost looked round. Most professors and scientists she knew wore simple clothing, but Dean O'Malley was wearing a **flamboyant** outfit that made him look more like a big, important movie **mogul** from the 1920s. He wore a long, silvery gray **mantle** over his plump shoulders, which was fastened at the neck with a glistening jeweled clasp. He carried a walking cane with a golden tip and wore sparkling rings on all of his fingers. His white hair and beard were carefully combed and styled. He had a friendly, pink face and a warm smile. Bridget could not help smiling at him.

"So, you have a lot to tell me, eh?" he asked, winking. "Splendid. But first, I have to tell Barnaby something. Barnaby? Where are you?"

Barnaby peeked out from behind the space ship and then nervously came forward.

"Y-y-yes sir?" he said.

"Barnaby! Didn't you get my **fax**? I've been trying to send you a note for hours! I finally decided that there must be something wrong with your phone line and that the message wasn't being received, so I came over myself. I see now that you probably just couldn't find the fax machine," said Dean O'Malley, looking around at the piles of paper and broken glass.

"Please do not be angry," urged Babette. "Let us explain. You see, we have just been traveling through time in order to save the world from destruction. Barnaby made an important scientific discovery that allowed us to return home from the future. We had to break the window to get in. I know you may not believe me, but it's . . ."

"It's true. I know," said the dean. "You see, I just got a visit from a scientist named Niels, who came from several decades in the future. He explained that it was Barnaby's research that allowed him to come, and he urged me to nominate Barnaby for membership in the Geneva Group. I am a member, you see, so I can invite new scientists to join."

Barnaby, Bridget, and Babette gazed at the stylish dean in amazement.

"Come, come, don't look so surprised!" laughed O'Malley. "Niels went over your notes with me and explained everything. I must say, I am impressed. You are certainly **entitled** to join the club. Yes, you definitely have earned the right. The **exclusion** of someone as brilliant as you are would be unpardonable."

"I am honored, Dean O'Malley," said Barnaby, blushing.

"Way to go, Barnaby!" said Bridget, slapping him on the back.

"That's wonderful!" agreed Babette.

Even Beauregard, who was stretched out on the floor, nuzzled Barnaby's foot fondly.

"Yes, congratulations, young man," continued the dean, taking on a look of seriousness. "In fairness, however, I should **qualify** my congratulations by warning you that the Geneva Group is pretty rough on its new members. There are some tasks that you will be forced to perform if you want to join."

Barnaby looked confused. "You mean the Geneva Group **hazes** its new members? I thought college students were the only ones childish enough to demand people to complete embarrassing tasks in order to qualify for clubs."

A smile crept across O'Malley's face as he reached into his vest pocket.

"Oh, no. I'm afraid you have to come with me right now. Your friends, too. And see if that **languid** cat has enough energy to stand up. If you want to be a member of the Geneva Group, you must come to tonight's Yankees game. And we have to see just how many hot dogs we can all eat," laughed the dean, waving several tickets in front of Barnaby.

Barnaby laughed. "Come to think of it, I am hungry," he said. "What do you say, guys?"

Bridget and Babette nodded eagerly, and Beauregard stood up grudgingly.

"Marvelous!" said O'Malley. "Oh! The **felicity** of this occasion almost made me forget my other news. Happy occasions always make me forgetful. Barnaby, I know you don't like to think about money matters, but luckily for you, I do like to consider the **fiscal** side of things. A **singular** invention like a time-traveling space ship will bring a lot of donations to the university, and of course you will share in the **bounty** you create. I have arranged to get you a new laboratory with all of the latest equipment. Something so fancy that it'll make this lab look **squalid** in comparison. Although I must say, this lab is so dirty, it is approaching squalor. Is that a half-eaten sandwich I see on the floor?"

Dean O'Malley poked at an old tuna sandwich with his cane. Barnaby blushed again.

"I know, I'm messy," agreed Barnaby sadly. "Maybe I don't deserve a new lab."

"Nonsense!" said the dean. "It's already settled. I decorated the new lab myself, and it's quite impressive, if you don't mind my saying so. I only hope you don't think I've gone overboard and made it too **grandiose**."

Barnaby laughed. "I'm sure you've done a **sublime** job. Your great taste in furniture and clothes is well-known in the department. Everyone is always in awe at how grand you make any room that you decide to redecorate. Of course, no one could accuse you of exercising **thrift**."

"No, I've never been one to pinch pennies in interior decoration, that's for sure," chuckled the dean. "It's a good thing I'm such a **canny** investor of money. I believe in investing carefully. As far as keeping your new lab neat, well, we'll leave that up to your students and your research team."

"Research team? Students?" asked Barnaby.

"Of course! And furthermore, I want you to design a new **curriculum** for the science department," said O'Malley. "Come up with a whole new set of science classes that will help students think about science in the truly unique way that you do. You will soon be recognized as a time-travel **guru,** the wisest and most knowledgeable in your field, and people everywhere will expect you to teach them and to set an example. But let's worry about that tomorrow. Today we're off to Yankee Stadium!"

Dean O'Malley turned dramatically on his heel and marched out the door, followed closely by Bridget, Barnaby, Babette, and Beauregard. Out on the street, the dean waved the children toward a shiny black van. It was not boxy, like old vans, but was **streamlined** to perfection, all of its slopes and angles were designed to help it cut through the air. Traffic, for once, was a breeze. None of New York's major **arteries** were clogged with honking cars, and they arrived at the ballpark in what seemed like no time at all.

This time, their seats were right behind home plate. The fans around them were mostly local police officers, firefighters, and other **municipal** workers still in their uniforms.

"All right!" said Bridget, when she saw the crowd near their seats. "They must have come straight from work. People who work for the city are the most **exuberant** fans there are. They really put a lot of energy into cheering for the Yankees. We're going to have some fun today!"

"Yes, those screaming men over there who have 'Go Yankees' and 'Kill the Red Sox' painted on their chests do seem to be **ardent** fans," agreed Babette.

"Yep, they really put their hearts into it," said Bridget.

"I am very glad the **dismal** weather cleared. Baseball weather should be cheery, not dreary," commented Dean O'Malley. "Come, Barnaby. Let's go to the snack stand. We need fuel."

The dean and Barnaby took off in search of food and returned a few minutes later with armloads of it. Even Bridget was impressed with the amount.

"Now then, this five-gallon tub of popcorn is for our **communal** enjoyment. We must all be polite and share it," explained the plump scientist. "I got each of us a separate super-giant soda. Mine is the grape drink without ice. I prefer my soda **tepid,** not cold. If the drink is just slightly warm, it is easier for me to smell it and enjoy its sweet, fruity **bouquet.** Besides, I hate it when the ice melts and **dilutes** my drink. I'm afraid the snack seller would only sell me fifty hot dogs at one time. We will have to **ration** our supply if we want to make it through the game. So only eat one per inning, okay? Dig in!"

The game began, and the fans were swept away with excitement. The Yankees fought hard, and managed to build a two-run lead early in the game. Before they knew it, the seventh inning arrived.

"The seventh inning already," remarked Dean O'Malley. "Time for that timeless, **perennial** favorite, 'Take Me Out to the Ballgame.' That's an old song that will stay popular forever."

"It's quite an **opus**," Bridget agreed, as she stood up and got ready to sing. "Not quite a symphony or opera or anything, but I do think it's a nice work. Hey, Babette, Barnaby, are you ready to sing? I sure hope we stay on the ground this time!"

Barnaby, Babette, Bridget, and Dean O'Malley joined arms and belted out the song with great energy. They were so happy and excited about Barnaby's good fortune, so glad to be home, and so caught up in the game, they didn't even notice the big, black cat quietly sneaking away into the gathering shadows of the evening.

✏ ✏ ✏ ✏ ✏

What can I say? I hate good-byes. All I wanted to do was make sure they made it safely through the seventh inning without being kidnapped by aliens. But I wasn't too worried—I think they had their fill of adventures for awhile. There was no need for me to keep such a careful **vigil** over them. O'Malley seemed like the sort who could keep three kids out of trouble.

Besides, I had a plane to catch. Ah, Trinidad! Ah, Consuela! Such a lovely time I had there! Consuela is a wonderfully **mercurial** cat—lively, high-spirited, and always keeping me guessing. She was such a **congenial** companion, with a personality so **engaging** and charming, most of the tomcats on the island were in love with her. We were so **compatible;** we were made for each other! I got so comfortable with my life there that I almost bought a **tract** of beach front property and settled down.

Almost. But then, along came a mysterious Siamese, with magical blue eyes and a mysterious past, who **derailed** my plans and put the whole island in an uproar. You see, she was a spy for a Burmese warlord named Chow who was trying to take over the sugar cane market in the Caribbean. And I became an unwilling **pawn,** completely under her control, in a plot to take over Trinidad and set up a secret outpost for Chow. Consuela tried to stop me, but I was caught in a web of lies, and Bridget, Barnaby, and Babette had to . . . well, perhaps we should save the details for later.

That's a story for another time.

✍ QUIZ #36 ✍
Relationships

Decide what relationship the following pairs of words have to each other. If they have similar meanings, write "S" next to the pair of words. If they have opposite meanings, write "O" next to the words.

1. ebullient : exuberant   _____
2. mogul : tycoon   _____
3. refract : straighten   _____
4. flamboyant : grandiose   _____
5. thrift : extravagance   _____
6. tepid : scalding   _____

✍ QUIZ #37 ✍
Relationships

Decide what relationship the following pairs of words have to each other. If they have similar meanings, write "S" next to the pair of words. If they have opposite meanings, write "O" next to the words.

1. congenial : engaging   _____
2. dismal : squalid   _____
3. guru : prophet   _____
4. dilute : strengthen   _____
5. stout : lanky   _____

✍ QUIZ #38 ✍
Fill in the Blank

For each sentence below, choose the word that best completes the sentence.

1. The _____ teacher soon learned that not everyone in the world liked to spend eighteen hours a day researching cockroaches like he did.

    a. singular   b. ardent

    c. compatible   d. languid

2. Unfortunately, Ben was unable to complete his two-hour _____ on the harmonica, "Schoolyard Blues," before his mother made him come inside for supper.

    a. mantle   b. vigil

    c. opus   d. tract

3. The new portable phone network used by the train engineers and station managers helped _____ the workings of the railroad and reduce commuter time by ten percent.

    a. derail   b. hover

    c. beam   d. streamline

4. Because they had no idea how long they would be shipwrecked, the crew decided to start _____ supplies immediately.

    a. rationing   b. christening

    c. excluding   d. entitling

5. The _____ singer would often start a concert in a sad mood, leave halfway through in a rage, and then come back at the end as happy as can be.

        a. perennial   b. mercurial
        c. municipal   d. communal

6. In our house, the making of the first cup of coffee was an elaborate _____ that involved multiple grinders, four different kinds of beans, and purified water.

        a. analogy   b. pawn
        c. curriculum   d. ritual

✍ QUIZ #39 ✍
Matching

Match each word on the right with the letter on the left that has a similar meaning.

1. fax	A.	electronic document transfer
2. sublime	B.	shrewd
3. increments	C.	increases
4. haze	D.	pleasant smell
5. canny	E.	supreme
6. bouquet	F.	joy
7. felicity	G.	fog

Matching

Match each word on the right with the letter on the left that has a similar meaning.

1. arteries
2. fiscal
3. bounty
4. compute
5. husky
6. qualify

   A. specify the meaning
   B. financial
   C. sturdy
   D. blood vessels
   E. calculate
   F. plentiful wealth

Cool Books for Cool Readers

Here's a list of books you may actually enjoy. You should know that reading is a surefire way to improve your vocabulary. But reading stories, novels, and poetry will help you do much more than improve your vocabulary. You can read for entertainment and for escape. You can also find out about the lives of young people like yourself who have grown up in places, cultures, or time periods different from your own. It's just like going on a trip, except that you don't have to worry about the driving.

The following list includes books recommended by teachers, librarians, and—most important—other young people. Check out the books in your library, and take home the ones that seem interesting to you. If you like a book, you can ask your parents, friends, teacher, or librarian to recommend others like it. But if you're not hooked after you've read a few chapters of a book, don't worry about it. Try something else. Nobody's grading you!

Adams, Douglas. *The Hitchhiker's Guide to the Galaxy.* (Science Fiction, Humor)
The first book in a series that includes *The Restaurant at the End of the Universe; Life, the Universe & Everything; So Long and Thanks For All the Fish,* and *Mostly Harmless.*

Alcott, Louisa May. *Little Women.* (Classic)

Block, Francesca Lia. *Weetzie Bat.* (Contemporary Fiction)
The first book in a series which has also been published in the volume, *Dangerous Angels: The Weetzie Bat Books.*

Blume, Judy. *Tiger Eyes.* (Contemporary Fiction)
Blume has written many other popular books for young people, including *Blubber* and *Just as Long as We're Together.*

Burnett, Frances Hodgson. *The Secret Garden.* (Classic)

Carroll, Lewis. *Alice's Adventures in Wonderland.* (Classic)
Alice's adventures continue in *Through the Looking Glass.*

Creech, Sharon. *Walk Two Moons.* (Contemporary Fiction)
Creech has written other novels for young people, including *Chasing Redbird* and *The Wanderer.*

Cooper, Susan. *The Dark is Rising*. (Fantasy)
The first book in a series that includes *Greenwitch*, *The Grey King*, and *Silver on the Tree*. *Over Sea, Under Stone* is the prequel to this series.

Cormier, Robert. *The Chocolate War*. (Contemporary Fiction)

Dorris, Michael. *The Window*. (Contemporary Fiction) Dorris also wrote about the main character of this novel, Rayona, in his debut novel, *A Yellow Raft in Blue Water*.

Hinton, S. E. *The Outsiders* (Contemporary Fiction) S. E. Hinton wrote this novel when she was a high school junior.

Fitzgerald, John D. *The Great Brain*. (Historical Fiction)
The first book in a series that includes *More Adventures of the Great Brain*, *Me and My Little Brain*, *The Great Brain at the Academy*, *The Great Brain Reforms*, *The Return of the Great Brain*, and *The Great Brain Does it Again*, and *The Great Brain is Back*.

George, Jean Craighead. *Julie of the Wolves*. (Contemporary Fiction)
George has written two other books about Julie, *Julie* and *Julie's Wolf Pack*, as well as *My Side of the Mountain*.

Hughes, Langston. *The Dream Keeper and Other Poems.* (Poetry)

Konigsburg, E. L. *From the Mixed-Up Files of Mrs. Basil E. Frankweiler.* (Contemporary Fiction)

Lee, Gus. *China Boy.* (Contemporary Fiction) Also read the sequel, *Honor and Duty.*

LeGuin, Ursula K. *A Wizard of Earthsea.* (Fantasy) The first book in a series that includes *A Wizard of Earthsea, The Tombs of Atuan, The Farthest Shore,* and *Tehanu.*

L'Engle, Madeleine. *A Wrinkle in Time.* (Science Fiction, Contemporary Fiction) L'Engle's series about the Murry family continues in *A Swiftly Tilting Planet, A Wind in the Door, An Acceptable Time,* and *Many Waters.* Also try *A Ring of Endless Light,* a favorite in her series about Vicky Austin and her family.

Lewis, C. S. *The Lion, the Witch, and the Wardrobe.* (Classic, Fantasy) The first book in the *Chronicles of Narnia.*

Montgomery, Lucy Maude. *Anne of Green Gables.* (Classic) Anne Shirley's story continues in *Anne of Avonlea* and *Anne of the Island. Rainbow Valley* and *Rilla of Ingleside* are about her children. Also try Montgomery's series about Emily Starr: *Emily of New Moon, Emily Climbs,* and *Emily's Quest.*

Myers, Walter Dean. *Hoops.* (Contemporary Fiction) Myers has written dozens of books, including *Fallen Angels* and *Monster.*

Nye, Naomi Shihab. *Habibi.* (Contemporary Fiction)

Paterson, Katherine. *Bridge to Terabithia.* (Contemporary Fiction) Other popular books by Paterson include *The Great Gilly Hopkins, The Master Puppeteer,* and *Jacob Have I Loved.*

Paulsen, Gary. *Nightjohn.* (Historical Fiction) Paulsen has also written a sequel, *Sarny,* as well as many adventure books, including *Hatchet,* the first in a series.

Rawls, Wilson. *Where the Red Fern Grows.* (Classic)

Rowling, J. K. *Harry Potter and the Sorcerer's Stone.* (Fantasy) The first book in a wildly popular series that includes *Harry Potter and the Chamber of Secrets, Harry Potter and the Prisoner of Azkaban,* and *Harry Potter and the Goblet of Fire.*

Salinger, J. D. *The Catcher in the Rye.* (Classic)

de Saint-Exupery, Antoine. *The Little Prince.* (Classic, Fantasy)

Soto, Gary. *Baseball in April and Other Stories.* (Contemporary Fiction)
Also try Soto's novel *Crazy Weekend,* and *Neighborhood Odes,* a collection of his poetry.

Staples, Suzanne Fisher. *Shabanu: Daughter of the Wind.* (Contemporary Fiction)
Shabanu's story continues in *Haveli.*

Taylor, Mildred D. *Roll of Thunder, Hear My Cry.* (Historical Fiction)

Tolkien, J. R. R. *The Hobbit.* (Fantasy)
The prequel to the *Lord of the Rings* series, which includes *The Fellowship of the Ring, The Two Towers,* and *The Return of the King.*

Voigt, Cynthia. *Homecoming.* (Contemporary Fiction)
The first book about Dicey Tillerman's family and friends; others include *Dicey's Song, A Solitary Blue,* and *Seventeen Against the Dealer.*

Wojciechowska, Maia. *Shadow of a Bull.* (Fiction)

Yep, Laurence. *Dragonwings.* (Historical Fiction)
Also try Yep's other novels about Chinese-American life, *Child of the Owl* and *Dragon's Gate.*

Zindel, Paul. *The Pigman.* (Contemporary Fiction)

Glossary

ABACK (uh BAK) *adv.* by surprise

I was taken *aback* when my grandmother answered the door dressed in her Grim Reaper Halloween costume.

Because nobody knew about my midnight phone calls to Guam, Father was taken *aback* when he received the long-distance bill for $4,700.23.

ABHOR (ab HOR) *v.* to regard with disgust or hatred

Mr. Simplet, who refused to change his clothes more than once a year, was *abhorred* by everyone in the neighborhood.

Juliet *abhorred* the task of cleaning out the bathtub and toilet, but she did it so that she wouldn't be grounded.

ABIDE (uh BYDE) *v.* to tolerate or put up with; to agree to go along with; to remain or stay

I could not *abide* my neighbor's rude manners, so I told him he could no longer borrow my lawnmower.

Because he would not *abide* by the other children's rules, Brandon was never asked to play Terminators vs. Cowboys again.

ABOMINABLE (uh BOM i nuh bul) *adj.* horrible or unpleasant

My teacher warned me that my grade on the test was *abominable*, but I had no idea that I could actually score a –80.

The salad dressing made by my brother was so *abominable* that we ended up using it to poison rats.

ABOUND (uh BOUND) *v.* to be plentiful; to be full

My mind *abounded* with compliments for Samirah's new hair, but I was tongue-tied and unable to voice any of them.

Our garden *abounded* with healthy tomatoes each summer so we made plenty of homemade spaghetti sauce all year round.

ABRIDGE (uh BRIJ) *v.* to reduce; to limit

The tough editor took my two-hundred-page novel and *abridged* it into a three-page pamphlet.

The new *abridged* dictionary contained none of the medical and scientific terms that had been included in the full-length version.

ABYSS (uh BIS) *n.* a seemingly bottomless hole or space

We threw a pebble into the *abyss* to see if we could hear it hit the ground, but no sound came back to us.

Morty Jenkins, whose stomach was like an *abyss*, was able to eat ten large pizzas and still be hungry.

ACADEMIC (ak uh DEM ik) *adj.* having to do with school or college

After years of writing long *academic* papers, Professor Propster had a hard time adjusting to his new job which involved writing snappy advertising slogans.

During her first year at college, Carol had a hard time focusing on her *academic* responsibilities because she was having so much fun with her new friends.

ACCESS (AK ses) *n.* the right to enter or use; the act of entering

Because I had *access* to the master set of keys, we were able to go backstage during the concert quite easily.

Once the man had spoken the secret password, the guard granted him *access* to the hidden military base.

ACCOMMODATE (uh KOM uh dayt) *v.* to help someone; to adjust or adapt; to have room for

We tried to *accommodate* our guests as best we could, but some of them still ended up sleeping on the floor of the kitchen.

Our new station wagon was so large that it could easily *accommodate* the entire family as well as a pair of German shepherds.

ACCORD (uh KORD) *v.* to grant or give; to be in agreement OR *n.* harmony or agreement

The king *accorded* Duchess Francesca a chest full of gold for saving the prince from drowning in his bowl of soup.

The negotiations ended after all sides reached an *accord* about how to solve the water shortage problem.

ACCUMULATE (uh KYOO muh layt) v. to collect or gain; to increase

My goal for the next five years is to *accumulate* all the money that I can so I can afford to buy the Australian continent.

During our vacation in Europe my family *accumulated* so many souvenirs that we had to buy an extra suitcase to bring them home.

ACQUISITION (ak wi ZISH un) n. the act of obtaining something; something added, like an addition to an existing collection.

My *acquisition* of the Omar Moreno baseball card meant that I now had the entire starting lineup of the 1979 Pittsburgh Pirates.

The art collector's most recent *acquisition* was a statue of a ballerina that was sculpted by the French artist Edgar Degas.

ADAGE (AD ij) n. an old saying that is usually considered to be true

The sight of Kyle moaning and clutching his twisted ankle reminded me of the old *adage*, "Look before you leap."

Uncle Nork firmly believed in the *adage* "Haste makes waste," so he would never complete any task in under three hours.

ADJACENT (uh JAY sunt) adj. next to or nearby; lying close by

All the kids in the neighborhood used to play dodgeball in the abandoned field that was *adjacent* to our apartment complex.

Unfortunately, Tammy's iced tea was *adjacent* to the glass containing Grandpa's dentures and when Tammy reached for her cool, refreshing beverage she ended up drinking teeth.

ADMONISH (ad MON ish) *v.* to scold or criticize in a friendly yet serious way

My grandfather *admonished* me every time I forgot to call him "Sir."

Jessica's parents *admonished* her for not calling them to say that she would be home late from the concert because of the traffic jam.

AFFECTED (uh FEK tid) *adj.* changed or influenced in some way OR behaving in an artificial manner

Luckily, the doctors were able to treat the *affected* area of skin with antibiotics, and thereby stop the disease from spreading deeper into the body.

Michael quickly stopped speaking in his *affected* English accent once everyone learned that he was born and raised in Brooklyn, New York.

AIL (AYL) *v.* to suffer from sickness; to cause to suffer

Medieval doctors believed that bleeding their patients helped to cure what *ailed* them.

I went to nurse my *ailing* grandmother in order to help her recover from a bout of the flu.

ALCOVE (AL cohv) *n.* a small room that opens into a larger room; no wall separates the two rooms

We hung our insect wings on a peg in the *alcove* and then joined the Halloween party that was in progress in the living room.

Visitors were asked to leave their shoes in the *alcove* before proceeding into the holy Mackinut shrine.

ALIGHT (uh LYTE) *v.* to settle down upon gently OR to leave or get off something OR *adj.* burning or lit up

The mosquito gently *alighted* upon my brother's cheek and bit him before I could smash it with my hand.

Realizing that this subway stop was our destination, we *alighted* from the train and headed out into the driving snow.

Once the bonfire was *alight*, all of the faces in the crowd seemed to glow with a warm, reddish tinge.

ALLEGE (uh LEJ) *v.* to declare that something is true without offering any proof

Although Olaf *alleged* that he knew nothing about the attempted robbery, the police suspected that he was the PEZ dispenser burglar.

While the prosecuting lawyers continue to *allege* that Heidi is guilty, the defense lawyers have already proven in a court of law that she was merely an innocent victim.

ALLIANCE (uh LYE uhns) *n.* a formal agreement between two or more groups to unite

After they formed an *alliance* with the auto workers at Tucker Inc., the windshield technicians demanded higher salaries from their company by threatening its management with a strike.

The *alliance* between the two rebel factions soon fell apart after a bitter dispute over who had to wash the dishes.

ALLY (AL eye) *n.* a country or person that is united or joined with another for a certain reason

France and England, who were political *allies* during the great wars of this century, seem to be completely culturally incompatible.

As I continued to push for longer work hours with less pay, I quickly discovered that I had few *allies* among my coworkers.

ALTRUISTIC (al troo IS tik) *adj.* showing concern for the well being of others

The *altruistic* efforts of Mother Teresa of Calcutta have saved thousands of poor people from starvation and disease.

Although at first I thanked the old man for his *altruistic* donation of fifty dollars, I soon learned that the money he had given me was fake.

AMASS (uh MAS) *v.* to gather or gain; to increase

Once the general had *amassed* all his troops in the field, he boldly led the charge against the fortress of Count Stoppmenau.

The billionaire had *amassed* so much wealth that whenever he sneezed, dimes came out of his nose.

ANALOGY (uh NAL oh jee) *n.* some form of similarity between two things that are otherwise unlike; an explanation that compares one thing to something else that is similar

To help us understand how some sea creatures breathe, our teacher made an *analogy* between gills on fish and lungs in mammals.

Poets have long seen an *analogy* between spring and youth, and between winter and death.

ANALYSIS (uh NAL i sis) *n.* the process of separating something into smaller parts to better understand the properties of the object as a whole

The laboratory completed its *analysis* of the foreign substance that was found on the last space shuttle mission and determined that it was an alien chewing gum.

Even after three years of careful *analysis*, I am still confused by the National Basketball Association draft system.

ANTISOCIAL (an tee SOH shul) *adj.* avoiding the company of other people OR interfering with society

The *antisocial* writer threw rocks at anyone who tried to walk up the path to his front door.

Marvin's shoplifting habit and bullying behavior are signs of an *antisocial* personality.

APPALL (uh POL) *v.* to shock or amaze; to horrify

Larry's ability to turn his eyelids inside out was truly *appalling*.

The woman was *appalled* to come home after the movie and find that her new curtains had been ripped to shreds by her dog Rocky.

APPARITION (ap uh RISH un) *n.* a visible spirit or ghost

My mother didn't believe in the haunted house's *apparition* until she walked into the kitchen one day and saw a shadowy form doing the dishes.

The *apparition* that I thought was trying to break through my upstairs window to take my soul turned out to be a large piece of cardboard stuck in our tree.

APPEND (uh PEND) *v.* to add on to something

Congressmen Debbs *appended* a paragraph to the crime bill that made it illegal to spit on penguins.

The manager wanted to *append* my contract so that I would have to pay for any food I ate while on duty, but I vowed not to sign the contract if he did.

APT (APT) *adj.* just right for the occasion OR quick to learn

As the snow began to fall, I discovered that my friend's decision to bring heavy jackets to the ball game was a very *apt* decision.

My sister's ability to perfectly construct a model of the Eiffel Tower using toothpicks showed that she was an *apt* student of architecture.

ARBITRATE (AR bi trayt) *v.* to agree to have a dispute settled by a third party; to settle a dispute

Judge Nervil once *arbitrated* a dispute between two neighbors over who had the right to play their stereo the loudest.

Fearing high legal costs, the two battling companies asked a local fortune teller to *arbitrate* for them.

ARDENT (AR dunt) *adj.* greatly passionate or enthusiastic

Corey was such an *ardent* lover of music that he once duct-taped his head to his stereo speakers.

Security guards finally had to go into the stands and throw the *ardent* fan out of the stadium, because the game had ended over three hours ago.

ARID (AIR id) *adj.* very dry; having little rainfall

The Empty Quarter of the Arabian Desert is so *arid* that no living thing can survive there.

Crops refused to grow in the *arid* soil, so the farmer was forced to go into the used-car business to make a living.

ARMADA (ar MAH duh) *n.* a great fleet of warships

Due to faulty navigation, a Finnish *armada* sailed into the wrong harbor and invaded their own country.

The astronauts watched as the vast *armada* of spaceships stopped outside the space station, rolled down a window, and asked for directions to the Pleiades.

ARTERY (AR tuh ree) *n.* a tube or vessel within your body that carries blood from the heart OR a major road or highway

Luckily for him, Jonathan's botched attempt at knife juggling did not sever any of his *arteries*, although he won't need to shave for a while.

The collision of two semi-trucks carrying manure clogged the main *artery* into town for over six hours, but it seemed like longer.

ASPECT (AS pekt) *n.* an element or feature; look or appearance

The fact that people are often forced to parallel park is one of the more annoying *aspects* of driving a car.

The warped glass in the old barn windows gave everyone standing outside a distorted *aspect*.

ASSAILANT (uh SAY lunt) *n.* a person who attacks someone else

Using what I learned in karate class, I was able to defend myself from the *assailant* by giving him a swift kick in the belly.

The cowardly *assailant* who tried to steal the old woman's purse soon found himself stunned by 10,000 volts of electricity from her taser.

ASSERT (uh SURT) *v.* to state a viewpoint definitively; to declare OR to defend or maintain

The students organized a boycott of the cafeteria to *assert* their opinion that the food was horrible.

In the town meeting, the Hendersons *asserted* their right to hang from trees in the park and scream at the top of their lungs, claiming that it was freedom of speech.

ASSESS (uh SESS) *v.* to evaluate; figure out the value or importance of OR to charge with a special payment

The baseball coach could *assess* a player's batting skills by watching him make just one swing.

My public speaking teacher *assessed* me one dollar every time I ended a sentence with "Ya know?"

ASSET (A set) *n.* a worthwhile object or quality that a person or thing possesses

While bravery is an honorable *asset* in any individual, sometimes cowardice is much more useful.

My ancient Greek coin, one of only three in the world, was definitely my most valuable *asset*, even though no one else could tell that it was valuable.

ASTRINGENT (uh STRIN junt) *n.* a cosmetic that cleans the skin and constricts the pores

The *astringent* I used to get rid of my pimples caused me to break out in an ugly purple rash.

ATMOSPHERE (AT muh sfeer) *n.* the mixture of gases that surround a planet and is held by gravity OR the mood of a place

Scientists speculate that Mars once had an *atmosphere* like Earth's, but something happened in the distant past to destroy almost all traces of it.

With its flashing lights, people in cages, and incredibly loud music, Zyggy's Fruit Stand had just the right *atmosphere* for our festive mood.

ATROPHY (AT roh fee) *n.* the wasting or withering away of parts of the body

The severe frostbite caused Ellen's smallest toe to *atrophy*, although the rest of her foot remained healthy.

Janice was so lazy that her leg muscles *atrophied* to the point where she couldn't get up off the sofa without the help of a crane.

AUDIBLE (AW di bul) *adj.* loud enough to be heard

The signal coming from the radio tower in Antarctica was a little fuzzy but still *audible*.

Much to my dismay, Clumsy Clyde's whisper of "I love you" in my ear was *audible* to the entire class.

AUTHENTIC (aw THEN tik) *adj.* genuine and true; not fake

The art expert concluded that the painting was an *authentic* Van Gogh and not a forgery.

I thought I'd found an *authentic* copy of the Declaration of Independence in our attic, but then I noticed that it had the word "suckers" in it.

AVANT-GARDE (ah vont GARD) *adj.* ahead of the times by being new and different, especially in the arts

A symphony composed of alarm clocks, airplane engines, and clanging pots and pans was too *avant-garde* for audiences in the 1920s.

The popular *avant-garde* coffee shop served thimbles full of thick, weird coffee at fifty dollars per drop.

AWE (AW) *n.* a feeling of wonder usually felt in the presence of something magnificent or majestic

I felt an incredible sense of *awe* while standing at the edge of the Grand Canyon, and then my brother sneezed on my hiking boots.

The other jugglers watched in *awe* as Jerry the Three-Handed Dude juggled thirty hacksaws at one time.

AWRY (uh RYE) *adv.* turned or twisted out of shape

Eleanor called room service for an iron when she discovered that her evening gown was all *awry* after it had been stuffed in a suitcase for three weeks.

My plans to skip school went *awry* when my mother saw my foot sticking out from under my bed.

BALEFUL (BAYL ful) *adj.* evil or harmful; threatening OR wretched and miserable

The *baleful* look I received from the python told me that my idea to pick up the snake and hug it was not a good one.

The child let out a *baleful* moan when the three
scoops of chocolate ice cream slipped off the cone
and fell in the dirt.

BALK (BAWK) *v.* to stop in the middle of something and
refuse to proceed

Much to the dismay of all the passengers, the
bus driver *balked* at stopping for lunch, and instead
informed us that he was going to drive straight to
our destination.

I was about to ask Richard to the dance, but I
balked at the last minute and instead talked about
particle physics.

BANDY (BAN dee) *v.* to throw back and forth; to
exchange

The two political candidates *bandied* threats and
insults most of the night, and then finally started
swinging punches at each other.

The crowd at the basketball game *bandied*
around a giant beach ball, which kept falling into
the court and interrupting the game.

BEAM (BEEM) *v.* to send a signal OR to smile proudly

We used a large reflecting mirror and a lighter to
beam a message in Morse code to the rescue ship
waiting in the harbor.

Father *beamed* with pride when he learned that
all three of his daughters had been accepted into
Yale University, but when he found out the cost of
its tuition, he cried.

BEARING (BAYR ing) *n.* the way in which you walk or handle yourself OR the knowledge of your general location (usually *bearings*)

King Stephanoupolous carried himself with such regal *bearing* down the stairs that no one had the nerve to tell him that his pants were unzipped.

After we got our *bearings* from the mountain peak and the angle of the shadows, we knew we could find our campground again.

BELLOW (BEL oh) *v.* to yell in a deep voice

The foreman at the cheese factory had to *bellow* in order to be heard over the loud noises coming from the huge cheese-shaping machines.

To me, the love call of a walrus sounds more like the *bellow* of a drunken sailor than a romantic love song, but then again I'm not a walrus.

BERTH (BURTH) *n.* a built-in bed on a ship or a train

The train did not have enough *berths* for all the passengers who wanted to sleep, so I was forced to take a nap in the luggage compartment.

BESIEGE (bee SEEJ) *v.* to surround a city in order to conquer it; to swamp or overwhelm

The invaders *besieged* the city of Carthage and vowed to keep fighting until all their demands were met.

Our office was *besieged* with phone calls after a local news station reported that we were giving away free turkeys for Thanksgiving.

BESTOW (bee STOH) *v.* to present a gift or honor

The National Committee of Birdwatchers *bestowed* the Grand Hoot Prize on Dr. Feldspar for his achievements in owl stalking.

In honor of the time she spent there in college, Lydia *bestowed* a gift of $50,000 on Zubazz University.

BEWILDER (bee WIL dur) *v.* to confuse greatly

The skinny, short taxi driver was *bewildered* when fourteen different people approached him and asked if he was Arnold Schwarzenegger.

We *bewildered* our dog by spinning her around in circles while shining a strobe light at her and playing industrial music. Obviously, we were bored.

BIAS (BYE us) *n.* a personal leaning or point of view in one direction OR *v.* to cause to have bias or be biased

Because she was unable to overcome her *bias* against livestock, Griselda was fired from her job as a cowgirl.

We suspect some sort of *bias* on the part of our teacher, because all the girls in my class receive A's and all the boys fail.

The Texan judges were *biased* against all the contestants from New York City.

BIPARTISAN (bye PAR ti zun) *adj.* made up of two political parties

The *bipartisan* committee was able to write up a contract that was satisfactory to both the Democrats and the Republicans.

It was going to be another strictly *bipartisan* election until Pete Newlywick, the world's wealthiest man, decided to run as an independent candidate.

BLASÉ (blah ZAY) *adj.* bored or uninterested due to constant exposure

The fans screamed wildly after Plonsky hit the home run, but the *blasé* expression on the sports announcer's face did not change at all.

During the climactic end of the movie, when most of the audience was cheering wildly, the *blasé* movie critic got up to get a root beer.

BLEARY (BLEER ee) *adj.* blurred and indistinct, usually by tears; fuzzy and vague

Stephon's *bleary* eyes and rumpled clothes were evidence that he had not slept for the past five days.

The chocolate stains left on the map by my little brother made the directions so *bleary* that I soon got lost.

BLOAT (BLOTE) *v.* to swell up

Eating an entire large triple-decker combo pizza all by myself caused my stomach to *bloat* and my belt to break.

Our schnauzer, Rex, became *bloated* immediately after eating the Alka-Seltzer tablets someone had left on the bathroom counter.

BLOCKADE (blah KAYD) *n.* to surround a place so that nothing can get in or out

The army of intelligent rats tried to *blockade* the city so that no news of their revolution could escape, but some cats escaped with the news anyway.

The *blockade* of Tyre soon caused a massive shortage of food within the city.

BOG (BOG) *v.* to be slowed down or hindered OR *n.* a damp, muddy place filled with decaying plants, somewhat like a swamp

I got so *bogged* down by reading the hundreds of footnotes in Henry's research paper that I forgot what the paper itself was about.

Our tennis shoes were so slimy after walking across the *bog* that we had to just throw them away.

BOMBARD (bawm BARD) *v.* to continuously strike at a place, usually using some kind of explosive; to fire at repeatedly

During World War II, citizens of London hid underground while German planes *bombarded* the city above.

My teacher *bombarded* me with so many different questions that I instantly regretted having raised my hand.

BORE (BOR) *v.* to drill into something, creating a hole

Because he knew that there was oil underneath him, Donald was determined to *bore* into the earth until he discovered it.

We *bored* holes into the flat piece of oak so we could place legs in them and create a table.

BOUNTY (BOWN tee) *n.* a reward for performing a special action OR plentiful goods or wealth

Once the millionaire offered a $10,000 *bounty* for the capture of the bluejay that stole her diamond necklace, people everywhere began climbing trees to look for it.

The peanut crops this year yielded so much *bounty* that we knew we would be able to eat peanut butter and jelly sandwiches for the rest of our lives.

BOUQUET (boo KAY) *n.* a group of flowers OR a pleasant odor, especially from wine or liquor

When he saw the wildflowers blooming by the roadside, Prakash stopped the car and picked a *bouquet* to give to his wife.

The wine expert inhaled, enjoying the *bouquet* of the expensive champagne.

BRAMBLE (BRAM bul) *n.* a shrub or plant with many thorns

I ripped my shirt in over thirty different places when I tried to walk into the *brambles* to retrieve my baseball.

The rabbit used to hide underneath the *brambles* where foxes couldn't go, until the real estate company sold the land and bulldozed the rabbit's hiding place.

BRETHREN (BRETH run) *n.* a group of relatives; associates within the same organization

The annual family picnic attracted so many of my *brethren* that we ran out of potato salad in under thirty minutes.

After Pinkerton and his work crew were fired unjustly, the rest of the miners went on strike in a show of support for their *brethren*.

BUCCANEER (buk uh NEER) *n.* a pirate

When the *buccaneers* had stormed the ship and taken the regular crew hostage, they stole all the rum that they could carry.

When I was young I heard the call of the sea and wanted to be a fierce *buccaneer,* but I ended up being an accountant instead.

BUNGALOW (BUNG uh loh) *n.* a small cottage with only one story

I left my *bungalow* on the beach and moved into a mansion after I won the lottery.

We thought the *bungalow* in the middle of the forest was a perfect spot to relax, but we soon found out that a family of three bears had leased the property through the summer.

BURLY (BUR lee) *adj.* very stocky and muscled

The *burly* police officer enjoyed towing away cars with his bare hands and a piece of rope.

The last time David started a fight, his *burly* opponent threw him out a window.

BURNISH (BUR nish) *v.* to rub a surface until it's smooth and shiny

Grandpa used to *burnish* his favorite brass spittoon so much that we could easily see our reflections in it.

The marble banister was *burnished* by the many hands that slid along it over the years.

BUSTLE (BUS ul) *v.* to hurry around; to walk around busily OR *n.* lots of activity

Eager to impress his new neighbors, Charles *bustled* around the kitchen for an entire afternoon preparing his favorite dish, Mongolian clams.

The boss was greatly impressed by the *bustle* in the mail room, although most people were simply hurriedly ordering lunch.

CACHE (KASH) *n.* a hidden supply of goods

I thought the attic would be a good place to hide my extra cookies, but some squirrels discovered my *cache* and ate them all.

The rebels found the *cache* of arms that were hidden in the mountains by the government and used the weapons to shoot down birds for their lunch.

CACKLE (KAK ul) *v.* to laugh in a high-pitched, unpleasant manner

The woman *cackling* in the front row bothered the comedian so much that he refused to tell any more jokes.

Kristin and John were happily married but had few friends because whenever they laughed, Kristin would *cackle* and John would snort.

CAJOLE (kuh JOHL) *v.* to influence someone by using flattery or lies

We attempted to *cajole* our mother into letting us stay up late by telling her that she was undoubtedly the most perfect human being who ever existed.

The foreign exchange student *cajoled* the teacher into letting him bake baklava instead of taking the final exam.

CANDIDATE (KAN di dayt) *n.* a person running for an award or political office

By informing voters that her opponent was no more than an ignorant clump of dirt, Laura Jackson proved that she was the better *candidate* in the race for governor.

Strangely enough, for once the *candidate* with the most political experience won the election instead of the candidate that had heaping bags of money to spend.

CANNY (KAN ee) *adj.* careful and shrewd; cautious

The mouse in our kitchen had the *canny* ability to avoid all of the traps we'd set and still find food for its entire family.

We took Bruce along on the camping trip with us because of his *canny* ability to always discover a source of fresh water.

CARCASS (KAR kus) *n.* the remains of a dead animal

Judging by the nasty smell coming from that raccoon *carcass*, I'd say the animal fought a wolf about two days ago and lost.

The *carcass* of the cow had been in the desert sun for so long that only its bones remained.

CATACLYSM (KAT uh kliz um) *n.* a terrible disaster; a violent change in the earth

The town of Greenville, California nicknamed itself "The Unluckiest Place on Earth" after a series of *cataclysms*, including two earthquakes and a typhoon, hit the town in one summer.

The island of Krakatoa was destroyed by a *cataclysmic* volcanic eruption in 1883.

CAVALCADE (kav uhl KAYD) *n.* a procession of notable events or people

We decided to call our school talent show "The *Cavalcade* of Laughs," because every single student planned on doing a comedy routine.

A colorful band of polka lovers danced down the streets behind the marching *cavalcade* of accordion players.

CAVORT (kuh VORT) *v.* to jump and leap about playfully

When we learned that school had been canceled for two weeks, my friends and I rushed outside to *cavort* in the waist-high snow.

Our family *cavorted* in the cool waters of the Pacific Ocean until someone yelled "shark!"

CELESTIAL (suh LES chul) *adj.* having to do with the stars or sky

According to my astrologist, whenever three *celestial* objects—for instance, Mars, Jupiter, and Venus—line up, I'll break out with acne.

Early sailors used *celestial* navigation to find their way around the oceans.

CEREMONY (SER uh moh nee) *n.* a formal activity performed in honor of a specific occasion

The *ceremony* for the opening of the new supermarket was attended by the mayor, the supermarket manager, and five townspeople who had nothing better to do that day.

The wedding *ceremony* was going along very well until the groom's tuxedo caught on fire and had to be extinguished with the contents of the punch bowl.

CHAR (CHAR) *v.* to burn until reduced to charcoal or to burn a little

The fire *charred* the groom's dress pants and transformed them into blackened dress shorts.

The hot dog had been *charred* so badly in the fire that I could eat it only after coating it in mustard.

CHARISMA (kuh RIZ muh) *n.* an exceptional ability to be liked and admired by a great number of people

Once the employees learned that their pension money had been stolen by their boss, even his well known *charisma* could not save him from their wrath.

Even though she wasn't the smartest girl in school, Adelaide had such *charisma* that she easily won the election for student council president.

CHERISH (CHAYR ish) *v.* to value highly; to affectionately care for

Although I had *cherished* my baseball card collection for many years, when a businessman offered me two million dollars for it, I sold it instantly.

Thelma and Louise *cherished* the friendship they had built by playing baseball together.

CHIDE (CHYDE) *v.* to scold

Natalie *chided* her friend Rachel for setting her up with Teddy "The Spaz" Zubazz without first asking her if she was interested in him.

When they finally saw his apartment at college, John's parents *chided* him for not cleaning the dishes in over three years.

CHRISTEN (KRIS un) *v.* to name at a Christian baptism; to name for the first time

Once the child had been dipped in the sacred water, the priest *christened* him "Newton Sigfrinnius IV."

Just before the freak hurricane wiped out the entire waterfront, the brand new yacht had been *christened* "The Invincible."

CHRONOLOGICAL (kron uh LOJ i kul) *adj.* arranged according to time of occurance, from earliest to latest

Unless you read them in *chronological* order, the seven books in the *Dark Lord of Emnon* series can be very confusing.

The detectives instantly knew who the real killer was, once they had figured out the *chronological* order of the night's events.

CINDERS (SIN durs) *n.* something burned down to the point where it can't be burned anymore; ashes

Following Dawn's cruel prank, all I had left of my Snooky Bear was a pile of *cinders* that I kept in jar.

We shoveled the *cinders* out of the fireplace and placed them in the garden as fertilizer.

CIRCULATE (SUR kyuh layt) *v.* to move around freely OR to spread widely

With my fake mustache, blonde wig, and dark sunglasses, I was able to *circulate* throughout the party without being recognized by my friends.

Rumors *circulated* throughout the town that the new mayor was actually an alien, but everyone soon learned that she was just a big *Star Trek* fan.

CIRCUMSTANTIAL (sur kum STAN shul) *adj.* not of main importance

I got a D on my essay about Albert Einstein because I focused on *circumstantial* facts, like his crazy hairstyle and love of wontons, and didn't mention any of his important scientific breakthroughs.

Note: *Circumstantial evidence* refers to facts offered as evidence in a trial from which jurors are supposed to draw conclusions and make decisions. Circumstantial evidence is not direct proof.

The prosecution offered plenty of *circumstantial evidence*—such as the fact that Evans owned a shotgun and the victim had been killed by a shotgun—but the jury found him innocent because there was no solid proof that he was guilty.

CITE (SYTE) *v.* to quote as an example OR to mention as a reward for honorable action

In an attempt to lessen his punishment, Brandon *cited* his previous punishment for not doing the dishes, which was only one day without TV.

The captain *cited* the brave sailor as having courageously wrestled the shark while the other crewmen swam for the lifeboats.

CLARIFY (KLAYR uh fye) *v.* to make something easier to understand; to explain in greater detail

After our mother had *clarified* the directions for changing the oil in the car, the task become much easier to do and far less messy.

We asked our teacher to *clarify* his directions on the final exam because he had only written, "Tell me everything."

CLINCHER (KLIN chur) *n.* the final, decisive act or point

Several things led me to believe that Brandy had eaten my grape-flavored popsicle. The fact that her tongue was purple was the *clincher*.

The *clincher* in the Super Bowl was when DuPont "Scrappy" Carruthers returned a kickoff 97 yards.

CLUTTER (KLUT ur) *n.* a bunch of things scattered around in a mess OR *v.* to fill up in a way that stops movement or action

I was unable to find my baseball glove in the *clutter* underneath my bed, but I discovered a three-year-old sandwich that I'd lost.

So many people were *cluttering* the exit to the movie theater that we decided to sit down and watch all the credits.

COALITION (koh uh LISH un) *n.* a group of people acting together for a specific goal

The sewer workers formed a *coalition* in order to demand higher pay and thicker boots.

The *Coalition* for Better Education was an assortment of teachers, parents, and community leaders who demanded more funding for public education.

COAX (KOHKS) *v.* to gently persuade

After a week of discussion, I finally *coaxed* my parents into letting me go on a camping trip with my friends.

By placing cat treats in the middle of the room, I was able to *coax* the kitten out from under the sofa.

COHERENT (koh HEER unt) *adj.* easily understood; logically connected

Once the gag had been removed from his mouth, the rescued prisoner was able to speak in a *coherent* manner.

The feverish patient kept blurting out sentences that were not *coherent*.

COMBUSTION (kum BUS chun) *n.* the act of burning

The car's *combustion* problems were soon traced to the fact that it was out of gasoline.

In an amateur science experiment, we learned that the *combustion* of firewood is not as smelly and nasty as the burning of plastic.

COMELY (KUM lee) *adj.* attractive and pleasant

The *comely* and smiling faces of the Everly triplets soon made me happy that I was in Mrs. Willenbring's class.

At our school's Thanksgiving dance, the *comely* lad had more than his fair share of willing dance partners.

COMMISSION (kuh MISH un) *v.* to grant authority to someone or some group for a specific purpose OR *n.* a group of people granted the authority to do something

The president *commissioned* a panel of chefs to review the contents of all Italian foods after a plate of spaghetti attacked a group of waiters in Atlanta.

The Italian Food *Commission* soon discovered that the combination of law-fat cheese and garlic was bringing out a violent streak in several traditional dishes.

COMMUNAL (kuh MYOO nul) *adj.* related to or serving every person in the community

The wait staff at the coffee shop had a *communal* tip jar, which they emptied and split evenly every night.

On the Fourth of July, our town holds a huge *communal* picnic, for which everyone brings one dish of food.

COMPATIBLE (kuhm PAT uh bul) *adj.* able to exist or work together in the same system

We quickly realized that the three-pronged electrical plug was not at all *compatible* with our two-pronged wall socket.

The software was not *compatible* with my computer, so when I tried to run it, the whole system crashed.

Sam and Sylvia were such *compatible* dance partners that they moved as a graceful unit.

COMPUTE (kuhm PYOOT) *v.* to work toward a solution through the use of math or a computer

Using his knowledge of physics and gravity, the scientist was able to *compute* the location at which the satellite would hit Earth.

The automated teller machine at my bank instantly *computes* how much money I have left in my account after each withdrawal.

CONCEDE (kuhn SEED) *v.* to give in; to surrender OR to grudgingly admit that something is true

Our team was forced to *concede* the football game after our quarterback ran home bawling for his mommy.

Seconds before the firing squad was going to shoot, the general *conceded* that he had made some mistakes during his career.

CONCOCTION (kun KOK shun) *n.* a mixture of different ingredients

While in the kitchen, Herb made a *concoction* of olive oil, molasses, grape juice, and tobacco, and then served it to us claiming that it was cola.

The powerful chemical *concoction* destroys mildew on contact, but unfortunately it also eats through porcelain and enamel.

CONDESCEND (kahn di SEND) *v.* to willingly do something that is beneath a person's dignity OR to act in a way that shows you think you are better than others

The Nobel Peace Prize winner *condescended* to clean up the auditorium after the awards ceremony.

Thurston is a great wrestler, but his teammates do not appreciate the way he *condescends* to them by constantly explaining what it means to be a champion.

CONFIDANT (KON fi dahnt) *n.* someone that you tell all your secrets to

The Silencers Club was a group of *confidants* that met in my treehouse after school to discuss all the juicy gossip we had learned that day.

You can imagine my dismay when I learned that Sheryl, my *confidant* since grade school, had been selling all my deepest secrets to the *National Tattler*.

CONFIGURATION (kun fig yuh RAY shun) *n.* the way in which the parts of an object are fitted together

By rearranging the *configuration* of his hands and fingers, Robert made the "bunny" shadow figure on the wall transform into a terrifying "Tyrannosaurus Rex."

Because of the careful *configuration* of the boulders at the ancient monument of Stonehenge, some scientists believe it was used as a tool for charting the stars and seasons.

CONFINES (KAHN fynze) *n.* the border or limits of a particular space

A suspicious family, the Alvertons protected the *confines* of their garden by placing land mines around the entire area and patrolling it with watch dogs.

Limited to the *confines* of his cell, the prisoner decided to give up his life of crime and violence and learn to paint with watercolors.

CONFIRMATION (kahn fur MAY shun) *n.* something that provides proof

When they received the battered royal crown through the mail, the police had *confirmation* that the kidnappers had taken King Muekus XIII.

Sylvia's bright orange tongue *confirmed* that she ate the rest of the orange-flavored ice pops from the freezer.

CONFOUND (kuhn FOUND) *v.* to puzzle, confuse, or bewilder

By switching among English, German, Japanese, and Hungarian throughout her speech, the speaker completely *confounded* her audience.

The more I learn about politics, the more *confounded* I become.

CONFRONTATION (kahn fruhn TAY shun) *n.* a direct encounter, especially with an opponent

After his *confrontation* with Mike "Crusher" Smith, Gerald "Yahoo" Johnson announced that he was retiring from boxing immediately.

Because the Mongols had a larger army, better fighters, and better equipment, their *confrontation* with the Chinese army was short.

CONGEAL (kuhn JEEL) *v.* to thicken; to change from a liquid to a solid

As it started to cool down, the top layer of the Thanksgiving gravy *congealed*.

The milk was left on the counter for a many days and eventually *congealed* into a chunky mass that looked like cottage cheese but smelled much worse.

CONGENIAL (kuhn JEEN yul) *adj.* pleasant, open, and friendly OR having similar habits and tastes

The neighborhood tax collector was so *congenial* that everyone on the block was glad to see her and give her their money.

The *congenial* roommates, Magnus and Mahmoud, shared a passion for Greek music, Jackie Chan movies, and record collections.

CONGREGATE (KAHNG gri gayt) *v.* to assemble; to come together and form a crowd

The whole town *congregated* in the town square when they heard that the two candidates for mayor were going to arm wrestle at 2:00 P.M.

Before the football game, the pastor asked all the members of his church to *congregate* in the east end zone and pray for a swift victory.

CONJECTURE (kuhn JEK chur) *v.* to make a guess; to form an opinion based on incomplete knowledge OR *n.* a statement or opinion based on guesswork

Judging by the huge number of feathers left at the crime scene, the detectives *conjectured* that the millionaire was killed by a flock of pillow-wielding ducks.

Early *conjectures* about life on the moon were proved false when astronauts landed there.

CONNOISSEUR (kahn uh SUR) *n.* a person who is an excellent judge in a specific field; an expert in a particular subject

The immense Marcel Roussaeu, a *connoisseur* of desserts, declared that Mrs. Finstin's chocolate fudge dip was the greatest food he had ever tasted.

The *connoisseur* of early European paintings was shocked to find a painting by Giotto at a garage sale in Poughkeepsie, New York.

CONSENSUS (kuhn SEN sus) *n.* an opinion or belief held by the majority of a group

The governor was hoping for support for his plan to become the first king of Vermont, but the *consensus* among voters seemed to be that he was a raving lunatic.

Because I had more brothers than sisters, the *consensus* among the children was that we would go to the wrestling match instead of the symphony.

CONTENTIOUS (kuhn TEN shus) *adj.* argumentative; easily bothered and ready to disagree

The *contentious* man asked me what time it was and then argued with me about the accuracy of my watch.

When she argued my statement that Earth was round, I knew that Sheryl was a *contentious* woman.

CONTRADICT (kahn truh DIKT) *v.* to express the opposite of a statement; argue against an earlier remark or belief

Innis knew it was rude to *contradict* people, but he had to protest when his friend started telling a story about how he had driven from California to Hawaii.

Phillip claimed that he loved to eat any kind of food but cornbread, but when he smelled the delicious yellow bread coming out of the oven, he *contradicted* himself and demanded a piece.

CONTRARY (KAHN trehr ee) *adj.* completely different; exactly opposite OR unfavorable

"On the *contrary*, Watson. Although you thought I was in London, I was in fact on the other side of the world!" exclaimed Holmes.

Even though the hurricane was still two hundred miles away, it created weather conditions that were too *contrary* for us to sail in.

CONTRITION (kun TRISH un) *n.* deep regret for doing something wrong

Hera doubted that her brother's *contrition* was real because he burst into giggles whenever he looked at her.

Note: *Contrite* (kun TRYTE) *adj.* means sorry or regretful.

At his trial, the robber seemed *contrite* for having taken part in the holdup of 343 different banks.

CONTROVERSY (KAHN truh ver see) *n.* a public dispute between two sides who have opposing views.

The city decided to hold an open debate with the hope that it would settle the *controversy* surrounding higher taxes.

Prince's album *Controversy* created a lot of *controversy* because of the racy lyrics in many of the songs.

CONVENE (kuhn VEEN) *v.* to assemble in one place

When their cars were complete, the soapbox derby racers agreed to *convene* at the top of the mountain at sunrise.

Most of our neighbors *convened* for the block party when they heard that our family was providing free barbecue.

CONVEY (kuhn VAY) *v.* to take from one place to another OR to make something known or understood

Henry rented a pick-up truck to help me *convey* my furniture to my new apartment.

The ambassador *conveyed* the deepest sympathies of his nation when he spoke at the funeral of the famous war general.

CONVICTION (kuhn VIK shun) *n.* a deeply held belief or opinion OR a guilty judgment from a judge or jury

It is my *conviction* that long hair and earrings are fine for men, but my mother disagrees.

Because the accused was so obviously guilty, the jury returned a *conviction* in under ten minutes.

CONVOLUTED (kahn vuh LOO tid) *adj.* difficult or complicated due to many twists and turns

Adele's *convoluted* scheme to take over the school involved four pieces of string, eighty-two assault helicopters, some peanut butter, and an android robot named McGyver.

Sam's fifty-seven step method for making a
peanut butter and jelly sandwich was too *convoluted*
for me to follow.

COPIOUS (KOH pee us) *adj.* plentiful; large in number
or quantity

Our family had prepared such a *copious* amount
of food for the party that I knew my mother
wouldn't mind if I gave a whole turkey to our dog.

After I saved my little brother from drowning,
newspapers and television news shows heaped
copious praise on me for my bravery.

CORRELATION (kor uh LAY shun) *n.* connection or
relationship of different factors or events

Over thirty years ago, doctors noticed a *correlation*
between cigarette smoking and lung cancer.

I learned in college that there is a definite
correlation between the amount of time you spend
studying and how well you do on tests.

CORROBORATE (kuh RAWB uh rayt) *v.* to provide
additional support for a statement by supplying new
evidence to back it up

The researchers need to *corroborate* their latest
findings with an additional series of tests before
they go public with their astounding breakthrough.

CORRUPTION (kuh RUP shun) *n.* wickedness, dishonesty
or bad behavior

The ace reporter finally uncovered the *corruption*
in state government when she photographed the
State Attorney accepting money from a gangster.

Note: *Corrupt* (kuh RUPT) *v.* means to cause to behave wickedly or immorally, *adj.* means wicked or immoral.

Mark had been a high school honor student, but he was *corrupted* by evil friends who encouraged him to take drugs.

COVERT (KOH vurt) *adj.* secret; concealed; kept hidden

Members of the CIA discussed their *covert* plan to replace the Libyan president with a cleverly designed cloth puppet.

The spy used the *covert* compartment of her briefcase to hide documents that she'd stolen from hostile countries.

COW (KOW) *v.* to scare by using force or threats

Jonathan gathered together his eight older brothers and *cowed* the bully into letting him play in the baseball game.

The short story "Tales of the Night Stalker who Ate Only Brains" *cowed* the Boy Scout troop into staying inside their tents at night.

CRAFTY (KRAF tee) *adj.* sneaky; sly; skilled in deception or trickery

The *crafty* card player was able to deal himself any card he needed from his specially-rigged deck.

I admired my sister's *crafty* plan to fake illness and avoid school by putting on some of our leftover Halloween makeup.

CRAG (KRAG) *n.* a steep thrust of rock that forms part of a cliff

The hang glider stepped off the *crag* and soared into the air above the canyon.

Desmond stopped himself from rolling off the side of the cliff by grabbing onto a *crag* at the last possible moment.

CREED (KREED) *n.* a belief system that helps guide a person's decisions and actions; a formal statement of the main beliefs of a religion

It was Lazy Larry's *creed* that chores and housework should be avoided at all costs.

According to a religion practiced only by himself and his parents, Sarfu's *creed* demands that he submerge himself in a vat of mustard during every full moon.

CREVICE (KREV iss) *n.* a narrow crack or opening, usually in a rock

While hiking, I lost my favorite watch when it fell so far down a deep *crevice* that there was no way I could retrieve it.

We watched dumbfounded as the earthquake first created a *crevice* in our ceiling, and then neatly split the entire room in two.

CRUCIAL (KROO shul) *adj.* of the greatest importance; highly decisive

With the score tied and two seconds left on the clock, the penalty kick against the Dragons became the *crucial* play in the soccer game.

I thought it was *crucial* that we tell my sister that we were keeping our new pet lizard in her bathroom, but my older brother locked me in the closet before I could get to her.

CRUSADE (kroo SAYD) *n.* a movement toward a specific goal or reform OR a series of expeditions that took place during the Middle Ages in which European knights fought Muslims in an attempt to recover the Holy Land

In the early seventies, Ralph Nader led a successful *crusade* for car safety when he demanded that seat belts be improved and used by everyone.

Although in some people's opinion the *Crusades* were mainly a waste of human life, the travel and communication between Europe and the Middle East did foster an exchange of ideas.

CUMULATIVE (KYOOM yuh luh tiv) *adj.* adding up through a series of increases or additions

Doctors warn that the *cumulative* effect of chewing tobacco is a tremendous increase in your chances for tongue disease.

Although one rotten tomato didn't hurt, the *cumulative* effect of all of them being thrown at him forced the lousy magician from the stage.

CUNNING (KUN ing) *adj.* skilled at fooling people; sly

By hopping on a streetcar and riding to the finish line, Rosie the marathon runner proved that being *cunning* is sometimes more important than athletic training.

The *cunning* burglar avoided the police by impersonating a newspaper reporter rushing to the crime scene.

CURDLE (KUR dul) *v.* to spoil or turn sour OR to thicken into clumps

When the mummy trapped the star of the film in a room, terror made my blood *curdle* and I could barely breathe.

When they were really bored one weekend, the farm kids took a glass of milk and watched it *curdle* over a four-day period.

CURFEW (KUR fyoo) *n.* a law or rule calling for a certain type of person to be indoors by a specific time

My parents let me stay out later than my midnight *curfew* as long as I call and tell them exactly where I am.

Due to the recent spread of smashed mailboxes, the city proposed a 6 o'clock *curfew* for all teenagers and a freeze on baseball bat sales.

CURRICULUM (kuh RIK yuh lum) *n.* the set of classes or courses offered at a particular school or by a specific department, like the math department

The bold high school proposed a *curriculum* that replaced geography class with a class called "Game Show History."

The small private college did not offer as broad a *curriculum* as the large state university, but the classes were smaller and more personal.

CURTSY (KURT see) *n.* a show of respect made by slightly bending one knee and then lowering the body a little, usually performed by women and girls

The princess gracefully *curtsied* toward the king and queen, then gave the order for the jousting tournament to begin.

Not only did the uppity schoolgirl refuse to *curtsy* to Mrs. Baba, she also refused to call the teacher anything other than "Yo, Lady."

CYCLONE (SYE klohn) *n.* a violent spinning windstorm with a calm center; on land also known as a tornado and at sea, a hurricane

The *cyclone* ripped through the trailer park on the edge of town and distributed the trailers over a five mile radius.

DAINTY (DAYN tee) *adj.* attractive and beautiful in a fragile, delicate way OR very choosy; fussy

Mother's collection of *dainty* blow-glass figurines is admired by all our neighbors, but it is a nightmare to dust.

The *dainty* young woman refused to eat anything that came out of a can, so the rest of the campers ate her ration of baked beans.

DAUNT (DAWNT) *v.* to scare and discourage

The steep 3,000-foot slope *daunted* the amateur climbers, who had only climbed up the side of their garage one time for practice.

Many of the tourists were *daunted* when the tour guide informed them that over half of the last tour never returned from the jungle.

DAWN (DAWN) *n.* the appearance of the first light in the morning; the beginning of specific event or activity OR *v.* to begin to be understood or noticed (usually followed by "on")

As the light of *dawn* cleared away the fog, I began to see the faint outline of the city.

It's easy for scholars to look back and say that the birth of Peter the Great marked the *dawn* of a great age in Russian history.

As I looked at my cat's wet paws and happy expression, the thought *dawned* on me that maybe she was responsible for the disappearance of my goldfish, Phil.

DAZZLE (DAZ ul) *v.* to momentarily blind with light OR to astonish, amaze, or impress

The huge spotlights arcing over the crowd *dazzled* fans who looked straight into them.

The Soaring Demplewolfs *dazzled* the audience as they juggled bowling balls while performing high-wire acrobatics.

DEBUNK (dee BUNGK) *v.* to prove or show that an exaggerated claim is false

Officials used video recordings of the race to *debunk* rumors that Willis had cheated by placing jet rockets on his shoes.

Hector's claim that he was the first man on the moon was *debunked* when NASA proved that he was participating in a state bowling championship on November 3, 1965 and was nowhere near outer space.

DECEPTION (di SEP shun) *n.* a form of trickery; something done to fool someone into believing a lie

Samer's neck brace and bandages were a *deception* that he hoped would convince the jury that he was badly injured when my shopping cart bumped his at the supermarket.

Note: *Deceive* (di SEEV) *v.* means to trick or fool.

"Your eyes can *deceive* you," warned Cherly, master of illusion, as she began to float off the floor.

DECOMPOSE (dee kum POHZ) *v.* to decay and rot; to break up into smaller, simpler pieces

Remember that poor raccoon from the "carcass" definition? Well, you can bet that its flesh is *decomposing*.

The chicken wing began to *decompose* when it was placed in the vat of acid, and soon only bits of floating chicken meat remained.

DECREE (di KREE) *n.* an order or command given by a person of authority OR *v.* to order or command something

In an effort to ease the effects of the drought that was sweeping the country, the government *decreed* that no person could waste water by showering.

The citizens were in a uproar when they heard of the king's *decree* that every first-born child would be named after him, King Blenny Blenblenneher.

DEFIANCE (di FYE uns) *n.* open disobedience to authority

In an act of *defiance*, the citizens from the sentence above started naming their children anything but "Blenny Blenblenneher," which, if you think about it, isn't hard to do.

The corporal was sentenced to five days in the army prison for his *defiance* of the direct order from the general.

DEFINITIVE (di FIN i tiv) *adj.* conclusive; having the ability to remove all doubt and end any debate

The *definitive* point in the championship boxing match came when Roberto slugged Al so hard that his teeth flew out into the fourth row of seats.

Taking the girl and tying her to the train tracks was the *definitive* action that convinced me that Dick Viper was a bad man.

DELUSION (di LOO zhun) *n.* a false opinion or idea

When Clark arrived at the Sahara Desert Motel with his snorkeling equipment, the staff realized that he had some *delusion* about the presence of an ocean nearby.

Brandon insisted that Cindy Crawford was his girlfriend and that he talked to her every hour, but his friends realized he was suffering from a *delusion* brought on by watching too many movies.

DEPLORE (di PLOR) *v.* to strongly dislike and disapprove; to condemn and hate

As much as my father *deplores* the violence going on in the world, he sure does love football.

The left-handed protesters *deplored* the new law which stated that only right-handed people could run for political office.

DEPLOY (di PLOI) *v.* to spread out and position in a systematic or strategic way

The search party *deployed* in a wide line across the field so that they could cover as much ground as possible.

DERAIL (de RAYL) *v.* to go off the tracks

The pickup truck that was stalled on the railroad tracks *derailed* the 8:23 northbound freight train, which was going too fast to stop in time.

Father's attempt at a quiet family picnic was *derailed* when Jonathan came across a drum set standing alone in the wilderness.

DERIDE (di RYDE) *v.* to laugh at and ridicule; to mock and scorn

Safe inside his house of brick, the third little pig *derided* the wolf for his wasted huffing and puffing outside the door.

At the school for geniuses, Natasha was constantly *derided* for her inability to understand how Boltzmann's constant applied to an eight-dimensional geodesic spatial causality.

DESOLATION (des uh LAY shun) *n.* a dreary condition or place where very little exists or is happening OR a feeling of sadness and isolation

One can never truly understand *desolation* unless one travels to Enid, Oklahoma, and stays in that drab wasteland for at least a week.

The Cherokee people felt great *desolation* when they were forced to leave their native land and begin the long, difficult journey to the west.

DESPAIR (di SPEHR) *n.* a feeling of absolute hopelessness OR *v.* to lose all hope

Our feelings of *despair* increased every day that we were stranded on that desert island, but we did have incredible tans.

After eight months in solitary confinement, the imprisoned writer *despaired* of ever seeing another human again.

DESPERADO (des pur RAH doh) *n.* a bold outlaw

After he had held up the stagecoach armed only with a banana, the *desperado* quickly peeled his weapon and ate it as he rode away.

The two *desperadoes* decided that they didn't need additional help to take over the fort and steal the eighteen tons of gold that were inside.

DETERIORATE (di TIR ee uh rayt) *v.* to lessen in value, condition, or character; to get worse

Once the termites really got down to business, the condition of the log cabin *deteriorated* rapidly.

The ancient portrait had *deteriorated* to such an extent that no one even knew whether the person shown in it was a man or a woman.

DEVASTATE (dev uh STAYT) *v.* to totally ruin or destroy; to lay waste

The bombing of Dresden, Germany, by the Allies in World War II *devastated* the city to the point where most of it had to be completely rebuilt.

Nikka was so *devastated* that she didn't get picked to be a cheerleader that she crawled under her bed and did not come out for three days.

DIABOLICAL (dye uh BAHL i kul) *adj.* concerning the devil; evil or wicked

Although the minister did admit that rock music was fun to dance to, he insisted that it was all part of a *diabolical* plot to steal teenagers' souls.

The entire staff of the Humane Society raided Mr. Wemberley's house when they learned of his *diabolical* treatment of canaries.

DIAGNOSE (DYE ug nohs) *v.* to study and examine carefully; to identify

The mechanic claimed that he would be unable to *diagnose* the problem until he could take the entire engine apart.

The dentist, who lacked experience with large reptiles, could not *diagnose* the alligator's illness.

DICTATE (DIK tayt) *v.* to say something out loud so that it can be recorded by another person OR to establish a rule or law with authority

While shaving at the sink in his office, the executive *dictated* his instructions for the day to his attentive secretary.

The queen *dictated* her new rules of government to the crowd of peasants below, who reacted by promptly storming the castle.

DIFFERENTIATE (dif uh REN shee ayte) *v.* to be able to tell the difference between two or more things; to make a distinction

Whenever the Pontifract twins dressed alike, no one was able to *differentiate* between them.

The snobby residents of Upper Roxbury Street *differentiated* themselves from the residents of Lower Roxbury by placing gold flamingoes in their lawns.

DILAPIDATED (di LAP i day tid) *adj.* worn down and in a state of disrepair

Just after the foreman of the demolition crew sneezed, the *dilapidated* building collapsed around him into a pile of rotten wood and dust.

The apartment building was so *dilapidated* that the landlord let me have the room for five dollars a month.

DILUTE (dye LOOT) *v.* to lessen the strength of a liquid by adding an additional liquid, usually water; to weaken the force of something

We *diluted* the lemonade by adding more water, but drinking it still made our mouths pucker up.

There was so much static coming from the old speakers that the power of the song was *diluted*.

DIMENSION (di MEN shun) *n.* the measurements of an object's length, width, and height OR the overall extent or scope

We misjudged the *dimensions* of the front door, and as a result we had to saw our new couch in half to get it inside.

The professor's in-depth discussion of variable quantum physics was well beyond the *dimensions* of my understanding.

DIMINISH (di MIN ish) *v.* to reduce or decrease

The noise from the plane's engines gradually *diminished* as it flew away from the airport.

My love for Nora Birloom has not *diminished*, even though she stuck a sign on my back that said "Kick Me."

DINGY (DIN jee) *adj.* dirty with grime or filth; dull and shabby

After a good scrubbing, the *dingy* old lace curtains came out shining and white.

The mirror in the hallway was so *dingy* that I couldn't even tell if the face I saw in it was my own.

DIRECTIVE (di REK tiv) *n.* an order issued by a central authority

Immediately after taking over, the new principal issued the *directive* that all students and faculty would be required to attend an early morning yoga class each day.

Once Central Command issued the *directive* that all guards were required to wear dresses, we knew someone was playing a joke on us.

DISCIPLE (di SYE pul) *n.* a person who trains with a specific teacher and spreads their particular beliefs

Kevin's quick method for doing long division in his head attracted many *disciples* who were eager to show the rest of the middle school the easier way.

Ziggy Zigmund, world-famous snake charmer, advises his *disciples* to use non-poisonous snakes when teaching his techniques to others.

DISCOURSE (DIS kors) *n.* conversation OR a formal, written discussion

By carefully listening to every bit of *discourse* during the embassy party, the spy was able to learn about the secret weapon.

Students recently complained that reading the ancient Greek philosopher Aristotle's *discourses* on nature was one of the most boring things they had ever done.

DISCRETION (di SKRESH un) *n.* caution and self-restraint in behavior OR freedom of choice

Knowing that the floors in the house were old, the colonel showed *discretion* by making a lieutenant walk in front of him.

This November, I will use *discretion* in voting for the next president of the United States.

DISMAL (DIZ mul) *adj.* depressing and miserable; gloomy

The *dismal* weather made the beach party a terrible flop.

Because she had not opened her textbooks all year, Janice knew that finals week would be a *dismal* time for her.

DISMAY (dis MAY) *n.* a quick loss of confidence or courage in the face of difficulty or danger

The bullfighter's confidence turned to *dismay* when he realized that his shoelaces were tied together.

The babysitter could not hide his *dismay* when little Mikey Munson came out of the bathroom and announced that he had shaved his sister's head.

DISPENSE (di SPENS) *v.* to distribute in parts; to deal out OR to do without (usually followed by "with")

The cool new plastic Pez head was able to *dispense* candy from both its mouth and eyes.

The dictator *dispensed* with justice and had the prisoner sentenced to death without a trial.

DISPERSE (di SPURS) *v.* to scatter in different directions OR to vanish and disappear

The mechanical seeder used a rotating arm to *disperse* wheat seeds over a large area of land.

The bright morning sunlight *dispersed* the fog that had been hanging over the bay.

DISPOSITION (dis puh ZISH un) *n.* the way a person usually feels, their mood OR an inclination or tendency

Wilhelm's bad-tempered *disposition* often made him punch any animal, vegetable, or mineral that crossed his path.

Although my sister is usually *disposed* toward green socks, that day she chose the black socks because it was almost Halloween.

DISTEND (di STEND) *v.* to expand or swell due to some form of internal pressure

After the Alka-Seltzer eating contest, the stomachs of both boys *distended* quite a bit.

Filling up the balloon with too much water *distended* it, and soon it exploded in the bathroom sink.

DISTORT (di STORT) *v.* to bend or twist something out of its normal shape

The weird mirrors in the carnival fun house *distorted* my reflection so it looked like I had a four-foot head and three-inch legs.

DNA (short for deoxyribonucleic acid) *n.* the molecule that is responsible for transmitting characteristics and traits in all life forms

The scientists used *DNA* samples from the orphan's blood to determine the identity of her real father.

The nuclear waste from the power plant damaged the *DNA* of the fish in a local stream, causing them to be born with no gills.

DOLEFUL (DOHL ful) *adj.* full of grief and sadness

The *doleful* family stopped by the cemetery one last time to pay their respects to the recently departed family cat.

The moviegoers were laughing and joking on the way in to see *Get Out Your Handkerchiefs,* but they were *doleful* on the way out.

DOMINION (duh MIN yun) *n.* the exercise of control over a specific area OR *n.* the area under control by a specific ruler

With the rebellion in the south successfully defeated, the emperor could once more claim *dominion* over the entire continent.

Signs posted along the border warned all travelers to stay out of King Vlad's *dominion,* or they would regret it.

DOUR (DOWR) *adj.* silent and ill-tempered; forbidding and harsh

When the schoolchildren began to taunt him, the *dour* woodsmen picked up his axe and chased them.

I wanted to buy a cookie, but the *dour* expression of the woman behind the counter made me decide to go across the street for some ice cream instead.

DREAD (DRED) *n.* a large amount of fear; utter terror OR *v.* to greatly fear

I *dread* going to sleep at night because for the past week I have been having a terrible nightmare about zombies who look like Frank Sinatra.

A shy child, Helena *dreaded* the moment she would have to present her book report to the whole class; the idea of speaking in front of the class filled Helena with *dread.*

DREARY (DREER ee) *adj.* dark and bleak OR dull and boring

The *dreary* look of the farm cellar was altered when we put in new light bulbs and hung bright streamers everywhere.

So many audience members had been put to sleep by the *dreary* play that you could hardly hear the actors over their snoring.

DRENCH (DRENCH) v. to soak thoroughly

After I was *drenched* in the rainstorm, I vowed to never again buy a five cent, paper umbrella.

The escape artist managed to free herself from the iron chest that had been thrown into the sea, but she was *drenched* in the process.

DRONE (DROHN) v. to speak in a monotonous tone; to make a continuous, low humming noise

My uncle would *drone* on about his experiences as a short order cook in the Gulf War until someone in the family changed the subject.

The farmhand would often go to sleep at night by listening to the steady *drone* of the cicadas outside.

DUPLICITY (doo PLIS i tee) n. deliberate trickery or deception

The man who impersonated the mayor and ordered that everyone pay him twenty dollars in city taxes, was arrested and convicted for his *duplicity*.

Jane was a bully who terrorized everyone at school, but she had a knack for *duplicity* that helped her convince all the teachers that she was the victim.

DYNAMIC (dye NAM ik) adj. exciting and vigorous OR rapidly changing; constantly active

The audience screamed for the *dynamic* performer to come back on stage and play some more.

The *dynamic* couple would often go on round-the-world vacations without a moment's notice.

EBULLIENT (i BOOL yunt) *adj.* high spirited, bubbly, and full of enthusiasm

Although no one was seriously injured, the *ebullient* mood of the festival was lost once the roof collapsed onto the dance floor.

Maxine's *ebullient* personality and charming smile made her the most popular girl at school.

ECLECTIC (i KLEK tik) *adj.* coming from a variety of different sources; choosing from a variety of sources

The Hammerboy's first album was an *eclectic* blend of Icelandic folk songs, Japanese heavy metal, and Brazilian samba music.

The restaurant's *eclectic* buffet featured eels dipped in peanut butter as well as roasted sheep's stomach filled with a frothy lime sauce.

ECOSYSTEM (EEK oh sis tum) *n.* a term used to describe the interactions between all living things and their particular environments

The oil spill caused massive damage to the Alaskan *ecosystem* by destroying countless birds and fish.

The fragile *ecosystem* of the swamp has been upset by acid rain and many types of frogs are dying off.

EDIBLE (ED uh bul) *adj.* fit for eating

We decided that the berries were *edible* after our dog ate some and did not get sick.

Sally's mom quickly determined that the four-month-old sandwich she found under Sally's bed was no longer *edible*.

ELABORATE (i LAB ur it) *adj*. created with great attention to details; intricate OR *v*. (i LAB uh rayt) to explain ideas or thoughts in even greater detail than before

The *elaborate* stitching and beading on the wedding dress took four seamstresses six months to complete.

Because Billy's answer to the Civil War question was rather short and vague, the teacher asked him to *elaborate* on his response.

ELEGANCE (EL i guns) *n*. grace and cultured beauty in appearance or style

The small apartment was decorated with such taste and *elegance* that visitors hardly noticed that it only measured six feet by ten feet.

When Odette, the Black Swan, appeared on the stage, her *elegance* and talent made the other ballerinas look like waddling penguins in comparison.

ELEMENT (EL uh munt) *n*. one part of a whole OR in chemistry, a substance that cannot be broken down into a simpler substance

A talented drummer is only one *element* of a good jazz band.

Silicon, which is found in sand, is the second most abundant *element* on Earth.

ELITE (i LEET) *n*. the very best or the highest group; what is thought to be the best or highest group OR *adj*. made up of the very best; belonging to or made up of a small, privileged group

Now that he was a member of the *elite,* the recently appointed knight refused to talk to any of his old "commoner" friends.

The *elite* country club only accepted millionaires as members.

ELONGATE (i LONG gayt) v. to stretch out or lengthen

The wad of chewing gum *elongated* as Billy held a part of it in his teeth while stretching out the rest with his hand.

Time seemed to *elongate* as I listened to the speaker drone on about her favorite type of garden beetle.

EMBED (em BED) v. to place something firmly within a surrounding mass

The explorer *embedded* the flagpole in the soil and proudly claimed this new land as part of France.

The splinter was so deeply *embedded* in her palm that tweezers couldn't remove it.

EMBROIDER (em BROI dur) v. to decorate an object using needlework

The once plain rug was *embroidered* with fine pearls so that it would be beautiful enough for the princess' room.

The biker's denim jacket was *embroidered* in an odd pattern that appeared to be rows of animal skulls.

EMPATHY (EM puh thee) n. the ability to understand another person's feelings or thoughts

The teacher's *empathy* for Robert did not stop her from giving him a failing grade, but she did offer to help him study for the next test.

Van's *empathy* for the refugees in Rwanda is so intense that he cries whenever he reads about them in the newspaper.

EMPHATIC (em FAT ik) *adj.* stressed with emphasis; forceful and striking

Kruschev made his declaration *emphatic* by taking off his shoe and pounding it into a table as he spoke.

EMULATE (EM yuh layt) *v.* to imitate someone in the hopes of equaling or exceeding their achievements

Walt tried to *emulate* the astronauts on a space flight by living in his closet for almost three weeks.

When I was in junior high school I spent hours teasing my hair and cutting off the sleeves of my T-shirts, in an attempt to *emulate* Madonna.

ENDEAVOR (en DEV ur) *n.* a serious attempt OR *v.* to attempt to do something

After long months of sleepless nights, we succeeded in our *endeavor* to transmit psychic messages to Elvis Presley.

The crew *endeavored* to please the captain, but nothing they did ever seemed to be good enough for him.

ENGAGING (en GAY jing) *adj.* likable and attractive; charming

Soon everyone in the party had gathered around one *engaging* man who was telling hilarious stories.

The audience was delighted by the *engaging* piece of music Claudia played at her recital.

ENHANCE (en HANS) *v.* to increase

The boxer hoped to *enhance* his reputation as one bad dude by claiming he once beat up a supertanker full of African killer bees.

The value of my Elvis Presley stamp was *enhanced* when all of the other Elvis Presley stamps in the world suddenly disappeared.

"Good lighting and good make-up *enhance* almost everyone's beauty," said the old movie star.

ENSURE (en SHOOR) *v.* to make certain; to guarantee

Father *ensured* that our luggage would not fly off the top of the car by wrapping eight steel cables around the suitcases.

The witch doctor *ensured* that the other team would lose the ball game by giving its entire starting offense the mumps.

ENTITLE (en TYTE ul) *v.* to give the right or privilege to somebody

The will clearly stated that the oldest sister was *entitled* to her mother's entire collection of sad-faced clown paintings but nothing else.

Although Morgan was actually *entitled* to receive the car next, she passed the Gremlin on to her younger brother.

ENTREPRENEUR (ahn truh puh NUR) *n.* someone who starts his or her own business

The young *entrepreneur* lost all his money when a national coffee shop chain opened a huge restaurant across the street from his small coffee stand and stole all of his customers.

The young *entrepreneur* soon transformed her tiny company into the worldwide leader in disposable bathtubs.

ERA (EER uh) *n.* a period of time marked by certain conditions or events OR a unit of time, usually hundreds of millions of years long, used by scientists to describe major stages in Earth's development

An *era* called "Reconstruction," which began after the end of the Civil War, saw many changes to the United States.

Geologist believe that all of the dinosaurs died off during the Mesozoic *era*.

EVACUATE (i VAK yoo ayt) *v.* to leave or withdraw, usually from an area that is dangerous in some way

When the fire alarm sounded, the school was quickly *evacuated*.

Visitors were forced to *evacuate* the zoo when the alligators broke loose from their pond and began to roam freely.

EVOKE (i VOHK) *v.* to summon or call forth OR to come to mind because of some type of stimulation or suggestion

The high priest of Kronhorst spoke the ancient chant that was supposed to *evoke* the spirit of the volcano god, but the spirit of Kronhorst's secretary answered instead.

Looking at the water lilies in the pond *evoked* memories of the Monet paintings I saw while in France.

EXASPERATE (ig ZAS puh rayt) *v.* to irritate greatly; to make impatient or angry

Bennie's inability to catch fly balls *exasperated* his teammates.

The loud music from the apartment next door *exasperated* the student, who was trying to study.

EXCLUSION (ik SKLOO zhun) *n.* the state of not being allowed to enter or to join

The continued *exclusion* of non-male, non-white people from high-ranking positions in our country is one of the most serious problems we face today.

Rudolph the red-nosed reindeer felt very sad because of his constant *exclusion* from all of the games that were enjoyed by the other reindeer.

EXEMPT (ig ZEMPT) *adj.* excused; free from obligation OR *v.* to release from obligation

Because she passed every one of her classes with an "A" average, Gia was *exempt* from final exams her senior year.

Phil's flat feet and partial blindness *exempted* him from having to serve in the army.

EXERTION (eg ZUR shun) *n.* strenuous effort or work

It's hard to imagine the amount of *exertion* that must have gone into the building of the Egyptian pyramids.

We started to build a four-story treehouse in our backyard, but the *exertion* of going up and down the tree soon wore us out.

EXILE (EG zyle) *n.* a person forced to live outside their native country OR *v.* to banish someone from his or her native land

While the *exile* yearned to return to his native Elvonia and continue the revolutionary struggle, he did admit that the television shows were much better in the United States.

Having been convicted of treason, Napoleon was *exiled* to the tiny island of Elba.

EXORBITANT (ig ZOR bi tunt) *adj.* far beyond customary levels or bounds

I thought that $50,000 was a little *exorbitant* for a pair of shoes, although they did have cool Velcro fasteners.

The forty-foot cake at movie star Tiffani Twinkle's wedding reception was *exorbitant* even by Hollywood standards.

EXOTIC (ig ZOT ik) *adj.* from a foreign land OR excitingly unusual and strange

The *exotic* vine imported from Japan grew so quickly in America that it soon destroyed most of the local vegetation.

Although Kelly has very ordinary features, her *exotic* perfumes and unique clothing give her an air of mystery.

EXPANSE (ik SPANS) *n.* a wide, open area

Travelers with good vision could see for three miles in any direction across the grassy *expanse*.

Each year, huge herds of wildebeest travel across the African *expanse* in search of food and water.

EXPLETIVE (EK spli tiv) *n.* a curse or vulgar word; profanity

Lola's mother washed her mouth out with soap when she overheard all the *expletives* she used during a phone conversation with her classmate.

The sailor kept quiet in polite company because the only words he knew were *expletives*.

EXQUISITE (EK skwi zit) *adj.* having a beautiful and intricate design OR intense; very powerful

The microscopic brush strokes, some smaller than the eye can see, give an *exquisite* brilliance to the painting.

The joy of the eighty-story roller coaster drop was mixed with an *exquisite* sense of terror.

EXTINCT (ek STINGKT) *adj.* no longer alive anywhere on Earth

The flightless dodo bird, killed and eaten in great number by Dutch sailors, has been *extinct* for over three hundred years.

African elephants were in danger of becoming *extinct* until international laws were formed to protect them from ivory hunters.

EXTRICATE (EK stri kayt) *v.* to get out of a situation; to remove or set free

Once the Mortons got the slide projector out, I knew it was time to *extricate* myself from their dinner party.

The famous magician, Harry Houdini, was able to *extricate* himself from handcuffs, straightjackets, and ropes with great ease.

EXUBERANT (ig ZOO bur unt) *adj.* overflowing with joy and happiness

The child was *exuberant* after receiving the Christmas gift she wanted most, a G.I. Hank Fort Impervious kit.

The *exuberant* feeling at the meeting of the Lucky People's Club disappeared when the black cat came in through the window.

EXUDE (ig ZOOD) *v.* to ooze out, give forth as if oozing; radiate

The sap *exuded* by the rubber tree is used to make . . . you guessed it, rubber!

The salesman *exuded* a friendliness that caused many people to buy his products without even looking at them first.

FATHOM (FATH um) *v.* to understand; to get the point OR *n.* a unit of length that equals six feet and is used by sailors to measure the depth of water

The professor's speech was so garbled and full of gaps in logic that I was unable to *fathom* what she was trying to tell the class.

Because the water near the left bank of the river was over three *fathoms* deeper than the water in the center, the steamship headed left.

FAWN (FAWN) *v.* to try to please someone by excessive flattery; to seek favor by showing attention

The cheerleaders used to *fawn* over the star quarterback until one of them found out the hard way that he never brushed his teeth.

The three brothers *fawned* over the new babysitter, hoping that they could convince her to give them ice cream for dinner.

FAX (FAKS) *n.* a machine which uses telephone lines to send and receive exact copies of paper documents; the copy produced by a fax machine OR *v.* to send someone a document by fax machine.

The *fax* machine in our office received a copy of the important contract that was sent from our Michigan office only moments before lightning struck the building.

I photocopied my face and then *faxed* it to a friend of mine who lives in Alaska.

FELICITY (fi LIS i tee) *n.* joy and great happiness

The *felicity* of the wedding reception was threatened when the bridesmaids got into a fist fight over the bouquet.

The beautiful sunrise and a swarm of colorful butterflies added to the *felicity* we felt as we strolled through the park.

FEND (FEND) *v.* to hold off, especially an attack OR to attempt to manage

By placing a wall of sandbags around the house, the Thompsons were able to *fend* off the rising flood waters for one more day.

When our hiking guide went mad after eating those weird purple berries, we knew we would have to *fend* for ourselves on the way back to camp.

FICTION (FIK shun) *n.* a piece of writing that is made up from the writer's imagination and is not factual; the category of writing that includes novels and short stories, but not plays, poems, or factual works OR a lie

Miranda's love of star-gazing and wild imagination help her write great *fiction* about visitors from other planets and travels through space.

My brother likes reading history books and biographies of famous people, but I think *fiction* is more interesting.

Myron's story about a giant ostrich breaking into his bedroom and eating his homework turned out to be complete *fiction*.

FIGUREHEAD (FIG yuhr hed) *n.* someone who is the head of a group by title, but who actually has no real power OR a carved figure, usually of a woman, on the front part (the prow) of a ship

After China lost its war with Japan, the once powerful Emperor of China became a *figurehead* controlled completely by the Japanese government.

The *figurehead* on the pirate ship looked like an Amazon warrior, bravely facing the dangerous seas.

FISCAL (FIS kul) *adj.* concerning money or finances; concerning the government's treasury or finances

Stan, who liked to shop and spent money freely, became cranky whenever his wife brought up *fiscal* matters or tried to set up a family budget.

The government hoped to solve its *fiscal* problems by printing ten trillion dollars in new money.

FISSURE (FISH ur) *n.* a long, thin split in a rock; any long, thin split

The horizontal *fissure* in the rock provided an excellent fingerhold during my climb up the face of Yosemite Cliff.

As the days grew warmer, *fissures* and cracks began to appear in the layer of ice covering the lake.

FLABBERGAST (FLAB ur gast) *v.* to amaze, astonish, bewilder

When the penguin at the zoo asked me for a cigarette, I was too *flabbergasted* to tell it I didn't smoke.

During the basketball game, when all the players started to float towards the ceiling, the referee was too *flabbergasted* to blow his whistle or call any penalties.

FLAG (FLAG) *v.* to lose strength; to weaken

As the malaria ran its course, the patient's health *flagged* dangerously.

As they reached the twenty-mile point in the marathon, the pace of the runners started to *flag*.

FLAMBOYANT (flam BOY unt) *adj.* very flashy, over-the-top, exaggerated

Although I didn't mind the diamond-studded suit and pants that Robert wore, I did think his eight-foot neon crown was a little *flamboyant*.

The *flamboyant* actor liked to burst into a room, scream, run around, and kiss everyone, and only then would he sit down for the morning meeting.

FLANK (FLANK) *v.* to move around and attack the side of something; to be placed at the side of another object OR *n.* the side of a body, just above the hip

By galloping around a hill to their left, the Huns were able to *flank* their opponents and attack them from two directions.

We decided that the two smaller stuffed bears should *flank* the larger Papa Bear who was in the middle of the bed.

The racehorse's muscular *flank* rippled as he rounded the first turn in the track.

FLATTERY (FLAT uh ree) *n.* excessive or insincere compliments

The reporters continued their *flattery* of the actress until she finally granted them an interview.

I was certain that *flattery* would put my mother in a good enough mood that she wouldn't get mad about the missing sofa, but I was wrong.

FLEDGLING (FLEJ ling) *n.* a baby bird that has just learned how to fly OR *adj.* new and inexperienced

The alley cat stood watch below the bluejay's nest, hoping that one of the *fledglings* would fall as it was trying to fly for the first time.

When our *fledgling* tour guide had trouble even turning on the microphone, I knew I was in for a long day at the museum.

FLEECE (FLEES) *n.* a sheep's coat of wool

Fleece makes an excellent jacket liner, but only after you wash the smell of sheep out of it.

Because they had some extra *fleece* left over after the shearing, the shepherds decided to knit warm gloves for everyone.

FLOTSAM (FLOT sum) *n.* floating wreckage and debris from a wrecked ship and its cargo

A jewelry box, a parasol, and some piano keys drifted among the *flotsam* from the sunken luxury ocean liner.

FLOUT (FLOWT) *v.* to scorn and show contempt for; to treat with contempt

Xander *flouted* his parents' authority by grabbing his father's car keys and speeding off to the Foo Fighters concert, even though he was supposed to be grounded.

The French waiter *flouted* my efforts to speak his language by calling my accent barbaric and covering his ears whenever I began to talk.

FLUCTUATE (FLUK choo ayt) *v.* to shift back and forth; to change irregularly

Fall weather in hill country *fluctuates* between eighty degrees and sunny one day to forty degrees and cloudy the next.

Pavel's weight *fluctuates* so wildly from month to month that he has to keep both extra-large and extra-small shirts in his closet.

FLUENT (FLOO unt) *adj.* able to express yourself smoothly; graceful

Because she was *fluent* in many languages, the translator had no problem interpreting everything the four foreign diplomats said.

Jordan's *fluent* movements on the basketball court make him a pleasure to watch.

FLUSTER (FLUS tur) *v.* to shake up and make nervous or excited

When told she was one of three finalists for the lottery, the woman was so *flustered* that she dropped the telephone.

The 3:00 A.M. surprise visit from the king *flustered* the farmer and his wife.

FLUX (FLUKS) *n.* continuous change; flow

Chrissie's career plans are always in *flux*; last week she wanted to be a mail carrier, yesterday she decided to become a ballerina, and today she announced that she intends to play golf for a living.

FOIL (FOYL) *v.* to prevent from being successful, to ruin

The villain's plan to kill the heroine was *foiled* when Pokey Slim arrived just in time to untie her from the railroad track and carry her to safety.

Meg *foiled* my dreams of becoming student class president by convincing everyone that I was a teacher's pet who secretly wanted to lengthen the school day by two hours.

FOLIAGE (FOH lee ij) *n.* a group of plant leaves

We stood next to the trunk of a tree so its dense *foliage* would shelter us from the rainstorm.

As they searched for the fabled gold howler monkey, the explorers used machetes to hack away the *foliage* of the jungle.

FOLLY (FAHL ee) *n.* lack of good judgment; stupidity and foolishness

Looking back, Edwin realized the *folly* of his plan to cross the Sahara Desert on rollerskates.

The daredevil's attempt to go over Niagara Falls in a barrel filled with deadly snakes was a *folly* for all concerned, including the snakes.

FOOLHARDY (FOOL har dee) *adj.* reckless and rash; bold without thinking

As she plummeted through the sky, Gabriella realized that it was *foolhardy* to go skydiving without a parachute.

The *foolhardy* soldier quickly volunteered to attack the German Seventh Tank Regiment armed only with a spoon and an old muffin.

FORAGE (FOR ij) *v.* to hunt or search for something

The raccoons that hang around our apartment complex love to *forage* for food in the dumpsters.

I *foraged* through my sock drawer looking for the one pair of tweed argyles that I wear whenever I need good luck.

FOREBODING (for BOH ding) *n.* a feeling that something bad is about to happen

A *foreboding* fell over the football crowd as they watched the mean-looking aliens descend from the sky and beat up the school band.

Milt Haaspand was a superstitious man who always had a sense of *foreboding* when his left knee started to ache.

FORGE (FORJ) *v.* to form (usually metal) by heating then shaping; to shape or mold carefully OR *v.* to head forward against resistance

Back in the old days, when peace returned to a country, blacksmiths would gather up the soldiers' swords and *forge* them into farm tools such as plowshares.

The skillful diplomat was able to *forge* a lasting peace between Israel and Egypt.

The candidate was determined to *forge* ahead with his campaign, despite the opinion polls that showed he was trailing far behind his opponent.

FORMIDABLE (FOR mi duh bul) *adj*. difficult to defeat; frightening or alarming; awe-inspiring

Lightning quick and over seven feet tall, Ed "Three Hands" Hroboski was one of the most *formidable* table tennis players around.

I think of Glenda as a *formidable* person because I once saw her uproot an oak tree with one arm.

FORTHRIGHT (FORTH ryte) *adj*. honest and open; straightforward and direct

Voters loved the *forthright* governor who always kept her campaign promises and never did anything unethical.

Because Charles was so *forthright* about his feelings for Karen, she agreed to go to the prom with him.

FOSSIL (FAHS ul) *n*. the bones or remains of an ancient lifeform

A farmer in England found a *fossil* that appears to be the footprint of the largest dinosaur ever discovered.

In the Museum of Natural History, I saw *fossils* of ancient plants and fish.

Note: Fossil fuel is any fossil material that burns. Coal, petroleum, and natural gas all came from fossils.

FRAIL (FRAYL) *adj*. weak and easily broken

Surgery had left Francine very *frail*, so her doctors kept her in the hospital for an extra week to make sure she was strong enough to go home.

It took only a mild gust of wind to smash the *frail* treehouse the boys had made out of toothpicks.

FRANK (FRANK) *adj.* open and direct; sincere

The queen liked *frank* advisers who pointed out her errors, not flatterers who always agreed with her and were afraid to speak their minds.

Note: *Frankness* (FRANK nes) *n.* means openness and directness

I admire Carol's *frankness* because even though she sometimes says unpleasant things, I always know she's giving me her true opinion.

FRENZY (FREN zee) *n.* a condition of wild excitement and agitation

Jonas, a huge Tampa Bay fan since birth, went into a *frenzy* after the Buccaneers' last-second win against the Chicago Bears.

The townsfolk went into a *frenzy* when they learned that Mayor Snide had tried to raise taxes by eighty percent and rename the town Snidesville.

FRINGE (FRINJ) *n.* the outer portion or margin; the edge OR a decorative edge with dangling or hanging threads

Salt *fringed* the little pool of sea water that was drying in the sun.

Teresa used tiny ribbons to create a *fringe* for her new dress.

FROCK (FRAHK) *n.* a large, loose outer garment, like a priest's robe; a woman's dress

I tried to listen to the priest's sermon, but I was distracted by the incredible number of mustard stains all over the front of his *frock*.

Diane's party *frock* was so loose and formless that it made her look like a human tent.

FUNDAMENTAL (fun dah MEN tul) *adj.* having to do with the basic level; primary or elemental

One of the *fundamental* rules of soccer is to never touch the ball with your hands.

Obedience to their commander is a *fundamental* requirement of all soldiers.

A *fundamental* knowledge of math is all you need in order to balance your checkbook.

FURTIVE (FUR tiv) *adj.* done in a quiet, secretive way

While her mother's back was turned, Sandy took a *furtive* peek inside the closet where she knew the Christmas presents were hidden.

Miguel had no hall pass, so he had to slide *furtively* along the wall and duck while passing the windows in the doors of classrooms so that none of the teachers would see him.

GALE (GAYL) *n.* an extremely strong wind OR a loud outburst

The rainfall from the thunderstorm wasn't threatening, but the *gales* ripped apart houses and knocked people off their feet.

Gales of laughter erupted from the club audience as the comedian went into his famous "Smashing Mushrooms" skit.

GALLEON (GAL ee un) *n.* a large ship with sails, used especially by the Spanish in the 1400s, 1500s, and 1600s

The sunset glowed off the *galleon's* white sails as it glided into port at Montevideo.

GARBLE (GAR bul) *v.* to mix up or distort

The poem is beautiful in the original Spanish, but this bad translation *garbles* its meaning.

The principal interrupted our classes to make an important announcement, but the intercom *garbled* his voice so badly that it was impossible to tell what he was saying.

GARLAND (GAR lund) *n.* a string of flowers, leaves, or other materials woven together to form a crown or some other ornament

I twisted the stems of the roses together to create a beautiful *garland*, but the thorns made wearing it a little painful.

The Pattersons always hung a *garland* of mistletoe and holly on their front door to show their Christmas spirit.

GARRISON (GEHR i sun) *n.* a military fort OR a group of soldiers stationed at a fort

The walls of the *garrison* had to be repaired after the fire started by the rebel soldiers burned most of them down.

Reinforcements from Adleyville boosted the *garrison's* strength, but the soldiers were still badly outnumbered by their enemy.

GAUNT (GAWNT) *adj.* bony and thin; undernourished OR bleak and stark

The *gaunt* cat looked like it was made of nothing more than furry paper stretched over a rib cage.

George Orwell's *gaunt* vision of the future in the book *1984* is enough to make anyone want to build a time machine and go live in the Paleozoic Era.

GENE (JEEN) *n.* a particular section of DNA that determines a particular hereditary characteristic that is passed down from one generation to the next

The color of your eyes is determined entirely by the combination of your parents' *genes*.

Scientists try to isolate the *genes* that cause hereditary diseases, like diabetes, so that they may some day be able to eliminate the disease.

GENRE (ZHAHN ruh) *n.* a specific type of literature or music, like science fiction or heavy metal

My father loves opera, but I think most of the music in that *genre* sounds like people screaming in some crazy language.

The writer Curly Pickins was a master of the Western *genre*, but critics hated his romances.

GIBBERISH (JIB ur ish) *n.* speech or writing that makes no sense; crazy talk

Walking bananas Tom bluebird in the dufflebeak nosehair mackinute soapdish von *gibberish* nork nork nork. (This is just an example.)

Foreign languages sound like *gibberish* unless you know how to speak them.

GIDDY (GID ee) *adj.* dizzy; feeling an unsteady, whirling sensation OR excited and light-headed

Riding the Doomhills of Tharg rollercoaster nineteen consecutive times left Jim *giddy* and unable to remember his own name.

I felt *giddy* as I rounded the bases after hitting my first home run ever in a Little League game.

GLARE (GLEHR) *v.* to stare angrily OR to shine very brightly OR *n.* a long, angry stare OR *n.* a bright, blinding light

The jealous student *glared* at Evelyn the whole time she was onstage accepting her award for being the Geography Student of the Year.

Evelyn noticed the *glare* of the jealous student, but she was too happy to care.

The sun *glared* down on the beach, making the sand look bright white.

The *glare* of the Sun, which was reflected off the sand made it hard for me to see who was approaching my beach blanket.

GLEAN (GLEEN) *v.* to gather or find something out piece by piece

After collecting and sorting through all the numerous fingerprints, the detectives began to *glean* the identity of the burglar.

Staring at the eight maps of Paris, Humberto was able to *glean* some idea of where the museums were located.

GLISTEN (GLIS un) *v.* to shine with a sparkling light; to sparkle

The light coat of dew caused the grass to *glisten* in the morning sunlight.

The sunbather *glistened* with sweat and suntan oil.

GNASH (NASH) *v.* to grind or strike teeth together

The weightlifter *gnashed* his teeth as he tried to bench press 600 pounds.

Hearing fingernails being raked across a chalk board makes me *gnash* my teeth in agony.

GOAD (GOHD) *v.* to urge or prod

We finally went outside and sat down in the backyard after our father *goaded* us to get off the sofa and do something with our lives.

The bully tried to *goad* Casey into fighting by spitting on him and then making chicken noises.

GOBLET (GOB lit) *n.* a drinking cup with a stem and a base and no handle

It took both of my hands wrapped tightly around the stem to lift the thick, gold *goblet* which weighed eighty pounds.

The Stanley Cup, a trophy given to be best pro hockey team each year, is a large *goblet*.

GOVERNESS (GUV ur nis) *n.* a woman whose job is to teach the children of a specific household

The strict *governess* told the Hansen kids to be at bed by eight with their teeth brushed and their toys put away.

GRANDEUR (GRAN jur) *n.* the state of being magnificent or grand

The tourists were so impressed with the *grandeur* of the German castle atop the snowy hill that they forgot to take a picture of it.

The redwood forests of California have as much *grandeur* as the palaces of Europe.

GRANDIOSE (GRAN dee ohs) *adj.* having a huge scope or intent OR being pompous; having a pretended grandeur

Kevin's teacher explained that his plan to write a report called "The Entire History of the World from Day One Until Now" might be a bit *grandiose*.

When Steve struck oil and got rich, he built a *grandiose* mansion with solid gold toilets, diamond doorknobs, and wall-to-wall zebra skin carpet in every room.

GRAPPLE (GRAP ul) *v.* to struggle to hold onto; to struggle to understand

When she jumped into the cold water of the lake, Gina learned that *grappling* with an eel should be avoided whenever possible.

After *grappling* with the idea that maybe he wasn't the most attractive man in the world, Brady understood why Sheila had rejected him.

GRIDLOCK (GRID lok) *n.* a complete stop of all traffic on a road; a complete halt in activity

The man turned off his car engine and started to read a book after being stuck in the *gridlock* downtown for two hours.

Negotiations reached a *gridlock* when each side refused to concede to further demands.

GUARDED (GAR did) *adj.* cautious or restrained

When asked if she knew anything about the secret missile base, the government spokesperson gave the *guarded* reply of "Maybe. No comment."

Mr. Johnson raised one eyebrow and gave a *guarded* welcome to his daughter's prom date, who came to pick her up wearing a black leather biker outfit and six nose rings.

GURNEY (GUR nee) *n.* a flat table with wheels used to transport patients around a hospital

The emergency room nurses quickly placed the injured man on a *gurney* and wheeled him away from the ambulance and into surgery.

GURU (GOOR oo) *n.* a person who is both teacher and leader to a group of followers

Thousands of believers traveled from all over the world to hear the *guru* speak about love, religion, and her new diet plan.

Zam Zamford, whose seminars and lectures are always packed full of farmers, is recognized as an agriculture *guru.*

HAPHAZARD (hap HAZ urd) *adj.* marked by chance or luck; random

The blindfolded children took many *haphazard* swings at the piñata, but Elwood finally landed a lucky blow and tore it open.

The librarian's *haphazard* approach to shelving and organizing books makes it difficult to find the materials you're looking for.

HAZE (HAYZ) *v.* to force someone to perform unpleasant tasks, usually in order for them to be qualified to join a club or fraternity

The young sailor was *hazed* by the older seamen, who painted his face and shaved his head while he was sleeping.

The Kappa Gnu Sigma fraternity *hazed* first-year students by forcing them to drink ketchup and mustard.

HEIST (HYSTE) *v.* to rob or steal OR *n.* a burglary

The thief *heisted* the wallet from the lady's purse and ran away down the street.

Once the train *heist* was over, the robbers split up and then met three weeks later at an abandoned farm to split up the goods.

Note: Heist is a slang term.

HIDEOUS (HID ee us) *adj.* extremely ugly; disgusting and revolting

The face of Medusa was reportedly so *hideous* that people would turn to stone just from looking at her. Needless to say, she seldom had a date.

The piece of rotting lasagna under Michael's bed is so *hideous* that I would rather burn his room than have to pick it up to throw it away.

HOARSE (HORS) *adj.* having a low, gruff sound; husky

My voice was *hoarse* after I spent the afternoon screaming for my team during the doubleheader baseball game.

Bruce Springsteen's *hoarse* version of the song "Pink Cadillac" blared from car stereos all across New Jersey when it was first released.

HOARY (HOR ee) *adj.* gray or white because of age OR very old

Fleming's great-grandchildren loved to pull at his long, *hoary* beard, but I don't think Fleming thought it was much fun.

The *hoary* gold digger told stories about the Wild West to the children until he fell asleep and his head fell forward into a bowl of soup.

HOBBLE (HOB ul) *v.* to walk with a limp or with difficulty OR to slow something down or get in the way of something

Sylvia *hobbled* around for three days after the Alaskan King Crab attacked her foot.

The heavy radio equipment and sleeping gear *hobbled* their efforts to reach the cabin before sunset.

HOMELY (HOHM lee) *adv.* not good-looking; plain or simple

Because they were both shy and *homely*, the Grinson girls didn't get many dates until they struck oil in their backyard.

The shirt was warm and comfortable, but its design was rather *homely*.

HOOPLA (HOOP lah) *n.* excitement and confusion

The rock star's surprise performance at the small local nightclub caused a lot of *hoopla*.

The players were quickly separated from each other in the locker room during the *hoopla* surrounding their amazing victory.

HORRID (HOR id) *adj.* extremely offensive; causing terror and disgust

The *horrid* display of bad table manners by the Embertons caused all of the other dinner guests to lose their appetites for several days.

Although my stomach was doing flip-flops and I wanted to run out of the theater, I just couldn't help watching the *horrid* film until it ended.

HOVER (HUV ur) *v.* to float in one place in the air OR to hang around close by

The flying saucer *hovered* silently in the air over a crowd of amazed campers, then blazed off over the mountains in a flash of blinding light.

My friend *hovered* eagerly outside the telephone booth while I called the radio station hoping to be the lucky listener who would win two backstage passes to the concert.

HUE (HYOO) *n.* the color of an object OR the shade or tint of a specific color

After it had been exposed to the air awhile, the white flesh of the apple took on a distinctly brownish *hue*.

The salesperson showed us lime and winter pine, but we were actually looking for a *hue* of green closer to emerald.

HUSKY (HUS kee) *adj.* strongly built and very sturdy OR having a hoarse, deep quality (of the voice)

Although the wooden casks each weighed two hundred pounds, the *husky* workers were able to lift two at a time off the barge.

Actress Demi Moore is famous for her *husky* voice.

HYGIENE (HYE jeen) *n.* practices related to good health, disease prevention, and cleanliness

Albert was a brilliant student, but his personal *hygiene* was so bad that the other students would not sit next to him because he smelled horrible.

Note: *Hygienic* (hye JEN ik) *adj.* means clean, sanitary, or related to good health.

It is important to keep newborn babies in *hygienic* surroundings because they catch diseases more easily than adults and older children.

HYPE (HYPE) *n.* exaggerated publicity OR *v.* to deceive or swindle

Braxo Detergent's claim that four out of five dentists use Braxo to clean their teeth as well as their laundry turned out to be nothing but *hype*.

The small-time poker player continued to *hype* himself as the greatest player of his time, although in truth he could only play Solitaire and Go Fish.

HYPODERMIC (hye puh DUR mik) *adj.* placed beneath the layer of skin OR *n.* an injection given under the skin

Using a *hypodermic* needle, the nurse was able to directly tap a vein to get a blood sample.

The patient was given *hypodermic* medication in her arm to settle her nerves.

IDEOLOGY (eye dee AHL oh gee) *n.* a set of beliefs shared by a group of people, such as a specific religion or political party

The Green Party's *ideology* centers around the belief that we must devote more energy to protecting our environment from the effects of pollution.

Non-violence is a central *ideology* of most religions.

IMPEDIMENT (im PED uh munt) *n.* something that blocks progress; an obstacle

My inability to speak or read German is a serious *impediment* to my quest to become the next chancellor of Germany.

Commuters braved such *impediments* as icy roads and fog to make it to work today.

IMPEL (im PEL) *v.* to drive forward; to urge into action

Brandon *impelled* his two daughters to study by denying them any television privileges until they finished all their homework.

Ginsberg tried to *impel* his roommates to go play basketball, but they preferred to lay around instead.

IMPERIOUS (im PEER ee us) *adj.* behaving like royalty; arrogant and snooty

Although she was only twelve, the princess fixed her *imperious* stare on the poor gardener and soon had him crying with fear.

The *imperious* club owner refused to let in anyone who earned less than one million dollars a year.

IMPLORE (im PLOR) *v.* to beg earnestly; to ask anxiously

The kids got down on their knees and *implored* their parents to take them to Wally's World of Wondrous Ice Cream.

Realizing that it was Christmas Eve and they still had no tree, Mr. Dwiley called the Christmas Tree Store and *implored* them to stay open a few minutes later than usual.

IMPORT (im PORT) *v.* to bring something in from a foreign country in order to sell it OR (IM port) *n.* significance or importance

The United States *imports* most of its oil from the Middle East.

Every reporter agreed that the fact that the president punched out two foreign leaders was a news event of *import*.

IMPOSE (im POHZ) *v.* to force yourself upon others; to place a burden upon others

Jonathan *imposed* on me by showing up on my doorstep and announcing that he was moving in with me.

The boss *imposed* on her secretary when she asked him to do her laundry for the rest of his natural life.

INAUGURATION (in aw gyuh RAY shun) *n.* a formal gathering to install a person into a position or office

Heavy rains prevented Governor Jubjub's *inauguration* from being held outdoors.

The speech that the new mayor gave at his *inauguration* was so boring that many people fell asleep.

INCARNATE (in KAR nayt) *v.* to embody in flesh, to put into or represent in concrete form OR (in KAR nit) *adj.* given human form; given bodily form

Some readers of *The Adventures of Huckleberry Finn* feel that Huck *incarnates* the free-spirited independence of nineteenth-century America.

The cat was so mean to everyone that we were convinced it was evil *incarnate*.

INCINERATE (in SIN uh rayt) *v.* to burn to ashes

Once the school year was over, I gleefully built a bonfire and *incinerated* my history textbook.

Although the kitchen fire *incinerated* almost everything in the room, amazingly enough the electric can opener was untouched by the blaze.

INCOMPETENT (in KOM pi tunt) *adj.* unable to do things correctly

The *incompetent* waiter managed to forget our lunch order seven times and then served us food that we didn't want.

The high school basketball team was so *incompetent* that their cheerleaders eventually had to suit up and play.

INCREMENT (IN kruh munt) *n.* an added amount; an increase

The tax increase came in such small *increments* that we didn't even know it was happening until one year we ended up owing more money than we earned.

As victory seemed within reach, the noise of the crowd increased in *increments* from a low whisper to a huge roar.

INCRIMINATE (in KRIM uh nayt) *v.* to cause to appear guilty of some crime

The presence of eight large lumps of wax in his kitchen was enough to *incriminate* the museum guard in the wax statue robbery.

The presence of O'Malley's fingerprints all over the gun and the crime scene *incriminated* him.

The defendant *incriminated* himself in the Bambi's Mom Trial when he admitted that he only liked to hunt deer out of season.

INCUMBENT (in KUM bunt) *n.* the person who currently holds a specific political office OR *adj.* holding a position or office

Senator Morst, the 106-year-old *incumbent*, easily won a tenth term in office and vowed to run for an eleventh term in six years.

Most experts agreed that the *incumbent* lost the debate with her challenger when she started crying on stage and asking for her mommy.

INDIFFERENT (in DIF ur unt) *adj.* showing no concern or interest; not caring one way or the other OR neither good nor bad, just so-so

The fact that the general started playing his game during my story made me think that he was *indifferent* to its ending.

While the cast of the play was known for putting on an incredible show, tonight's performance was *indifferent* at best.

INDIGNANT (in DIG nunt) *adj.* feeling angry or upset about a perceived injustice or wrongdoing

Ms. Shropshire was *indignant* when the health department declared her pet mosquitoes a health hazard and ordered her to kill them.

When the lawyer suggested that Judge Jaasma was part of the cover-up, the judge became *indignant* and had the lawyer tossed from the building.

INDUCE (in DOOS) *v.* to influence or lead on; to coax OR to cause something to happen

We finally *induced* the cat to come out from under the couch by putting a plate of tuna on the floor in the middle of the room.

Syrup of Ipecac *induces* vomiting when swallowed, which is good if you've just been poisoned and bad at any other time than that.

INDULGENT (in DUL junt) *adj.* characterized by giving in to needs or desires; pampering

Unable to stick to his diet any longer, the *indulgent* clerk broke down and ate twenty chocolate bars in a row.

Even though he already worked at three jobs, seventy hours a week to support his family, the *indulgent* father told his ten children that he would buy them ponies.

INDUSTRIOUS (in DUS tree us) *adj.* hard working and consistent

The father in the sentence above is very *industrious*.

When told she would have to work through the entire Christmas break, the *industrious* employee merely grinned and started filing.

INFERENCE (IN fur uns) *n.* the act of figuring something out by looking at all the facts OR a conclusion drawn from looking at the facts in a situation

The old detective preferred to figure out the identity of the bank robber by *inferring*, based on the clues at hand, but his young assistant simply watched the security video, which had recorded the whole crime.

Pinkerton *inferred* that a man dressed as a pigeon must have robbed the bank because there were a few feathers at the crime scene.

INFERNO (in FUR noh) *n.* a confusing, chaotic place, usually on fire; someplace that resembles Hell

When a gas valve exploded and everything caught on fire, the calm dining room of the ship was transformed into an *inferno*.

Working in the hot, windowless basement of the department of motor vehicles was as close to an *inferno* as Joe wanted to get.

INFINITE (IN fuh nit) *adj.* having no end or limit; boundless

When I look up at the stars and think about how far away even the closest one is, I have no trouble believing that the universe is *infinite*.

I thought my mother had an *infinite* supply of patience until one day, when I was thirty-six years old, she finally lost her temper and yelled at me.

INFUSE (in FYOOZ) *v.* to fill or put into

William *infused* a little humor into the annual board-of-directors meeting when he arrived dressed as a circus clown.

The coach *infused* some energy into his sagging football program by hiring seven new players.

INGENUOUS (in JEN yoo us) *adj.* honest and open, without trickery OR innocent and simple

In the story "The Emperor's New Clothes," an *ingenuous* little boy points out that the emperor is naked while everyone else is pretending that he is wearing the finest outfit they have ever seen.

The *ingenuous* country girl was easily tricked into giving her life savings to the fast-talking con artist from Chicago.

INITIATIVE (i NISH uh tiv) *n.* the first step of an action; the lead OR the ability to start your own projects

The boxer seized the *initiative* in the match when he ran over and started punching his opponent as soon as the bell rang.

Sandy's plan to build a rocket and travel to the moon on her sixteenth birthday required a lot of *initiative*.

INLET (IN let) *n.* a body of water, like a bay, that points in toward land OR a narrow passage of water between two islands

The thin strip of land protected the *inlet* from many of the high waves caused by the ocean storm.

The two boys, eager to see their girlfriends, built a makeshift raft to cross the *inlet* between Kwaje Island and Lein Island.

INORDINATE (in OR dn it) *adj.* going way too far; excessive

The police commissioner admitted that using two hundred armed officers to arrest one man who was speeding was an *inordinate* display of force.

Spending eighteen hours on the same math problem seemed like an *inordinate* waste of time to me, but I tried telling that to my teacher and was suspended from school.

INQUIRY (in KWYRE ee) *n.* a request for information OR an in-depth search into a matter

Joan made an *inquiry* at the state department about the whereabouts of her brother who was a diplomat, but officials there claimed he was still missing.

The reporter's *inquiry* into the counterfeiting ring unearthed startling evidence that the entire city council was involved the crime.

INSINUATE (in SIN yoo ayt) *v.* to suggest something in an indirect manner; to sneak something into conversation

Graham was constantly *insinuating* that Jeanne was mentally unbalanced; whenever she spoke in groups of people he would silently rotate his finger at his temple and roll his eyes.

The mild accountant tried to *insinuate* himself into the local motorcycle club by wearing a leather jacket and army boots, but he had no luck.

INSOLENT (IN suh lunt) *adj.* boldly rude or disrespectful

When asked to apologize, the *insolent* prisoner spit in the judge's face and then put a curse on the next three generations of his family.

The *insolent* child walked through the front door six hours after her curfew and refused to answer any of her parents' questions.

INTEGRATE (IN ti grayt) *v.* to bring all different parts together

Researchers had to *integrate* the many pieces of clay into one single block before they could decipher the ancient message written on it.

The community leaders hoped to *integrate* the town, which had been severely racially divided.

INTEGRITY (in TEG ri tee) *n.* a person's moral character; honesty OR togetherness and unity; completeness

Mr. Colright's *integrity* was damaged in our eyes when we learned that he was the one responsible for all of the illegal gun sales.

The *integrity* of the ship's hull remained intact
when the torpedo failed to detonate.

INTERVAL (IN tur vul) *n.* the amount of time between two
events; the space between two things

There was such a brief *interval* between the first
and second act of the play that I couldn't even get
up to buy a soda.

INTRIGUE (IN treeg) *n.* a secret plot or scheme OR (in
TREEG) *v.* to fascinate and excite curiosity

Movies in the fifties were full of drama and
intrigue because filmmakers relied more on
stimulating personal interactions and less on
special effects.

My father was so *intrigued* by the juggling bears
that he didn't even notice when I slipped away and
joined the high-wire act.

INVARIABLE (in VAR ee uh bul) *adj.* always the same;
never changing

Few plants grow in the desert because it is
invariably hot and dry.

Because of Victor's immense bad luck and utter
lack of experience, something *invariably* went
wrong whenever he tried to fly a helicopter.

JABBER (JAB ur) *v.* to speak rapidly but without making
much sense; to chatter

The crazy man on the corner *jabbered* about
whales and tuxedos living together until somebody
threw him some money.

The gossipy old women *jabbered* for so long at the coffee house that the waitress was certain their jaws were going to fall off.

JAR (JAHR) *v.* to have an irritating effect; to bother OR to knock off balance; to frighten and upset

The sound of fingernails being scraped down the chalkboard was horribly *jarring*.

The news that I was about to speak in front of three million people *jarred* me out of my relaxed mood.

JARGON (JAHR gun) *n.* a specialized language for a specific trade or industry, like "computer jargon" or "medical jargon" OR a mixture of several different languages

The paint salesmen used *jargon* like "coat factoring" and "color distortion effect" in the hopes that it would impress people and inspire them to buy paint.

The Caribbean sailor spoke *jargon* which was made up of French, English, and Dutch words all mixed together.

JOSTLE (JAHS ul) *v.* to bump or come into contact with roughly while you're in motion

I *jostled* my way through the crowd on the train in an attempt to reach the luggage compartment and look for my lucky suitcase.

The rude baseball fan used his elbows to *jostle* people out of his path and reach his seat.

KALEIDOSCOPE (kuh LYE duh skohp) *n.* a series of changing events or ideas, or a little, telescope shaped object that you can look through to see a blend of changing colors

The *kaleidoscope* of events that led up to the first World War has long been a hot topic among historians.

KARMA (KAHR muh) *n.* a belief put forward by certain religions that a person's conduct and actions during life determines his/her destiny in the world; a person's fate

Natasha kept good *karma* by always helping sick animals and, according to her, because of this she won the lottery.

Brent knew that it was bad *karma* when he broke his arm after stepping on a piece of gum, because at school he would always try to put gum in his classmates' hair.

KEEN (KEEN) *adj.* having a sharp edge; intense OR very intelligent and bright

The *keen* scissors were able to cut through the thin piece of steel like it was butter.

The Student of the Year award went to Adrian Gilcutty, whom everyone agreed was one *keen* thinker.

KNOLL (NOHL) *n.* a small, rounded hill

Jack and Jill started to climb up the *knoll* to fetch a pail of water, but then Jack said, "Hey, this doesn't rhyme, let's go up that hill over there instead."

The Zimberts built their house on top of a *knoll* so that they could go sledding in the winter.

LADEN (LAYD un) *adj.* weighed down with a heavy load; burdened

With a loud snap, one wheel of the cart, which was *laden* with crowbars, broke off under its weight.

When mom walked in with her shoulders slumped and her face drooping, we knew that she was *laden* with bad news.

LANGUID (LANG gwid) *adj.* slow-moving, usually because of a lack of energy; weak

My stupid older brother once took too much cold medicine by accident, and he moved *languidly* about for three days.

The film was shown in slow motion, and the Olympic sprinters were transformed into *languid* walkers out on a stroll.

LARCENY (LAR suh nee) *n.* a robbery; taking someone else's possessions unlawfully

Police suspected that the *larceny* committed at the Peanut Storage Facility was the work of rogue elephants.

Miles Keenan was convicted of *larceny* after police found thirty-two TV sets stamped with "Property of the Governor" in his living room.

LARGESS (lar JES) *n.* generous giving and generosity

Every Halloween the Hamiltons demonstrate their *largess* by giving each child in the neighborhood a chocolate-covered tricycle.

LARVA (LAR vuh) *n.* the wormlike stage of an insect's development

Caterpillars, which are *larva*, are the wormlike stage of development between egg and butterfly.

I found the white, wriggling *larva* disgusting to look at, but the adult butterflies were quite beautiful to see.

LINGER (LING gur) v. to be slow in leaving or acting

Curious onlookers *lingered* at the scene of the crime, hoping to catch a look at the person that police arrested.

Marcus *lingered* in the doorway in a final effort to get invited to the slumber party, but the cheerleaders ignored him.

LIVID (LIV id) *adj.* discolored and bruised OR white or ashen from fright OR very angry; furious

Mom's left arm was *livid* after she accidentally dropped the large cooking pot on it.

Mom's face was *livid* as she watched the final scary scenes from the movie *Jaws*.

Mom was *livid* when she found out we used her wedding dress to clean up the orange soda we spilled on the floor.

LOFT (LOFT) *n.* a large, open, upper floor of a building; an open space under a roof, like an attic

Because the light was better in the *loft*, the artist climbed into it from the living room and placed her painting supplies there.

Last night I climbed up the ladder and discovered that the odd noises coming from the *loft* in the garage were being made by a family of feisty raccoons.

LOGO (LOH goh) *n.* a symbol or trademark designed for easy recognition of a specific company or group

When we saw a McDonald's *logo*, which is the golden arches, appear on the horizon we knew that our prayers for fast food had been answered.

LOOM (LOOM) *v.* to come into view, usually in a threatening way; to stand over someone threateningly

The huge gym teacher *loomed* over the frightened second grade students and ordered them to start playing dodgeball.

The entire ocean *loomed* up before us as we drove over the last sand dune.

LOPE (LOHP) *v.* to run using long, easy strides

The timberwolves *loped* across the snowy mountainside, while the trappers in pursuit of them struggled to keep from sinking into snowdrifts.

Gary changed his *lope* into a dead run when he saw that the student known only as Mucus Child was approaching to give him one of his famous "gifts."

LOUT (LOWT) *n.* a stupid, awkward, foolish person

Even members of Vince's own family considered him a *lout* and would cross the street so that they wouldn't have to stop and talk to him.

Darryl admitted that he was a *lout* for selling all of his sister's furniture so that he could raise the money to take a trip to the Bahamas.

LUG (LUG) *v.* to carry something with great difficulty

The bellboy *lugged* Howard's two suitcases full of igneous rocks all the way from the car to the third floor room.

The workmen *lugged* the grand piano up one flight of stairs before they agreed to quit their jobs and join the French Foreign Legion.

LUSH (LUSH) *adj.* covered with a great amount of plant life OR juicy and tender

There were so many different plants and animals living in the *lush* jungle that destroying even one acre of it affected hundreds of species.

The *lush* bananas tasted even better than they looked and Weiss ate one hundred of them.

LUSTER (LUS tur) *n.* fame and glory OR a soft reflection of light; gloss

The general knew that the *luster* of victory would fade if he admitted that he had been in the bathroom during the final battle.

The antique brass platter regained its beautiful *luster* after we polished it for an hour.

MAGISTRATE (MAJ i strayt) *n.* a civil servant with the authority to enforce the law

Because the two neighbors couldn't agree about where one's yard ended and the other's began, they took their dispute to the *magistrate*.

Bob Pickle promised that if he was elected *magistrate* of Boone County, he would eliminate all unpaid parking tickets from everyone's record.

MAGMA (MAG muh) *n.* liquid rock heated to great temperatures inside Earth's core

After *magma* reaches the surface of the earth, it cools and forms new landscapes.

The miner boasted that he once drank *magma* and an X-ray showed that his throat was indeed lined with rock.

MAHOGANY (muh HOG uh nee) *n.* a tree with a hard, reddish-brown wood well-suited for furniture because of its strength; wood from such a tree

Although the *mahogany* bow looked beautiful, no one was able to bend it because the wood was too stiff.

While my baby brother wanted to make a desk out of spit, we ended up using *mahogany* because I thought it would last longer.

MANE (MAYN) *n.* the long hair which grows from the neck of certain animals

The long golden *mane* of the lion helps it to blend into the grassland, and protects its neck from injury during fights over territory and mates.

Terrified by the knowledge that I was a city girl, I held on to the horse's *mane* for dear life as we galloped across the field.

MANGY (MAYN jee) *adj.* looking shabby; covered with bare spots and appearing worn and rundown

The *mangy* dog inspired pity in every person who saw it because it lived in an alley and ate whatever scraps of food it could find.

Henderson mistreated his cat to the point where it started looking so *mangy* that many people thought it was an rat with patches of heavy fur.

MANIFEST (MAN uh fest) *adj.* obvious and clear OR *v.* to show or display or to be the physical proof of something

Gene's feelings toward Gwen *manifested* themselves on Valentine's Day, when Gwen received eight dozen roses from him.

MANTLE (MAN tul) *n.* a loose, cape-like coat without sleeves OR the layer of rock between Earth's core and the upper crust

Asmara put on her uncle's thick wool *mantle* and went out into the cold, driving rain.

The explorers hoped to find the lost land of dinosaurs that they saw in an old space movie by mining Earth's crust and boring into the *mantle*.

MAR (MAR) *v.* to damage or ruin; to deface

Terrance *marred* the surface of the birthday cake when he raked his fingers through the icing.

The large scratch marks all over the hood *marred* the beauty of the 1964 Corvette, which was otherwise in perfect condition.

MEDDLESOME (MED ul sum) *adj.* interfering in others' business

The entire town of Nash wrote and signed a letter that asked the *meddlesome* Mr. Banks to either sew his lips together or mind his own business.

The *meddlesome* dentist was constantly sneaking up to me at the mall and trying to floss my teeth.

MEGAPHONE (MEG uh fohn) *n.* a funnel-shaped device through which people speak in order to amplify their voices

The cheerleaders held their *megaphones* to their mouths and began leading the crowd in the popular chant "Go, team, go!"

Even though his voice was terrible even at a normal volume, Principal Murdoch liked to stand in the halls every day and sing "Good Morning to You" through a *megaphone* as the students headed for their classes.

MELODRAMA (MEL uh drah muh) *n.* a play, book, or movie characterized by exaggerated emotions and feelings; behavior or actions full of exaggerated emotions and feelings

During the entire four-hour *melodrama*, not one moment passed where some actor or actress wasn't shrieking, crying, or shrieking onstage.

Watch any episode of a soap opera for dozens of examples of *melodrama*.

MERCURIAL (mur KYOOR ee ul) *adj.* rapidly changeable in thought, feeling, or opinion; fickle

That night, my *mercurial* roommate decided to leave for Guam, then changed his mind and decided to stay, and then left to become a priest in Ireland.

MIDST (MIDST) *n.* the center or middle position; right in the middle of something

As loyal Green Bay Packers' fans, we were disappointed to learn that our seats were located in the *midst* of the Tampa Bay section.

In the *midst* of all of the confusion resulting from the fire in the banquet hall, the waiter sat down at a table and ate someone's ham sandwich.

MINGLE (MING gul) *v.* to combine by mixing together; to join with others

Trey and Kelly were worried that the party would be a flop, but Kelly's lawyer friends easily *mingled* with Trey's friends, who were mainly toll booth operators.

We *mingled* in the crowd standing at the front of the ferry because we wanted to get a good look at the Statue of Liberty as we passed it.

MINUTE (mye NOOT) *adj.* incredibly small; insignificant OR characterized by a close study of all small details

Always a pig, Tommy ate an entire large pizza and left a *minute* portion that wouldn't even feed a starving cricket.

It was only after a *minute* inspection of the car that the police found a piece of hair that belonged to the kidnapped prize-winning hamster.

MIRTH (MURTH) *n.* happiness and good cheer

Even though it was quite cold, the group singing Christmas carols door-to-door was warmed by the general *mirth* of the season.

The *mirth* of the vacationing couple quickly ended when the real owners of the condo arrived and found strangers using all of their things.

MODE (MOHD) *n.* a manner or style OR the latest fashion or trend

Brent's strange *mode* of speaking made it necessary for his friends to translate what he said to his teachers.

The *mode* of traveling around town on rollerblades ended soon after the first winter storm covered the roads with a thin layer of ice.

MOGUL (MOH gul) *n.* a very rich and influential person

Every year, the *moguls* of the movie industry get together and decide who they want to make the next big star.

A *mogul* of the car industry, Marlene once bought eight hundred Volkswagons and gave them away as stocking stuffers on Christmas.

MOLECULE (MOL i kyool) *n.* the smallest unit of a chemical that still maintains all of the properties of that chemical

A long time ago, scientists learned that one atom of sodium combined with one atom of chlorine forms a *molecule* of ordinary table salt.

Diatomic oxygen makes up only twenty percent of the *molecules* found in ordinary air.

MONSTROUS (MON strus) *adj.* abnormal and horrifying; frightening and shocking OR really large

The *monstrous* creature that rose up out of the radioactive tar sludge terrified everyone except Dan, who was hoping to write a great screenplay based on his experience.

My older sister once had a pimple on her nose that was so *monstrous* that we needed a brace to support her head from falling forward under its weight.

MOOR (MOR) *v.* to secure or fasten something, usually a ship OR *n.* a broad stretch of land with low-lying shrubs and patches of wetland

Sailors on the boat threw ropes to people waiting on the dock, who tied them around large wooden poles to *moor* the ship in place.

After wandering across the *moor* for hours, Heathcliff was forced to admit that he had lost his left contact lens for good.

MOTIVATE (MOH ti vayt) *v.* to provide with an incentive for action; to get things moving

Gavin *motivated* the normally lazy group by promising to pay each of them five thousand dollars if they would help him fix his car.

The opening band *motivated* the crowd to dance.

MUCK (MUK) *n.* a moist, sticky pile of dirt, manure, rotting matter, or all three

No amount of water or scrubbing got rid of the *muck* that was stuck to the bottom of my boots.

While most animals stayed away from the offensive pile of *muck*, the pigs enjoyed rolling in it and squealed happily.

MULTILINGUAL (mul ti LING gwul) *adj.* able to speak more than one language well

The *multilingual* diplomat was able to hold a conversation in Belgian, Swahili, Portugese, and pig Latin all at the same time.

Donald needed to use his *multilingual* skills almost every day while working at the immigration department.

MUNICIPAL (myoo NIS uh pul) *adj.* relating to a municipality, which is just a fancy word for a town or city

The *municipal* council worked closely with county and state officials to plan the construction of the new dam.

A successful *municipal* council member, Maxine decided to up the stakes and run for state senator.

MURMUR (MUR mur) *v.* to speak in a low voice; to speak unclearly

The *murmurs* of discontent from the audience got much louder as the assembly for cardboard waste went on and on.

"Speak up or shut up!" was what my brother would tell me whenever I started to *murmur*.

MUSE (MYOOZ) *v.* to consider for a long time; to meditate on a subject

The philosophy teacher *mused* about the student's research paper for almost an entire day, and then he gave the student an F.

We *mused* for so long about how to spend our Saturday afternoon that it was nighttime before we had reached a decision.

MUSKET (MUS kit) *n.* a primitive shoulder firearm that was used before the modern rifle was invented. It was invented in the late 1500s and used into the 1900s

During the Battle of Bunker Hill, rebel soldiers were ordered not to fire their *muskets* until they could see the whites of the British soldiers' eyes.

MUSTER (MUS tur) *v.* to bring together into one place; to call to come together, to summon

The sounds of the morning trumpet solo *mustered* the sleeping troops together in the main plaza.

We *mustered* all of the family members to the spring picnic by promising free hot dogs for everyone.

MUTILATE (MYOOT ul ayt) *v.* to damage or seriously ruin, usually by cutting off or destroying some part

The lawn mower plowed over the toy monster truck and *mutilated* it beyond all recognition.

My jealous sister *mutilated* my soldier-shaped gelatin dessert by eating his arm.

MUZZLE (MUZ ul) *v.* to prevent from speaking or expressing an opinion OR *n.* a device that fits over an animal's nose and mouth to keep it from opening its mouth

When I see a dog walking down the street wearing a *muzzle*, I instantly feel safe because it can no longer freely bite people.

MYSTIFY (MIS tuh fye) *v.* to confuse or stump

The complex string of mathematical equations written on the chalkboard totally *mystified* Earl, who had trouble even remembering his own age.

The talking sheepdog *mystified* us with its incredible knowledge of history, although it did confuse the Battle of New Orleans with the Battle of Bunker Hill.

NARRATOR (NAR ray tur) *n.* the person telling a particular story

The comments made by the *narrator* of the book were much funnier than the things that were said by the main characters in the novel.

NAUGHT (NAWT) *n.* zero; nothing

When we learned that the plane flight had been delayed for three hours, my family realized our mad dash to get to the airport on time had been for *naught*.

Ron believed that wishing for something really hard would make it happen, but his efforts to become world ruler proved to be all for *naught*.

NAUTICAL (NAW ti kul) *adj.* related to ships or sailing

Although he was eighty years old and blind, the old sailor's great store of *nautical* knowledge was extremely helpful to us on our voyage to the South Seas.

The researcher read every book on *nautical* history that exists, in an attempt to learn who had constructed the first ship in a bottle.

NIGH (NYE) *adj.* or *adv.* near or close in some way

The fact that my stomach was growling indicated to me that the time was *nigh* for me to go and get some lunch.

It was *nigh* onto seven o'clock at night when the advanced English class decided that their teacher wasn't going to show up for class, and reluctantly left.

NIMBLE (NIM bul) *adj.* quick and agile in movement or thought

The *nimble* child was able to complete the obstacle course in a new world record time.

Petra *nimbly* solved the question "What is three pi times seven-tenths minus eighty?" in less than thirty seconds.

NONDESCRIPT (non di SKRIPT) *adj.* without any qualities that stand out, rendering something difficult to describe

The bank robber's *nondescript* clothing allowed her to fade into the crowd easily and escape detection by the police.

Uncle Ted had such a *nondescript* face and appearance that most people would only refer to him as "You know, that guy."

NOOK (NOOK—pronounced like "book") *n.* a hidden spot OR a corner or recess that is part of a larger room

Billy kept all of his expensive baseball cards in a *nook* at the far end of the garage so that his little brother wouldn't find them and chew on them.

Before leaving for work, the young couple always had coffee together in the breakfast *nook* just off the kitchen.

NOTION (NOH shun) *n.* an idea of how something should be; an opinion

A fanatic about American nationalism, the patriot had the *notion* that everyone should only wear red, white, and blue clothes.

I had a *notion* that I should call my sick girlfriend after eight of her friends cornered me and said, "Contact Becky at home or you won't make it to sixth period."

NUANCE (NOO ahns) *n.* a small, subtle change in something

Adding just a pinch of pepper gave a spicy *nuance* to the strawberry cheesecake.

The Australian boys' accents gave an interesting *nuance* to words like "shrimp" and "leather tuxedo" that I found quite exciting.

OATH (OHTH) *n.* a promise to behave in certain way, calling on God or using some sacred item as your witness

Placing his hand on the Bible, the witness gave his solemn *oath* that he would tell the whole truth and nothing but the truth.

With all nine of us holding onto our only baseball bat, our team made an *oath* that we would practice at least once before next season.

OBLIGE (uh BLYJE) *v.* to do a favor for OR to make thanks

Father felt *obliged* to invite Timmy over for supper after he mowed our lawn every week during the summer that we were away.

The engaged couple felt *obliged* to listen to their parents' request not to have their wedding take place in zero gravity on the space shuttle.

OBSTINATE (OB stuh nit) *adj.* stubborn; unwilling to change from a particular course or belief

Even though she didn't have a ticket for the seat that she was in, the *obstinate* woman refused to get up and go where she was supposed to be seated.

The *obstinate* family was convinced that cars were just a fad and refused to give up their horse and carriage.

ODIOUS (OH dee us) *adj.* disgusting and nasty; causing repulsion

Several passengers on the train took out perfume bottles and sprayed furiously in order to cover up the *odious* smell from the dead skunk that had been found in the cargo area.

Carlos had such an *odious* reputation as a student that most teachers failed him before he even reached their classroom door.

OPTIMAL (OP tuh mul) *adj.* the best or most favorable

Clear skies and a constant mild breeze are the *optimal* conditions in which to fly a kite.

Lawrence soon learned that the *optimal* time to ask his Dad for some cash was every other Friday, just after he came home from work.

OPULENT (OP yuh lunt) *adj.* characterized by great wealth and abundance; rich

When we stepped into the mansion we were immediately surrounded by incredible *opulence*; there were even huge, uncut diamonds being used as doorstops.

OPUS (OH pus) *n.* an artistic work of some kind, usually musical

My favorite Beethoven *opus* is probably his Ninth Symphony, which he wrote when he was deaf.

After eight years of hard work, the writer finally completed her six hundred page *opus* about a family who moves from Maine to Kuala Lumpur.

ORATION (aw RAY shun) *n.* a formal speech given at a special event

During the governor's *oration* at the black-tie dinner, he continually thanked Semartech's leaders for building their new plant in his city.

Marc Antony gave a brilliant *oration* at the funeral of Julius Caesar.

ORCHESTRATE (OR ki strayt) *v.* to arrange a performance of an orchestra; to arrange something that has many different parts

Adding kazoos and whistles made it harder to *orchestrate* Mozart's Great Symphony, but the conductor did the best she could.

The travel agent tried to *orchestrate* the vacation plans of the four families so that they would all be in Paris at the same time.

ORGANISM (OR guh niz um) *n.* a living thing of any kind

Scientists recently discovered small bacterial *organisms* that live at the bottom of the ocean and consume sulfur that rises up from underground vents.

Insects make up over fifty percent of all the different kinds of *organisms* living on this planet.

OSTENTATIOUS (os ten TAY sus) *adj.* flashy or showy for the sake of being impressive

Wearing fourteen brightly-colored glass rings on each hand is a little *ostentatious* for a trip to the local convenience store.

Because the old man was blind, the *ostentatious* costumes worn by the parade-goers did not effect his belief that the parade was dull.

PACT (PAKT) *n.* a formal agreement between two countries; a bargain

The A.N.Z.U.S. *pact* between Australia, New Zealand, and the United States pledged that each country would come to the aid of the others in times of economic or political crisis.

I made a *pact* with my brother to stop calling him "four eyes" if he would stop telling Janine Strong that I loved her.

PAINSTAKING (PAYNZ tay king) *adj.* involving great care and thoroughness

The triple-bypass heart surgery on the hamster took five *painstaking* hours for the veterinarian to perform.

Our *painstaking* search of the entire house finally ended when we found Mom's lost ring in the clothes hamper.

PALPABLE (PAL puh bul) *adj.* able to be touched or felt; very obvious

There was a *palpable* bump on Tracy's head after she accidentally hit herself behind the ear with the baseball bat.

The tension in the air between the two rivals was almost *palpable*.

PANHANDLE (PAN han dul) *n.* a small strip of land extending like the handle of a pan from a larger area of land (look at a map of Oklahoma or Texas) OR *v.* to beg for handouts or money on the street

Any good student of geography knows that the *panhandle* of Florida extends west all the way to Alabama.

The city council passed a law that made it illegal for beggars to *panhandle* on any public property.

PANORAMA (pan uh RAHM uh) *n.* a view of everything over a wide area; a view of a long series of events or a period in time

The family pulled over at the scenic overlook in order to gaze at the *panoramic* view of the Valley of Sponges that sprawled below them.

The historian wanted to write a book that viewed the entire *panorama* of World War II through the eyes of a common Russian soldier.

PARADOX (PEHR uh doks) *n.* a statement that seems to contradict itself, but still might be true

Some people might consider the phrase "military intelligence" a *paradox*, but if so they probably aren't in the military.

After I failed to make the cross-country skipping team, Dad comforted me with this rather meaningless *paradox*: Sometimes you have to fail in order to succeed.

PARCEL (PAR sul) *n.* a package; something bundled up to be sent for delivery OR a section or piece

The post office representative claimed that the *parcel* from Aunt Bea containing her famous brownies was lost in the mail, but I could hardly understand him because his mouth was full at the time.

The farmer bought the *parcel* of land between his property and the river so that he could take his cows down to the river to drink without trespassing on someone else's land.

PARCH (PARCH) *v.* to make very thirsty and dry, usually by intense heat

Playing a soccer game without stopping, in the Texas sun in July makes my mouth so *parched* that I feel like I could drink an ocean.

Try eating eight saltines in one minute without water, and by the end of that minute your mouth will definitely be *parched*.

PARIAH (puh RYE uh) *n.* someone who has been kicked out of society; an outcast

Jody became a *pariah* at work when her fellow employees learned that every day she stole her lunch from someone.

The villagers tarred and feathered the *pariah* before throwing rocks at him and running him out of town.

PARODY (PEHR uh dee) *n.* a comic piece that exaggerates the actions or characters of some other piece to the extent that it becomes absurd and ridiculous OR a poor, weak imitation

While I thought my *parody* of Principal Hawkins as a ruthless dictator was quite amusing, I changed my mind after he gave me ten hours of detention.

The hearing before the Student Council was a *parody* of justice because the council slept through our explanations and then promptly ruled against us.

PARSON (PAR sun) *n.* a religious leader in charge of a specific area called a parish

Parson Collins had administered all of the weddings in Somerset County for the past thirty years.

The young couple went to the *parson* to find out the meaning of the sign "John 3:16" that they saw at the football game.

PAWN (PAWN) *n.* someone used and controlled by others

The foot soldiers knew that they were merely *pawns* used by the government for purposes that they couldn't understand, but, at least it was a job.

The boss of the huge corporation liked to give the "Employee of the Month" award to the lowly *pawn* who made the best coffee.

PECULIAR (pi KYOOL yur) *adj.* strange or unusual; weird OR belonging specifically to one area or region (usually followed by "to")

Saul thought it was *peculiar* that he lost his pack of blueberry gum right before he saw his two younger brothers blowing huge purple bubbles from their mouths.

Fortunately, the custom of greeting one's neighbors with a hard slap is *peculiar* to a very small southern region of France.

PEDDLER (PED lur) *n.* someone who travels around selling goods

At first the *peddler* made fairly good money selling kitchen supplies to households in eastern Mississippi, but then people started ordering their supplies through catalogs.

On his way into town the farmer stopped a *peddler* and traded his basket of eggs for a new rake.

PEEVISH (PEE vish) *adj.* irritable; easily annoyed

A single mosquito bite was enough to make the *peevish* child bawl for hours.

The *peevish* roommate erupted in anger when he saw that his CD collection was no longer in alphabetical order.

PENICILLIN (pen i SIL in) *n.* a compound found in a kind of mold that is used to cure a variety of bacterial diseases

Although a shot of *penicillin* can cure strep throat, the administration of the shot makes it uncomfortable for the patient to sit down for several days.

The doctors weren't certain what kind of bacteria was causing the high fever, but they figured that *penicillin* would probably kill it.

PERENNIAL (puh REN ee ul) *adj.* living indefinitely; perpetual; appearing again and again

Until dams were built, flooding on the Colorado River was a *perennial* problem that prevented settlers from building anywhere near the river.

Even though old Stasson was ninety, the *perennial* candidate ran for president for the twentieth consecutive time.

PERPETRATOR (PUR puh tray tur) *n.* someone guilty of committing a crime

The police knew that Gomez was the *perpetrator* of the tobacco store robberies when they saw that he was slowly building a house for himself out of cigars.

The *perpetrator* admitted to having stolen the puppies, but she claimed that old show tunes were speaking to her and was instructed to do it.

PERPLEX (pur PLEKS) v. to confuse or bewilder; to puzzle through excessive complication

The strobe light, fog machine, and deafening music of the disco completely *perplexed* the simple goatherder who had never seen a lightbulb before.

The question of how the escape artist was able to free herself from the iron trunk that had been shot into space *perplexed* everyone in the audience.

PERSISTENT (pur SIS tunt) *adj.* refusing to give up; stubborn and undaunted

Although they failed the first eighty-three times, the *persistent* movers tried once more to carry the grand piano up the stairs.

Shawna acknowledged the fact that Horatio was *persistent* when he asked her out every day for three years, but she still refused to go to the movies with him.

PETULANT (PECH uh lunt) *adj.* ill-tempered and spoiled; bratty

Realizing he was no longer the center of attention, the *petulant* child screamed at the top of his lungs.

The *petulant* child demanded that anyone who stayed overnight at her house address her as "your Highness."

PHENOMENON (fi NOM uh non) *n.* an unusual occurrence or event; something wacky that happens

The *phenomenon* of the glowing lights over Farmer Ben's wheat field was explained when Benny was caught painting moths with glow-in-the-dark paint.

The *phenomenal* child wrote her first major symphony when she was only two years old.

PHILOSOPHY (fi LOS uh fee) *n.* a study of the basic truths that govern the world and society OR a value system by which you live

The college freshmen chose to study ancient *philosophy* because she wanted to have a better understanding of why humans exist.

It was against the rock star's *philosophy* to wake up before 2:00 in the afternoon.

PIGMENT (PIG munt) *n.* a specific substance that provides a characteristic color to an object, such as hemoglobin (red) in blood

Chlorophyll converts sunlight into food in plants, and is also the *pigment* that makes them green.

Determined to find the *pigments* that make the chewy candies different colors, the amateur doctors took out their microscopes and a kitchen knife.

PIT (PIT) *v.* to set against in a competition OR to mark with depressions

The opening round of the karate competition *pitted* Frank "Walking Pain" Fantos against Maurice "Choppy Dog" Smoot.

We used an icepick to *pit* the pumpkin with holes that made it look as though it had two eyes, a nose, and a very small mouth.

PLAUSIBLE (PLAH zuh bul) *adj.* appearing to be reasonable and true

Judging by the empty bed, open window, and missing car, the only *plausible* explanation for Angela's disappearance was that she sneaked out to see her friends.

While my excuse that I was too lazy to do my homework was certainly *plausible* to my teacher, it didn't prevent her from giving me an F for the assignment.

PLUMAGE (PLOO mij) *n.* the feathers on a bird

The male peacock spread out its colorful *plumage* in an effort to attract a certain female peacock he had his eye on.

The brown *plumage* of the owl allowed it to blend well into the tree trunk.

PONDER (PON dur) *v.* to think about something for a while; to carefully consider

I spent the whole afternoon *pondering* why cats and dogs don't get along, but then I realized that I would never be able to figure it out and that I didn't care anyway.

The coach *pondered* the score, the field position, and time remaining in the game before he signaled for a field goal attempt.

PRECISE (pri SYSE) *adj.* exact in execution; direct and clear; right on the nose

Walter's estimate of the baseball crowd at 32,743 people turned out to be *precise.*

The space shuttle pilot's calculations were so good that she landed the shuttle on the *precise* spot from which it had taken off six days before.

PREDATOR (PRED uh tur) *n.* an animal that hunts and eats other animals for its survival

Humans are the only *predators* that kill other animals for reasons other than survival.

Mountain lions are fierce *predators* that are becoming scarce as more of their natural habitat is being converted for human use.

PREDECESSOR (PRED i ses ur) *n.* the person who came before another person in time, such as the former person to have a certain job

My *predecessor* had been fired so suddenly that a half-empty cup of his coffee was still on the desk when I arrived for my first day of work.

PREDICAMENT (pri DIK uh munt) *n.* a difficult, unpleasant situation that is hard for you get out of

After my sister faked an illness, I knew there was no escaping the *predicament* of baby-sitting my eight cousins for the whole weekend.

PREMISE (PREM is) *n.* a fundamental fact or facts

Once the witness admitted he was lying, the whole *premise* of the case against K.O. Hertz fell to pieces.

The brother's accusation that his little sister was a thief was based on the *premise* that a child was more likely than a dog to steal his last chocolate bar.

PRESUME (pri ZOOM) *v.* to assume that something is true; to take for granted OR to do something without asking permission

When he heard the knock on the door, Derek *presumed* that it was his next-door neighbor returning the rake that he'd borrowed.

Because I had finished all my chores and homework, I *presumed* that my father wouldn't mind if I took the car. Boy, was I wrong.

"How could you *presume* to take my car without asking me?" Dad demanded.

PRETENSE (PREE tens) *n.* a false action or reason that's used to deceive; an unsupported claim

Citing national security as his *pretense*, the brother stole his sister's diary and ran off to read it to his friends.

Our mother used the *pretense* that she had to ask us a question in order to try and find out what we were talking about in our Secret Treehouse Club meeting.

PRETENTIOUS (pri TEN shus) *adj.* trying to assume a position of status or wealth that is false; showy without a reason to be

The *pretentious* host took two tin statues, painted them with gold paint, and then told her guests that they were priceless works of art.

The other customers felt that driving the limousine to the Stop-N-Drive to get a carton of eggs was a little *pretentious*.

PREVAIL (pri VAYL) *v.* to triumph OR to be most common or frequent

The Union *prevailed* over the Confederacy during the Civil War because they had a greater number of troops and more supplies.

When the teacher took a survey of the class he learned that the *prevailing* desire was for there to be no homework assigned over the weekend.

PRIM (PRIM) *adj.* stiffly proper and correct in manner

The *prim* secretary was shocked when the boss announced that Friday would be shorts-and-T shirt wearing day at the bank.

Bridget offended some of her *prim* relatives when she hugged Grandpa Anka instead of curtsying to him.

PRINCIPAL (PRIN suh pul) *adj.* first in rank or degree

The manager discovered that the double overtime football game on Monday night was the *principal* reason that half of his workers were late to work on Tuesday.

Most of the nation agreed that the *principal* achievement of the Lunos 6 space probe was the discovery of the intelligent alien named Shamus.

PRISTINE (PRIS teen) *adj.* remaining in a pure, original state, unspoiled by humanity

After watching one week of daytime soap operas, the child no longer had a *pristine* mind.

Sheldon quickly jumped into the *pristine* snow of the backyard and started making a snow angel.

PROCESSION (pruh SESH un) *n.* a group that moves forward together in an orderly line; the act of moving forward

The wedding *procession* walked gracefully up the aisle but then the bride tripped on her dress and fell forward into the priest.

The problem with the ticket machine caused the *procession* of people waiting to see *Toy Story 4* to halt.

PROFESS (pruh FES) *v.* to claim openly; to state aloud OR to claim knowledge or skill in

Using a megaphone, Xavier stood on a table and *professed* his love for Claire to everyone at lunch.

Although Morton had originally *professed* to be skilled at surgery, he later confessed that he had learned everything he knew through playing the game *Operation*.

PROLIFERATE (pruh LIF uh rayt) *v.* to multiply and increase at a fast rate; to grow rapidly

With no predators and unlimited food, a male and female rabbit would *proliferate* so fast that you'd be swimming in bunnies in no time at all.

The idea of a rebellion *proliferated* in the countryside, where the people had been overtaxed by the government for decades.

PROPHETIC (pruh FET ik) *adj.* predicting the future

Harold started to think his choices *prophetic* after he picked the winning team in ten basketball games in a row.

The flower salesman was *prophetic* when he told the man that his wife would be mad if he came home without a gift for her birthday.

Note: A *prophet* (PRAH fit) is someone who can tell the future.

PROSPEROUS (PROS pur us) *adj.* economically successful; enjoying success and good fortune

During a gold rush, people who sell mining and digging equipment are virtually guaranteed to *prosper*.

Every year on Valentine's Day, the *prosperous* rose seller thanked the huge number of romantics in the world.

PROTOTYPE (PROH tuh type) *n.* the first example of an object or idea, upon which later models are based

Instead of using gasoline as fuel, the new engine *prototype* ran on sea water.

Once the rocket exploded on the launch pad, the scientists knew that their *prototype* fuel was a little too dangerous to use at that point.

PROVISIONS (pruh VIZH uns) *n.* stockpiles of food or other supplies OR measures taken to prepare for a certain event

A steady stream of supply boats from the mainland kept the tiny island stocked with *provisions* the whole year round.

Deepening the moat and adding more guards were the only *provisions* the king took to protect the castle from the invaders.

PRUDENT (PROOD unt) *adj.* sensible in handling common matters; level-headed and wise OR careful about your own conduct; cautious

Screaming "Fire!" in a crowded movie theater is only a *prudent* action when there actually is a fire.

The college sophomore knew that it would not be *prudent* to date the fifty-year-old dean of admissions, even though she was cute.

PUNGENT (PUN junt) *adj.* a sharp, biting smell or taste

The homemade cheese Wanda kept in her kitchen was so *pungent* that you could smell it as you walked up to the front door of her house.

The *pungent* smell coming from the kitchen warned me that Jonathan's pizza would not be ordinary.

QUAINT (KWAYNT) *adj.* unfamiliar and odd OR odd in an old-fashioned way

One of the *quaint* things about the Dzudombi Sand People is their custom of shaking each other's ankles fiercely as a way of saying "hello."

The time travelers from the twenty-second century thought that our use of calculators was incredibly *quaint*.

QUALIFY (KWAHL uh fye) *v.* to limit the meaning OR to soften; to make less extreme

The governor quickly *qualified* his remarks about a tax increase by stating that only the top five percent of all companies would be affected.

QUELL (KWELL) *v.* to stop by using force OR to calm

By quickly putting on heavy boots and stomping, the oil workers were able to *quell* the Great Mouse Riot of 1827.

Valeria *quelled* our fears about walking into the haunted house by showing us the patented Ghost Zapper she bought through the mail.

QUIBBLE (KWIB ul) *v.* to complain about little things; to gripe for small reasons

Even though he was about to become the first person to walk on Mars, Morton kept *quibbling* about the unflattering color of his space suit.

Everyone left the party when the Hendersons started to *quibble* about who had made the better bean dip.

RADIANT (RAY dee unt) *adj.* sending out light or heat OR bright with happiness

The *radiant* sign in the window glowed brightly on the dark street and indicated that the restaurant was open.

Salma flashed a *radiant* smile at her parents after she finished playing the difficult song on the piano without making any mistakes.

RAMBLE (RAM bul) *v.* to walk around with no purpose or direction OR to write or speak for a long time, constantly wandering off the topic

If I were to write a sentence that *rambles*, I would probably want to talk about that one time I was in Chicago, not the first time I was there but the second, because the first time I was there was really just a layover at the airport, and normally I wouldn't count that as a stop except the flight I was supposed to be on was delayed, I think they had engine problems, or maybe it was something wrong with the wing, and so I had to spend more time than usual, something like three hours, I think, and so...

RANCID (RAN sid) *adj.* having a nasty smell or taste due to rotting

In February, Emile found that the *rancid* smell coming from the trunk of his car was caused by the leftover Thanksgiving turkey which they'd decided to take home from his mother's house.

Remember that raccoon carcass from the "carcass" sentence earlier? Well, you can bet that animal smelled *rancid*.

RASCAL (RAS kul) *n.* someone who misbehaves in a playful way OR a dishonest person

Although he was certainly a *rascal*, Noah had such a cute smile that most adults rarely punished him for his pranks.

When the townsfolk learned that the *rascal's* scheme to form a high school band was all a fake, they quickly located him and demanded back their money.

RASPY (RAS pee) *adj.* rough and grating

The *raspy* sound coming from the shed told me that my father was scraping the barnacles off of the bottom of our boat.

After smoking three packs of cigarettes a day for ten years, the singer's voice was so *raspy* that she could no longer perform her songs well.

RATION (RASH un) *v.* to make available in set amounts, especially during a time when a supply is scarce

The county started to *ration* everyone's water supply when the drought was in its third month.

After cunning thieves stole over 75 percent of the nation's rubber trees, the government had to start *rationing* car tire sales.

REBUFF (ri BUF) *n.* an unfriendly rejection; a snub OR *v.* to reject briefly and rudely

I received my *rebuff* from Anderson Industries in the form of a quick slap in the face from its owner, Wiley "Snapper" Anderson.

Natalie *rebuffed* my request for a date by screaming "No!" and throwing her sandwich in my face.

RECEDE (ri SEED) *v.* to move away; to become smaller

As our annoying guests drove away down the road, we made sure that their car had *receded* far enough into the distance before we started to celebrate.

Once my fear of the new neighborhood dog had *receded*, I was able to resume my paper route.

RECIPIENT (ri SIP ee unt) *n.* a person who receives something

Although she was listed as the *recipient* of the package, Angela denied that she knew that there was stolen artwork inside it.

RECKONING (REK uh ning) *n.* the process of computing or calculating; the settling of all accounts, debts or otherwise

Using only a compass and a old map for *reckoning*, the guide was able to locate the site of the ancient stone carvings for us.

After my *reckoning* with the debt collector, all I had left was one pair of blue jeans and twenty-three cents.

RECUPERATE (ri KOO puh rayt) *v.* to get healthier after an illness; to return to normal health

I was able to *recuperate* from the chicken pox faster than my sister because I continued to take walks outside and get fresh air, while my sister refused to get out of bed.

When he had *recuperated* from his eighty broken bones, the stunt man decided not to ever jump over twenty flaming buses again.

REEDY (REE dee) *adj.* tall and thin, like a reed OR sounding like a reed instrument.

The giraffe's *reedy* neck allows it to reach branches that no other animal can get to for food.

Malcolm's *reedy* voice could be heard above all of the other voices in the choir.

REEL (REEL) *v.* to be thrown off balance; to stagger OR to pull inward using a winding motion

After spinning in place for over thirty minutes, I was *reeling* all over the park, bumping into slides and other kids as I attempted to regain balance.

Grandpa slowly *reeled* in the hooked fish, which we would see occasionally jump out of the lake about twenty yards from shore.

REFRACT (ri FRACT) *v.* to deflect or bend light

Swimming underwater at the pool's deep end, I saw how the water *refracted* the sunlight into wavy shapes along the bottom.

Anyone can use a prism to take a beam of sunlight and *refract* it into a rainbow.

REFRAIN (ri FRAYN) *v.* to hold back; to restrain OR *n.* a phrase that is repeated throughout a song or poem

I tried to *refrain* from causing a disturbance, but when they brought out the cat jugglers, I had to rush the stage to try to stop the performance.

A local disc jockey noted the Fweeb's new song, which was called "Cake Tango," repeated the *refrain* "dance on the icing" over seventy times in four minutes.

REGAL (REE gul) *adj.* very fancy, beautiful, and expensive; kingly or queenly

Unlike most dresses, the *regal* gown had large diamonds for buttons, which made it sparkle brilliantly in the sunlight.

The *regal* manner in which the king addressed the merchant made him tremble out of fear and respect.

REGIMENT (REJ uh munt) *n.* a group of soldiers OR *v.* to conform to a highly-ordered system

During World War II, the eighty-third *regiment* became famous for stopping over two divisions of German soldiers by themselves.

My life at the summer camp was so *regimented* that even the times at which I brushed my teeth were strictly regulated.

REGRESS (ri GRESS) *v.* to go back to a previous state of development

Although the talking chimp experiment was successful, the monkey soon *regressed* to its normal state once the scientists stopped the injections.

Even though he was a mature, forty-year-old businessman, Chan would occasionally *regress* into childlike fits of rage.

REIGN (RAYN) *n.* the time period during which a king or queen is in power OR *v.* to rule as a king or queen (usually followed by "over")

The *reign* of King Henry VIII of England spanned four decades.

Emperor Charlemagne *reigned* over much of what is now Europe.

RELISH (REL ish) v. to greatly enjoy; to take immense pleasure in

Even though the drive was over three hours, all the kids *relished* the chance to go to the amusement park.

Sigmund *relished* the thought of playing tennis against Jung because since Jung's serve was so weak.

REPARATION (rep uh RAY shun) n. something done or paid in order to repay a debt or earlier mistake

The government paid over fifty million dollars in *reparations* for people who were wrongly imprisoned during the last war.

After testifying against them in the trail, the brother tried to make *reparations* to his family by offering them the best legal service money could buy.

REPLENISH (ri PLEN ish) v. to fill again; to restock or resupply

Luckily the thunderstorm *replenished* most of the water that had been lost from the pond during the days of the drought.

The parents knew they had to *replenish* their stock of batteries after Gerald bought a portable stereo that used sixteen C batteries at a time.

REPOSE (ri POHZ) n. a state of mental peace; freedom from anxiety or unrest

Once she had completed her eighth and final midterm exam, Maeve kicked back her chair and assumed a position of *repose*.

The quiet *repose* of the little fishing village was shattered when the army of sea monsters appeared with high tide.

REPRESS (ri PRES) *v.* to hold back; to keep down or hidden away OR to force out of the conscious mind

Government officials rapidly tried to *repress* the information that the president liked to wear women's clothes, but the photos had already been taken.

The three days I had to spend with smelly Uncle Stan were so horrible that I've *repressed* the entire event in my memory.

REPROACH (ri PROHCH) *v.* to blame or criticize OR *n.* blame or contempt; disgrace

The boss *reproached* her secretary Ross for forgetting to mail paychecks out to any of the employees except himself.

After I burned down the house by trying to bake cigarettes, my wife gave me a dark look of *reproach*.

REPUGNANT (ri PUG nunt) *adj.* highly disgusting; offensive

The mixture of spam, bacon grease, motor oil, and vanilla sprinkles was so *repugnant* that I couldn't imagine why anyone would want to eat it for dessert.

Killeen's *repugnant* personal habits were attractive only to flies and a certain type of carrion beetle.

RESENT (ri ZENT) *v.* to be angry about something unfair or unjust

Myra deeply *resented* the fact that her best friend Sheila had stolen her boyfriend Mehke away from her during the Valentine's Day dance.

Because they played Irish folk songs loudly until three A.M. every night, most of the Dwiskson's neighbors *resented* them.

RESIDUE (REZ i doo) *n.* the remains of something after a larger part is removed

Once we removed the plant from its pot, all that remained was a tiny *residue* of the dirt.

The snail left a *residue* of slime as it traveled across my face while I was taking a nap in the garden.

RETROSPECT (RET ruh spekt) *n.* the review of a past event; hindsight

Now that I am old and very ill, in *retrospect* I realize that it was a bad idea to smoke two packs of cigarettes a day when I was younger.

In *retrospect*, Dan realized that selling one of his legs for only $50 was a poor decision.

REVELATION (rev uh LAY shun) *n.* the act of revealing; a surprising disclosure

Our teacher Mr. Mieszkowski's *revelation* that he was a sheepdog trapped in a man's body came as quite a surprise to all of us.

REVENUE (REV uh noo) *n.* income; the money collected by the government for public expenses

With the *revenue* from my international chain of lasagna restaurants steadily increasing, I could not help but become more and more wealthy.

The state government created a tax on all pet goldfish in order to raise *revenue* for a new convention center.

REVERENCE (REV ur uns) *n.* a feeling of respect, admiration, and love

Our *reverence* for the holy hermit diminished when we learned he had used church funds to buy a satellite TV dish for his cave.

The old men talked about football with so much *reverence* and seriousness that you would have thought they were discussing philosophy.

REVILE (ri VYLE) *v.* to denounce using abusive language

The manager of the construction crew *reviled* his workers for falling asleep on the job and threatened to seal them in cement if it ever happened again.

RHETORIC (RET ur ik) *n.* the study of how to use language persuasively and expertly OR insincere, snobbish, and boorish speaking or writing

Many of today's successful politicians study *rhetoric* so that their speeches and beliefs will affect a greater number of people.

The student's self-evaluation was full of *rhetoric* and the teacher threw it away in disgust.

RHEUMATISM (ROO muh tiz um) *n.* a disease that affects the muscles and joints, causing pain and disability

Now that my grandfather has *rheumatism*, he never goes to the second floor because the walk up the stairs is too painful.

A daily massage and visit to the whirlpool helps Aunt Bea cope with her *rheumatism*.

RHYTHM (RITH um) *n.* a movement or action that occurs over and over again in a regular pattern

The *rhythm* of the waves against the sides of the lifeboat eventually lulled me to sleep.

Leo discovered that the pulsing *rhythm* of Cuban music made him want to dance.

RICOCHET (rik uh SHAY) *v.* to bounce off at least one surface

Fortunately, the bullet *ricocheted* off of my belt buckle, bounced off a wall, and hit the robber in the foot.

RIFT (RIFT) *n.* a narrow break, as in a rock; a split

A brown lizard that had been sunbathing on a boulder quickly ran into a *rift* in the rock when it saw us coming.

By flirting with both of them openly, Jeannie created a *rift* in Bob and Doug's friendship that never closed until they met the beautiful Klein twins.

RITUAL (RICH oo ul) *n.* a ceremony; a specific procedure or method

Only yellow candles made from the pollen of Siberian bees may be used in the ancient *ritual* of blessing Kronhorst the Rice God.

The purification *ritual* in Jed's church was so complicated that everyone received a twelve-page manual describing the procedure.

RIVALRY (RYE vul ree) *n.* a competition between two parties

Although the two colleges often worked together on academic projects, there was a fierce *rivalry* between their football teams.

The intense *rivalry* between the two soccer teams sometimes resulted in fights between their overly enthusiastic fans.

ROMP (ROMP) *v.* to goof off and have fun in an energetic, lively way

Our playful *romp* in the nearby field ended once we realized that we were jumping around in poison ivy.

The three brothers were having such a fun *romp* in the local mall that security eventually threw them out for "disturbing the serious shoppers."

ROUT (ROUT) *n.* an overwhelming defeat; a blow-out OR *v.* to drive away; to scatter

Once the other team hit its eighteenth home run in a row, the coach of the home team admitted that the softball game was a *rout*.

Because of their superior weapons and technology, the Romans were able to *rout* the invading barbarians from their country.

ROVE (ROHV) *v.* to wander around a large area

After *roving* around the valley for several hours, Jakob had to admit that his lucky picnic basket was lost for good.

The cows spent the day peacefully *roving* around the west pasture until some high school kids showed up and tried to tip them over.

RUBBLE (RUB ul) *n.* fragments of material left after a building collapses or is destroyed

In the spirit of recycling, the villagers used the *rubble* from the old castle to build a rock wall around their new town.

RUDDY (RUD ee) *adj.* characterized by a healthy, reddish look

The mother's habit of making her kids eat only healthy foods was manifested in the *ruddy* faces of her three daughters.

RUFFIAN (RUF ee un) *n.* a thug or tough guy

Ever since the two *ruffians* beat him up in an alley and took his wallet, Cuttrell never leaves the house without wearing a full suit of armor.

Yesterday, the police arrested the *ruffian* who broke into the zoo and started a fight with the baboons.

RUMINATE (ROO muh nayt) *v.* to spend time thinking about something

While I was *ruminating* on which flavor of chewing gum I should buy, my friends left the store and went to play without me.

After three days of *ruminating* on his choice of colleges, Terrance decided he should just flip a coin and choose one that way.

RUSE (ROOS) *n.* a sneaky trick or deception

By lowering my voice, I had convinced the principal that I was my father, but then my mom walked in and destroyed my *ruse*.

Their *ruse* of getting into the movie as adults was foiled when the eight-year-old at the top fell off of the shoulders of his friend below.

RUSTLE (RUS ul) *v.* to act quickly and energetically OR to move with a soft, fluttering sound

When the pioneer finally found his way home he *rustled* around in his kitchen in order to get some real food.

As I heard the *rustle* of the geography worksheets being handed back, I prayed that I had remembered the capital of the United States correctly.

SALLOW (SAL oh) *adj.* characterized by a sickly, yellowish color

After eating one hundred bananas in five days, Brent's face was *sallow* and his vision was failing.

The once-purple grapes in the refrigerator appeared *sallow*, so we threw them away.

SATURATE (SACH uh rayt) *v.* to fill or load to capacity; to soak thoroughly

The air had become so *saturated* with smoke from our fireplace that we had to leave the house and spend Thanksgiving in a nearby hotel.

Tammar *saturated* his towel with pool water and then snapped it at people as though it were a whip.

SAUNTER (SAHN tur) *v.* to walk at a casual pace; to stroll OR *n.* a leisurely walk

The newlyweds *sauntered* through the park at sunset without a care in the world.

Once we realized that we'd be late for the game, we changed our pace from a *saunter* to a quick jog.

SCAMPER (SKAM pur) *v.* to run quickly and lightly

The rabbit *scampered* through the bushes and disappeared into its den when it saw the fox coming toward it.

The running back was only five feet tall but he was incredibly fast, and was often able to *scamper* past all the defenders and score touchdowns.

SCARCE (SKEHRS) *adj.* hard to find; rare; not enough

The fact that gold is so *scarce* means that many people go to great lengths in order to get their hands on it.

In a town completely filled with vegetarians, ham and turkey sandwiches are rather *scarce*.

SCENARIO (si NAR ee oh) *n.* an outline of an expected series of events OR the outline of a story or play

A team of Pentagon generals worked overnight to come up with all the possible *scenarios* that might occur now that Kubekstan has declared war on Canada.

Julia tried to write a *scenario* of the book, but because she'd only read the title and the jacket cover, she wasn't very successful.

SCHOONER (SKOO nur) *n.* a sailing ship with two or more masts

Because of the strong wind that was blowing steadily from the east, the *schooner* made excellent time on its voyage to New Spain.

I broke both of the masts on my model *schooner* when I tried to force the ship into a glass bottle.

SCORCH (SKORCH) *v.* to burn the surface of; to burn intensely

Although the skin of the hot dog had been *scorched* in the barbecue, the insides were still edible.

The toasted marshmallow was so badly *scorched* that it was just a black lump.

SCORN (SKORN) *v.* to treat something as unworthy or inferior OR *n.* a strong feeling of dislike and contempt

The governor *scorned* the salesman's offer by slapping him in the face and instructing the butler to beat him up.

The *scorn* that Allison felt for Ms. Taylor was obvious after she put her photograph on the dartboard and started playing.

SCOUNDREL (SKOWN drul) *n.* a villain; a wicked person

The *scoundrel* broke into the animal shelter, took a litter of puppies, and trained them to be vicious attack dogs.

When Edward stole a wallet from a sleeping priest, I knew that he was definitely a *scoundrel*.

SCOUR (SKOWR) *v.* to clean by scrubbing vigorously OR to search thoroughly; to search over a large area

We had to *scour* the bathtub with heavy-duty cleaner after we gave our dog Rufus his annual bath.

The search party *scoured* the forest around the cottage for any sign of the woodsman.

SCOURGE (SKURJ) *n.* a cause for widespread loss and suffering, like a war or disease

The Hundred Years War was a *scourge* that left most of central Europe in ruin.

Almost half the people in London died when the *scourge* of bubonic plague struck the city centuries ago.

SCRAWNY (SKRAW nee) *adj.* very bony and thin, often due to lack of adequate food or exercise

The fierce wind actually knocked the *scrawny* dog off of its feet and into a ditch.

Although he was too *scrawny* to play any other position, Harrison's incredibly long arms made him an excellent goalie.

SCUFFLE (SKUF ul) *n.* a rough, unorganized fight in close quarters

The *scuffle* in the bar started near the pool table in the back but soon spread to the karaoke stage near the front window.

The *scuffle* in the Boy Scouts' tent arose from a disagreement over who should have to go outside and fight the bear.

SCULLERY (SKUL uh ree) *n.* a room next to the kitchen where dish washing and other cooking-related chores are done

The water used to clean dishes was so dirty that a fire started in the *scullery* when someone dropped a match into it.

The new owner of the house decided to convert the *scullery* into a cozy little breakfast nook.

SECRETE (si KREET) *v.* to exude or produce a substance, usually a fluid

Everyone for miles around knew that the Johnsons' pet skunk had just *secreted* her warning scent.

SENTIMENT (SEN tuh ment) *n.* a general emotion or attitude; an opinion or feeling

Although the jury found the CEO innocent, public *sentiment* held that he had indeed stolen the shareholders' money for personal use.

My father's *sentiments* in baseball are still with the Chicago Cubs, even though they haven't won a World Series in a hundred years.

SHARD (SHARD) *n.* a fragment, often of glass or metal OR a broken piece of pottery like those found at archeological digs

At a contest booth in the carnival, Donovan threw the tennis ball so hard that it smashed the milk bottles into *shards* of glass.

Once the *shard* was identified as Fourth Millennium Axumite clay, the two professors knew that they had made a major discovery.

SHREWD (SHROOD) *adj.* very clever and smart; tricky

The *shrewd* coach had one of his players jump to the ground and bark like a dog to distract the other team while his teammates scored the winning basket.

By deftly evading the actual question, the *shrewd* politician avoided exposing his ignorance.

SHRILL (SHRIL) *adj.* high-pitched and piercing

When little Klaus throws a temper tantrum, everyone in the house puts cotton in their ears to muffle his *shrill* screams.

SHUN (SHUN) *v.* to avoid deliberately; to stay away from

Incredibly shy, Jonas *shunned* the company of other people and spent most of his free time talking with his pet fern.

After her third bout with food poisoning, Frances decided to *shun* Ishmael's House of Raw Clams.

SIDLE (SYDE ul) *v.* to walk or move sideways; to move in a quiet, sneaky way

The repairman *sidled* around the corner of the building on a thin ledge to fix the drainpipe.

SIMPER (SIM pur) *v.* to smile in a goofy, self-conscious manner

My little brother's *simpering* revealed to us who had actually cooked the mystery waffles that morning.

Horace continued to *simper* uncontrollably while the three supermodels thanked him for saving them seats on the plane.

SINGULAR (SING gyuh lur) *adj.* being one of a kind; unique OR remarkable; peculiar

Historians agree that Abraham Lincoln was a man of *singular* courage and determination.

Crossing the Swiss Alps with a brigade of war elephants was a *singular* experience for most of Hannibal's troops.

SIPHON (SYE fun) *n.* a U-shaped tube used to transfer liquid from one container to another OR *v.* to draw off liquid by using a siphon; to drain in some way

Because I ran out of gas while mowing the front lawn, I *siphoned* some gas from the car into the lawnmower.

SKULK (SKULK) *v.* to creep around so that no one notices you

Looking for the best house to rob, the burglar *skulked* around the neighborhood peering into windows.

Determined to become an international spy, Laura practiced *skulking* around the house and ambushing the poodle.

SLACKEN (SLAK un) *v.* to slow down; decrease; to make something less firm or tense

At the end of a long day of walking across the desert, our pace had *slackened* from a brisk walk to a slow crawl.

As the kite plummeted toward the earth, the tension on the kite string *slackened* considerably.

SPASM (SPAZ um) *n.* a sudden involuntary twitch of a muscle OR a sudden burst of activity

Before he realized that he was allergic to shellfish, Michael would eat oysters and then immediately have violent *spasms* in his arms and legs.

My brother cleaned the entire house and washed both cars during a brief *spasm* of activity one Saturday afternoon, and then he took a five-hour nap.

SPECTACLE (SPEK tuh kul) *n.* a remarkably impressive sight; a grand public display OR a regrettable display or action

The Fourth of July fireworks display near the Washington Monument is truly an awesome *spectacle* of light and sound.

Keith made a *spectacle* of himself at the wedding when he punched out the bride and then proceeded to leg wrestle the priest.

SPECTRUM (SPEK trum) *n.* a band of colors that together make up visible light OR a broad range of related ideas or qualities

Our science teacher used a prism to break up a beam of white light into a *spectrum* of colors.

Although the conference was designed only to discuss lasers, a broad *spectrum* of scientific topics came up in conversations.

SPITE (SPYTE) *n.* ill feelings that cause one person to harm or hurt another

Widow Bellson was so full of *spite* for everyone that not a day passed when she didn't try to hit someone with her umbrella.

When I learned that he had ruined my science project just for fun, the amount of *spite* I felt toward Teddy increased substantially.

SPORADIC (spuh RAD ik) *adj.* happening infrequently or on an irregular basis; having no pattern or order

Thunderstorms in this part of the country are so *sporadic* that no one's ever prepared for the rain when it comes.

Because their parents liked to look in on them *sporadically* at night, the kids were never able to sneak out.

SPRAWL (SPRAHL) *v.* to sit or lie down with your body spread out in every direction; to spread out awkwardly

Sprawled all over the floor, the basketball team made the living room look a bird's nest built of thin human arms and legs.

Heather fell down the stairs and was *sprawled* on the second floor landing.

SPREE (SPREE) *n.* a carefree outing OR the overdoing of a certain activity

Our shopping *spree* at the Lego factory left us completely broke but with enough Legos to build ourselves a three-story ranch house.

Father decided to go on a spending *spree* at the mall and buy three items from every single store.

SPRY (SPRYE) *adj.* lively and active

Over the weekend, the *spry* kids played hide-and-seek in the neighborhood for eighteen hours in a row.

Although he was fifteen years old and practically blind, the *spry* cat still liked to fight with rattlesnakes in the backyard.

SPURN (SPURN) *v.* to reject something with a scornful air; to refuse something with disdain

Tomasson *spurned* the offer of a truce by ripping up the document and then force-feeding the paper to its messenger.

Brad *spurned* my offer of a date and asked me never to come within fifty yards of him again.

SQUALID (SKWAHL id) *adj.* appearing dirty and repulsive; wretched

Even rats and cockroaches were disgusted by the things they saw in the *squalid* apartment.

The refugees were forced to live in *squalid* conditions until the fighting in their homeland stopped.

STAMINA (STAM uh nuh) *n.* the ability not to get tired when working or laboring hard; endurance

It was a salute to the *stamina* of the troops that they were able to march for four days in a row and then start fighting immediately.

The police officer knew that it would take a lot of *stamina* to fingerprint the 10,000 criminals by the next afternoon.

STAMMER (STAM ur) *v.* to speak with involuntary pauses or repetitions, usually caused by nervousness

Frightened of gorgeous Russian women, the normally calm Stan would begin to *stammer* badly whenever Svetlana entered the room.

STARK (STARK) *adj.* bare; without any decoration or adornment OR *adv.* completely and totally

The bachelor's *stark* two-bedroom apartment contained only a stereo system, a mattress, and a "Stone Cold" Steve Austin poster.

When our neighbor asked us to stop insulting cheese because it interfered with her psychic communication with goats, we knew she was *stark* raving mad.

STATELY (STAYT lee) *adj.* characterized by formality and dignity; impressive due to its size; majestic

The *stately* opening ceremony consisted of a parade, several speeches, and a formal blessing.

The nine-story mansion was even more impressive because of the *stately* mountain range that loomed behind it.

STENCH (STENCH) *n.* a very unpleasant smell

We soon discovered that the *stench* coming from the closet was a mixture of dirty gym socks and a forgotten piece of pizza.

No amount of soap seemed able to get rid of the *stench* of our car after Billy filled the back seat with pig manure.

STEREOTYPE (STEHR ee uh type) *n.* a conventional and oversimplified idea, usually about a group of people

The teenager's *stereotypical* view of teachers as boring was shattered when Ms. Eubanks decided to introduce a class in bungee jumping.

The beauty contestant who was unable to tie her own shoelaces was a perfect example of the dumb blonde *stereotype.*

STERN (STURN) *adj.* hard and severe in manner; firm and unwilling to change OR *n.* the rear part of a ship

The *stern* principal said that saving a busload of nuns from certain death was no excuse for being two minutes late to class.

The captain sent the prisoners back toward his cabin, which was located between the middle mast and the *stern* of the ship.

STIFLE (STYE ful) *v.* to keep something in or hold something back OR to smother by depriving of air or oxygen

Everyone in the meeting had to *stifle* a laugh as the chairman stapled a bundle of documents to his tie.

The bully threatened to stick smelly socks into my mouth and nose and *stifle* me if I didn't give him my lunch money.

STILTED (STIL tid) *adj.* having an artificially formal quality; pompous

Jeffrey's *stilted* speech showed how desperately he wanted to become part of the wealthy class.

The *stilted* manner of the announcer at the square dance showed how self-important he felt he was.

STOUT (STOWT) *adj.* sturdy and bold; bulky; strong and determined

It took four men to lift up the *stout*, unconscious sailor and carry him from the bar.

The *stout* courage of the team members allowed them to rally and win the world hopscotch championship.

STREAMLINED (STREEM lyned) *adj.* designed and built to offer the least resistance to air; modernized and more efficient

The Edsel's new *streamlined* hood increases the car's mileage considerably.

The new, *streamlined* post office has faster jeeps and can deliver packages anywhere in the world in only three hours.

STRIDE (STRYDE) *v.* to walk quickly and take long steps; to take a single long step over something in your path

The two children had to run to keep up with the long *strides* taken by their seven-foot tall father.

Nancy was able to *stride* over the mud puddle with her long legs without getting any part of her shoes wet.

STRIVE (STRYVE) *v.* to put in a great deal of effort and work; to struggle against

Everyone in the village, even young children, *strove* to build the wall around the city before the invading tax collectors arrived.

Jim was forced to *strive* against a strong current for two miles in order to find his lost swim trunks.

SUBLIME (suh BLYME) *adj.* inspiring awe and admiration; supreme and without any equal

Salma's *sublime* ability to convince anyone to stop fighting made her the ideal person to head the peace party.

Many people consider the first major rock concert they see a *sublime* experience, especially if it was the Grateful Dead.

SUBSIDY (SUB si dee) *n.* financial assistance, like a loan from the government to a small company

The Florida sugar farmers would have been forced into bankruptcy years ago if they hadn't received a sizable government *subsidy*.

Pick, Inc. used the *subsidy* to buy new equipment that would allow them to build better, stronger toothpicks.

SUFFICE (suh FYCE) *v.* to adequately meet present needs; to satisfy; to be enough

While I really wanted glow-in-the-dark moon boots, the vintage green army boots *sufficed* to keep my feet warm during the winter.

SULLEN (SUL un) *adj.* characterized by ill-humored brooding; having a morose and sulky personality

The *sullen* ex-cheerleader liked to go to football games and root against her own school.

Although everyone else could see that the sky was clear, the *sullen* child continued to believe that a huge comet was about to hit their town.

SUMMIT (SUM it) *n.* the highest point, usually the top of a mountain; the peak

The hikers reached the *summit* of the mountain and looked down at the forest below them, which spread in all directions.

Going to school for a summer at Oxford was the *summit* of my educational experience.

SUPPLE (SUP ul) *adj.* easily bent and manipulated; moving easily; limber and adaptable

After it had been in the refrigerator for a week the *supple* stalk of celery could be tied into a knot.

While many other trees were uprooted, the *supple* trunk of the coconut tree allowed it to withstand the hurricane's force.

SUPPLICATION (SUP li kay shun) *n.* begging; earnest appeal

After "Dangerous" Drederick Tatum lost the heavyweight championship, his whiny *supplications* for a return match seemed a bit out of character.

Note: To *supplicate* means to ask humbly.

The baseball fan *supplicated* himself in front of his boss in the hope that he would be allowed to leave work early to go watch the game.

SWAGGER (SWAG ur) *v.* to walk with a boastful air; to strut about with excessive pride

After making the move that would win him the game, the nerdy chess player *swaggered* around the room like she had just gained world dominion.

I thought that *swaggering* down the aisle would show my history classmates how cool I was, but then I tripped and dislocated my jaw.

SWAY (SWAY) v. to move from side to side OR to have influence over something

After riding in the Spinning Teacup Ride at the state fair, I found myself *swaying* back and forth as I attempted to regain my balance.

Sylvia's persuasive speeches, when combined with her ability to entertain people by juggling, *swayed* all of the voters in the district in her favor.

SWOON (SWOON) v. to lose consciousness; to faint

Unable to overcome his stage fright, Sam *swooned* onstage and had to be carried off by a teacher.

When the New Infants in the Community took the stage, many of the girls in the audience *swooned* with delight.

SYNCHRONIZE (SING kruh nyze) v. to plan something so that it occurs at the same time; to happen at the same time

The four police units surrounding the stadium *synchronized* their watches so that they would all move forward at exactly the same time.

The twins *synchronized* their dance movements so well that some people in the audience thought they were seeing double.

TANGIBLE (TAN ju bul) *adj.* something real; something you can actually touch

Because Bronson could show us no *tangible* evidence of his friend Luke, we all agreed that Luke was probably imaginary.

While sadness is not *tangible*, tears are.

TANTRUM (TAN trum) *n.* a fit of anger in which you behave badly and sometimes even throw things

Kerri threw such a *tantrum* at the picnic that it took six people to subdue her.

Denied her yellow duck, the toddler went into a *tantrum* that only a trip to the amusement park could stop.

TAPESTRY (TAP i stree) *n.* a large, heavy cloth decorated with a design or scene and then hung on the wall as decoration

Once the *tapestry* in the hallway caught fire, I knew I shouldn't have tried to barbecue inside the old castle.

We found a secret doorway behind one of the *tapestries* in the hallway of the old mansion.

TARPAULIN (tar PAH lyn) *n.* a waterproof piece of fabric used to cover and protect something from getting wet

After the grounds crew removed the *tarpaulin* that had covered the infield, game one of the Little League World Series was officially underway.

Dad loved his new lawn furniture so much that he would cover it with a *tarpaulin* each night, despite the odd looks his neighbors gave him.

TAUT (TAHT) *adj.* pulled tight

The tug-o-war game between the ten rival weightlifters made the rope so *taut* that I was certain it was going to snap.

When I popped the paper bag behind her back, my sister's *taut* emotions finally snapped and she shrieked wildly.

TEEM (TEEM) *v.* to be full of things; to abound

Holding the gun at my side, I looked in and saw that the barrel was *teeming* with fish. This was going to be easy, I thought.

The soup was *teeming* with bugs and I couldn't stick my spoon into it without hitting a fly.

TEMPERAMENT (TEM purh ment) *n.* how a person acts; his/her attitude toward all events and situations

I thought that the sight of his wrecked car would send my dad into a rage, but his *temperament* was more composed than I had predicted and he only cried.

Charles' cat, Loki, had such a nervous *temperament* that simply slamming a door too hard would send her running under the bed for cover.

TENDRIL (TEN drul) *n.* something long, slim, and curling, like a vine

The *tendrils* of ivy that covered the sides of the building had completely changed its color from brick red to dark green.

Within days after planting the magic beans, the little *tendrils* of the plants had transformed into a huge forest of towering trunks.

TEPID (TEP id) *adj.* neither hot nor cold; lukewarm

The *tepid* water of the pond was not as satisfying as we'd thought it was going to be when we jumped in to escape the summer heat.

Bill was able to chug down his entire mug of coffee once the liquid became *tepid*.

TERRAIN (tuh RAYN) *n.* the surface characteristics of a specific piece of land

The flat Oklahoma *terrain* allowed the farmers to set up an outdoor bowling lane that was 2,000 yards long.

Because no cars could cross over the rocky *terrain*, we were forced to unload the supplies and start walking.

TERRESTRIAL (tuh RES tree ul) *adj.* originating from the planet Earth

Once the blue-skinned creatures started speaking some crazy moon language, I knew they were extra-*terrestrial*.

All *terrestrial* forms of life, from bugs to people to whales, share many of the same characteristics.

TESTY (TES tee) *adj.* irritable or impatient

During a faculty meeting, the *testy* principal started screaming at a teacher for chewing his gum too loud.

Because waiting in lines made my parents *testy*, we always went to the movies fifteen minutes late.

THATCH (THACH) *n.* roofing material made out of plant stalks or leaves

Hurricane Jerry easily blew away the *thatch* roofs in the village, but the brick roofs remained intact.

Once the *thatch* roof got soaked and started rotting away, the smell convinced us that it was time to install a slate roof.

THERAPY (THEHR uh pee) *n.* a procedure used to heal people who are physically or mentally ill

The daily *therapy* of a hot bath and a massage eventually cured the athlete of the muscle pains in her back.

As part of my *therapy* to overcome a fear of heights, I have to climb a mountain each week and then stand at the edge and look off of the steepest cliff I can find.

THRESHOLD (THRESH hold) *n.* the lowest level at which something can be heard or recognized OR the place of beginning

I knew I was near the *threshold* of understanding my weird dream that involved penguins at my senior prom, but I still couldn't put it into words.

As I opened the secret door leading into Queen Nuputoopoo's tomb, I was certain I was on the *threshold* of a great scientific discovery.

THRIFT (THRIFT) *n.* the ability to handle money wisely

Gwendolyn demonstrated her *thrift* by transforming her lemonade stand into a multimillion dollar company.

Although she was from a poor family, Sophie's purchase of $10,000 socks showed that she lacked *thriftiness*.

THRIVE (THRYVE) *v.* to grow vigorously

With no predators and abundant flowers, the African bees *thrived* in the jungles of Central America.

A born daredevil, Winston *thrived* in the high-speed, high-risk world of flaming motorcycles races.

TIMID (TIM id) *adj.* very shy; easily scared

The *timid* cat refused to leave her litter box whenever strangers would enter the house.

By telling him that these vitamins pills were actually Instant Hero Capsules, we transformed *timid* Gary into a fearless football player.

TINGE (TINJ) *n.* a slight hue, a little bit of color

Although it was originally painted bright yellow, the car now had a *tinge* of red to it as small spots of rust started to become visible.

TORRENTIAL (tuh REN shul) *adj.* resembling a massive downpour of water

As the *torrential* rainstorm showed no sign of letting up, I began to appreciate the fact that I worked in the canoe store.

The *torrential* flow of information into the computer's circuits caused it to crackle, shoot sparks, and then shut down.

TRACT (TRAKT) *n.* a specific stretch of land OR a document written to declare a political or religious viewpoint

The *tract* of land between the river and the dirt road was known throughout the county as Farmer Anse's famous turnip patch.

In open defiance of the military leaders, Suu Kyi wrote a fiery *tract* outlining the reasons that democracy must prevail in her country.

TRAIT (TRAYT) *n.* a recognizable characteristic or feature

Oddly colored hair and multiple body piercings are two *traits* that most Californian surfers have in common.

A common *trait* among all Mongolian types of clothing is a lack of pockets.

TRAJECTORY (truh JEK tuh ree) *n.* the path of a moving object, like the arc of a ball through air

By watching games that were recorded on film, the coaches were able to study the *trajectory* of their star pitcher's fastball, and then give advice to the other pitchers.

The cannonball traced a graceful *trajectory* through the air before it smashed into the fortress wall.

TRANQUIL (TRANG kwul) *adj.* very calm and peaceful; without anxiety or stress

Our *tranquil* day at the lake was destroyed by the four power boats that came roaring down the river.

Although it didn't pay much, the job of snail babysitting was certainly very *tranquil*.

TRANSFIX (tranz FICKS) *v.* to pierce something firmly OR to pin something so that it is unable to move

Freddie would *transfix* the butterflies in his collection with a pin through the abdomen and then mount them on a board.

I was so *transfixed* by the lead character's god-like looks that I barely blinked during the entire three-hour film.

TRANSGRESSION (trans GRESH un) *n.* a violation of a law or order

After being caught asleep while on sentry duty, the White House guard was fined $50 for her *transgression* and demoted to the position of guard of the vice-president's dog.

I knew that staying out past my curfew was a *transgression* of the rules, but because I had just won the lottery, I didn't really care.

TRAVAIL (truh VAYL) *n.* difficult and painful work; a really tough task

Feeding liver soup to the six Mackenzie brats was hard enough, but my *travails* weren't over until I got them all to sleep.

The mountain climber knew that her *travails* were not over until she successfully climbed all the way back down the mountain.

TREND (TREND) *n.* a current fashion or style OR the general direction in which something seems to move

The recent *trend* of dancing the Macarena finally ended once people realized just how idiotic they looked doing it.

The car dealer was forced to admit that there was a *trend* toward buying more compact vehicles.

TRIFLE (TRY ful) *n.* a little thing that's not very important OR *v.* to play around

The color of the alien's shoes was a *trifling* issue compared to the great scientific knowledge and many exotic board games they brought to Earth.

When I learned that Gladys had only gone out with me because of a one-dollar dare, I knew she was just *trifling* with my feelings.

TUNDRA (TUN druh) *n.* a cold region of the earth, without trees and with only small, stunted shrubs and mosses for plant life

While trekking across the open *tundra* of Siberia during our expedition, I couldn't help wishing for the warmth and comfort of my hometown shopping mall.

The mouse hoped to hide from the swooping hawk, but the *tundra* offered nothing to shelter it.

UNFURL (un FURL) v. to open up or spread out

Before raising the flag, we *unfurled* it so that our drill sergeant could inspect the material to make sure that it was spotless.

The banner proclaiming the Houston Rockets as national basketball champions was *unfurled* from the ceiling and everyone applauded wildly.

UNIFORM (YOO nuh form) adj. always exactly the same; never changing

Because all the tables were of *uniform* size and color, it didn't really matter where we sat to eat our Big Brother burgers.

Every saxophone reed produced by the highly advanced machine was *uniform* in shape and size.

UNPRECEDENTED (un PRESS i den tid) adj. with no previous example

The ice skater's quadruple upside-down somersault with a twist was such an *unprecedented* move that the judges awarded her the gold medal instantly.

In an *unprecedented* move, the government spokesperson refused to answer any questions unless the reporter would agree to play Charades.

UTMOST (ut MOHST) *adj.* of the greatest amount or degree

This Friday, getting home in time to watch the season premiere of *The X-Files* is of the *utmost* importance, so I'm planning on leaving work two hours early.

It took the *utmost* amount of courage for the spectator from the audience to place her head into the lion's open mouth.

UTOPIA (yoo TOE pee uh) *n.* a perfect, ideal place; a land where everything is perfect

Jimmy's idea of *utopia* was a really awesome couch in front of a television that had over two million sports programs playing every day.

Listening to the radio announcer talk about pollution alerts and crime statistics serves to remind us of how far we really are from *utopia*.

VACCINE (vak SEEN) *n.* a drug given before the onset of a specific disease that helps prevent the disease from occurring

In the United States, few people die from polio anymore because more than ninety percent of the population now receives a *vaccine* against it when they're very young.

Unfortunately, science has yet to create a *vaccine* that prevents people from acting like jerks in a movie theater.

VANTAGE (VAN tij) *adj.* having a superior position or state of events OR *n.* an advantage of some kind

From our *vantage* point in the weather balloon, we could look down and see the entire countryside below.

The country of Hyborea used its *vantage* in trade to destroy the economy of its enemy, Emorial.

VEHEMENT (VEE uh munt) *adj.* forceful or intensely emotional; vigorous and energetic

In a *vehement* response to the reporter's question, Jacob hurled his microphone at the reporter and jumped into the crowd and attacked him.

It took four nurses and two doctors to hold down the patient after his *vehement* reaction to what he'd read in a tabloid while waiting for his appointment.

VENTRILOQUIST (ven TRIL oh kwist) *n.* someone skilled at projecting his/her voice so that it sounds as if it were coming from someplace else

A skilled *ventriloquist*, Loren would often appear to be having a serious conversation with her lampshade.

The prolonged case of laryngitis signaled bad times for the *ventriloquist* and his hopes for a national tour.

VENTURE (ven CHUR) *n.* a risky undertaking OR *v.* to take a risk; to guess

Diving into shark-infested waters was not a *venture* I was willing to make.

With the polls showing that the two delegates were almost dead even, I would not *venture* to say who will win the election for dogcatcher.

VERANDAH (vuh RAN duh) *n.* a covered porch that wraps around the outside of a house

Grandfather liked to sit out on the *verandah* of his home in Georgia, sip lemonade, and watch the sunset at the river.

While the plants inside our house always died, the ones we had on the *verandah* did quite well.

VETO (VEE tow) *n.* the right of the president to reject a bill that has been passed by Congress

By law, Congress can override a presidential *veto* if over two-thirds of Congress approve the bill.

VEX (VEX) *v.* to really irritate; to greatly annoy

The constant buzzing of a fly near my ear *vexed* me so greatly that I couldn't get back to sleep all night.

The Mustard Game, which consisted of spraying mustard on every carpet in the house, *vexed* our parents greatly.

VIABLE (VYE uh buhl) *adj.* capable of success or continued growth; workable

Although we had yet to win a game that season, our upbeat coach still believed that a shot at the playoffs was *viable*.

The commission declared that only candidates without a prison record were *viable* choices for the office of police chief.

VIGIL (vij uhl) *n.* to guard or watch over something for an extended period of time

FBI agents maintained a constant *vigil* around the house of Stones "The Hammer" Pugolowski, key witness in the Kronhorst murder trial.

Despite my unending *vigil* in the kitchen, the pot of water that I had been watching started to boil.

VINDICATE (VIN di kayt) *v.* to clear someone of wrongdoing by providing evidence that shows their innocence

After the secret witness told her story, the defendant was immediately *vindicated*.

Finding my sister's lost ring in the crow's nest *vindicated* me of the crime of brotherly theft.

VIRTUE (VUR chyoo) *n.* moral righteousness and excellence

Our image of Mr. Ertel as a man of great *virtue* was destroyed when we learned that he had four different wives.

Try as they might, the witches were unable to corrupt the *virtue* of the gallant knight.

VISTA (VIS tuh) *n.* a view, usually of things far away

Standing on top of the island's highest mountain, we gazed with wonder at the endless *vista* of the Pacific Ocean.

VIVID (VIV id) *adj.* very distinct and sharp; very realistic

The *vivid* use of red, black, and blue in the center of the painting greatly contrasted with the soft browns and yellows around the edge of the canvas.

The experience of Smell-o-Vision was so *vivid* that I almost believed I had actually been walking inside the cheese factory myself.

VOID (VOID) *n.* a place of nothingness, seemingly without end

We dropped a pebble into the *void*, but we never heard it hit the bottom.

Looking out into the *void* of space that surrounded the spacecraft, the astronaut was suddenly very glad that she had brought her lucky rabbit's foot.

VOLATILE (VOLL uh til) *adj.* easily changeable; quick to explode

The actor's *volatile* moods were such that he would sometimes laugh, cry, and then laugh again in the space of a minute.

Nitroglycerin is such a *volatile* liquid that just looking at it the wrong way will sometimes cause it to explode.

VOLLEY (VOL ee) *n.* a group of shots fired at the same time

The revolutionary soldiers waited until they could see the whites of the British troops' eyes before they released their *volley* of shots at them.

The candidate's statement that she was an alien caused a *volley* of questions to erupt from the gathered reporters.

VOUCH (VOWCH) *v.* to provide support; to give supporting evidence

Because his principal personally *vouched* for Leroy's commitment to learning, he was accepted as a student at Harvard Barber College.

Because no one but fish could *vouch* for her story that she had been at the lake, Gwendolyn was arrested by police on the charge of bank robbery.

WAFT (WAHFT) *v.* to float gently through the air or on water OR *n.* a light breeze or scent

The tiny leaf *wafted* slowly down from the tree until it reached the lava flow below and was burned to a crisp.

After having been stranded on the sea for ten days, the sailors cheered wildly when a *waft* of air struck the sails and began to slowly move the ship.

WANE (WAYN) *v.* to decrease; to approach an end to something

My hope for a quick visit *waned* when the Hendersons brought out eighteen video cassettes that they filmed during their trip to Milwaukee.

As the distance separating the two approaching clowns *waned*, each began to see distinct features of the other.

WHET (WET) *v.* to sharpen; to stimulate

I *whet* the blade of my lucky knife by running it along the edge of a nearby rock.

Although the chips and salsa were only supposed to *whet* my appetite, I ate so many of them that I was full by the time the main course arrived.

WHIRL (WURL) *v.* to spin rapidly; to turn around suddenly OR *n.* a state of confusion; a swift round of events

As the merry-go-round *whirled* faster and faster, the kids found it harder and harder to hold onto the bars.

After the tear gas canister exploded by accident, events were in such a *whirl* at the police station that the criminal was able to walk out the front door.

WILY (WYE lee) *adj.* crafty or cunning

Even though the coyote was *wily* and dangerous, he never was able to catch that speedy roadrunner.

The *wily* general devised a plan to fool the enemy troops which involved placing uniforms on mannequins so that they looked like real soldiers.

WISTFUL (WIST ful) *adj.* full of hopeful wanting; mildly sad

The kid with the broken leg had a *wistful* look on her face as she watched the marathon runners reach the finish line.

It was a *wistful* moment in the movie when we realized that Tinkerbell had always loved Peter Pan, but could never tell him.

WONDROUS (WUN drus) *adj.* brilliantly remarkable; extraordinary

The *wondrous* movie won every Academy Award possible that year, and its lead actress was given the Nobel Peace Prize.

When the aliens showed up with free lottery tickets for everyone, I knew it was a *wondrous* time to be alive.

WRATH (RATH) *n.* violent anger

Rather than face the queen's *wrath*, most of the people in the castle jumped into the moat and started swimming for their lives.

The *wrath* of the umpire was so great that he threw the entire baseball team out of the game, as well as their fans.

WRETCHED (RECH id) *adj.* very miserable and unhappy; hateful OR inferior in quality

I soon realized that working twenty hours a day making pickles in a cellar was a *wretched* way to live.

The *wretched* car could not even be sold for scrap metal, so we dug a large hole and buried it.

WRY (RYE) *adj.* funny in an understated way OR twisted into an expression of distaste; crooked or twisted

The *wry* play produced a lot of chuckles from the audience, but no huge bouts of laughter.

George's expression was *wry* after he ate the entire rotten lemon, skin and all.

YEARN (YURN) *v.* to want something greatly; to feel deep concern or pity

Walter *yearned* to be a Air Force pilot so badly that he memorized every word of the movie *Top Gun*, even though we told him that it wasn't required.

While the townsfolk *yearned* for the poor prairie dogs whose homes would be ruined, the greedy developer continued with his housing project enthusiastically.

YONDER (YON dur) *adv.* in or at a place indicated usually by pointing OR *adj.* at a distance but within sight

"The town lies directly over *yonder* hill," replied the old man, pointing at a large, rocky hill directly ahead of us.

"I'll meet you over by that tree *yonder*," said the girl, pointing to a willow at the edge of the meadow.

Answer Key

CHAPTER 1

QUIZ #1
1. O
2. S
3. S
4. O
5. O
6. S
7. S
8. S
9. O
10. O
11. S

QUIZ #2
1. O
2. S
3. O

4. S
5. S
6. O
7. S
8. O
9. O
10. S

QUIZ #3
1. B
2. B
3. D
4. C
5. B
6. A
7. A
8. D
9. C
10. D

QUIZ #4

1. F
2. H
3. A
4. E
5. J
6. C
7. I
8. D
9. B
10. G

QUIZ #5

1. C
2. J
3. I
4. E
5. A
6. H
7. F
8. B
9. D
10. G

CHAPTER 2

QUIZ #6

1. O
2. O
3. O
4. S
5. S
6. S
7. O
8. S
9. O
10. O
11. S

QUIZ #7

1. O
2. S
3. S
4. O
5. S
6. S
7. O
8. O
9. S
10. O
11. S

QUIZ #8

1. B
2. C
3. A
4. D
5. C
6. B
7. C
8. D
9. A

QUIZ #9

1. C
2. A
3. I
4. F
5. B
6. D
7. G
8. E
9. H

QUIZ #10

1. E
2. C
3. I

4. D
5. G
6. A
7. F
8. H
9. B

CHAPTER 3

QUIZ #11

1. S
2. O
3. O
4. S
5. O
6. S
7. S
8. S
9. O
10. S
11. O
12. O

QUIZ #12

1. S
2. O
3. S
4. S
5. O
6. O
7. O
8. S
9. S
10. O
11. S
12. O

QUIZ #13

1. C
2. B
3. A
4. C
5. C
6. D
7. B
8. A
9. D
10. D
11. A
12. A

QUIZ #14

1. F
2. H
3. A
4. L
5. D
6. M
7. B
8. I
9. C
10. E
11. G
12. J
13. K

QUIZ #15

1. D
2. A
3. H
4. K
5. F
6. M
7. B

8. I
9. L
10. C
11. E
12. G
13. J

CHAPTER 4

QUIZ #16

1. S
2. O
3. S
4. O
5. S
6. O
7. O
8. S
9. O
10. S

QUIZ #17

1. S
2. O
3. S
4. S

5. O
6. O
7. S
8. O
9. O
10. S

QUIZ #18

1. A
2. C
3. D
4. A
5. B
6. C
7. C
8. D
9. B

QUIZ #19

1. J
2. B
3. G
4. H
5. A
6. I
7. C

8. F
9. D
10. E

QUIZ #20
1. F
2. A
3. G
4. B
5. J
6. D
7. I
8. E
9. H
10. C

CHAPTER 5

QUIZ #21
1. S
2. O
3. S
4. O
5. O
6. S
7. O

8. S
9. S
10. O

QUIZ #22
1. S
2. S
3. O
4. O
5. S
6. O
7. O
8. S
9. S
10. O

QUIZ #23
1. A
2. C
3. A
4. B
5. D
6. B
7. C
8. D
9. D

QUIZ #24

1. B
2. D
3. H
4. C
5. A
6. J
7. E
8. F
9. I
10. G

QUIZ #25

1. H
2. I
3. C
4. F
5. A
6. J
7. E
8. B
9. G
10. D

CHAPTER 6

QUIZ #26

1. S
2. S
3. O
4. S
5. O
6. S
7. O
8. O
9. S
10. O

QUIZ #27

1. S
2. S
3. S
4. O
5. O
6. O
7. S
8. S
9. O
10. O

QUIZ #28

1. C
2. C
3. A
4. B
5. C
6. A
7. B
8. B
9. D

QUIZ #29

1. G
2. B
3. I
4. F
5. A
6. D
7. H
8. J
9. E
10. C

QUIZ #30

1. D
2. I

3. E
4. B
5. H
6. F
7. C
8. A
9. G

CHAPTER 7

QUIZ #31

1. O
2. S
3. S
4. O
5. O
6. S
7. S
8. O
9. O
10. S
11. O

QUIZ #32

1. S
2. S

3. O
4. S
5. O
6. O
7. S
8. O
9. S
10. S
11. S

QUIZ #33

1. C
2. C
3. D
4. D
5. B
6. B
7. A
8. B
9. D
10. C

QUIZ #34

1. F
2. I
3. A

4. D
5. B
6. K
7. G
8. J
9. C
10. H
11. E

QUIZ #35

1. J
2. E
3. A
4. G
5. B
6. K
7. D
8. I
9. C
10. H
11. F

CHAPTER 8

QUIZ #36

1. S
2. S
3. O
4. S
5. O
6. O

QUIZ #37

1. S
2. S
3. S
4. O
5. O

QUIZ #38

1. B
2. C
3. D
4. A
5. B
6. D

QUIZ #39

1. A
2. E
3. C
4. G
5. B
6. D
7. F

QUIZ #40

1. D
2. B
3. F
4. E
5. C
6. A

ABOUT THE AUTHOR

C.L. Brantley has worked for The Princeton Review since 1991 as an editor and author. Prior to teaming up with them, she worked in the software, telecommunications, and entertainment industries as a copywriter and speech writer. Her other books include *Word Smart Junior*, *Writing Smart Junior*, and *Kids Go! Austin*, a travel guide for children visiting the Austin, Texas area.

Brantley holds a B.A. in English, an M.S. in mass communication, and is working toward a Ph.D. in Computers and English Studies. She currently lives in Texas, where she studies, teaches, and writes. Her favorite color is red, and her favorite saying is, "Hey, at least I'm not dead." She sincerely hopes that you enjoy this book.